The Road to Positive Advocacy for Your Gifted Child

A Family Handbook

Carol Malueg

Routledge
Taylor & Francis Group

NEW YORK AND LONDON

Designed cover image: Nora Malueg, 2025

Illustrations by Nora Malueg, 2025

First published 2025
by Routledge
605 Third Avenue, New York, NY 10158

and by Routledge
4 Park Square, Milton Park, Abingdon, Oxon, OX14 4RN

Routledge is an imprint of the Taylor & Francis Group, an informa business

Library of Congress Cataloging-in-Publication Data
Names: Malueg, Carol, author.
Title: The road to positive advocacy for your gifted child:
a family handbook / Carol Malueg.
Description: New York, NY: Routledge, 2025. | Includes bibliographical references.
Identifiers: LCCN 2024058521 (print) | LCCN 2024058522 (ebook) |
ISBN 9781032740287 (paperback) | ISBN 9781003467441 (ebook)
Subjects: LCSH: Gifted children--Education. | Education--Parent participation. | Educational acceleration. | Gifted children--Social conditions. | Parent and child.
Classification: LCC LC3993 .M32 2025 (print) | LCC LC3993 (ebook) |
DDC 371.95/6--dc23/eng/20250130
LC record available at https://lccn.loc.gov/2024058521
LC ebook record available at https://lccn.loc.gov/2024058522

ISBN: 9781032740287 (pbk)
ISBN: 9781003467441 (ebk)

DOI: 10.4324/9781003467441

Typeset in Palatino
by Deanta Global Publishing Services, Chennai, India

The Road to Positive Advocacy for Your Gifted Child

The journey from preschool to independent adulthood can present a tricky route to navigate when you are the parent or caregiver of a gifted or multi-exceptional child. The job of advocating for these children is not about providing the "perfect" education, but about making the best choices within the given constraints.

Starting with the earliest school years, this book provides caregivers with the resources they will need to positively advocate for their gifted child and to help their child become strong self-advocates. Full of practical tips, this book answers questions such as: How can I meet other parents raising kids like mine?, Why can't schools meet the needs of my child?, How can I productively communicate with the educational team?, and more!

Providing expert guidance on collecting resources, expanding your network, and practicing and modeling positive advocacy skills, *The Road to Positive Advocacy for Your Gifted Child* will empower caregivers of gifted and twice-exceptional children to trust their instincts and understand their options when it comes to their children's education.

Carol Malueg is the founder of Gifted Roads, a company that offers services for gifted and multi-exceptional people throughout the lifespan. She works as a Learning Coach and Educational Consultant, specializing in gifted and twice-exceptional K-College education and support.

To my parents for paving the way, my siblings for sharing the driving, my husband for being the best travel partner, and our kids who make the journey well worthwhile.

Contents

Foreword

Observing your child interact with same-age peers, you wonder, "Is my child more or less advanced in some ways?" Observing your child behave differently than others in your neighborhood pre-school, you wonder, "Does my child have unique learning strengths or weaknesses?" Observing your child in kindergarten, do you have a tinge of concern about his or her future? Fortunately, Carol Malueg has written a caring and well-resourced guidebook, a comprehensive yet practical road map that addresses the questions and concerns of parents who have unique children we call gifted or twice-exceptional.

Having known and worked with Carol Malueg for several years, I know that she brings many experiences as a parent, advocate, and consultant in working with parents of twice-exceptional children when developing this road map. In addition to working with parents, she has tutored and mentored students who demonstrate giftedness and twice-exceptionality. This book is just what many parents and caregivers need to address their fears and anxiety about raising and advocating for children with exceptional gifts. The book provides parents with information that will help them recognize and understand the unique needs of their children, address the many challenges along the way, and celebrate their talents.

Among the strengths of this guidebook is its comprehensiveness in addressing many aspects of a parenting journey, and it does not come across as "preachy" in the least. Her experiences have provided insight into the anxieties and experiences that many parents have when raising children with gifts and talents. Readers will learn strategies for becoming effective advocates, techniques for managing expectations, and tools for achieving goals. The book is particularly helpful because she includes sections such as advice from others (called Mile Markers), stories from her own practice, and responses to frequently-asked questions.

In addition to being a helpful, informational guidebook, the book is a delightful read because of the manner in which it is written. Carol's creativity is evident in the chapter titles and sections. She cleverly uses the road trip metaphor throughout the entire book, from "meeting your tour guide" to "enlisting a good pit crew" to "having a spare tire." She also includes several humorous examples of situations that support the points she makes. For example, the photo of her newborn brother being transported in the backseat of a car with only a lap belt illustrates her argument for advocating for change.

The best feature of this book is its realistic advice for individuals who want to make life better for children demonstrating giftedness and twice-exceptionality, as well as for their caregivers. For example, in addition to providing advice on how adults can become advocates, she includes information on how to help children learn self-advocacy. This reminds me that this book is not only an excellent read for parents and caregivers, but provides useful information for educators as well.

When we embark on a road trip, what do we hope to experience? We expect to have a pleasant journey, one in which we learn new things and arrive safely at our destination. This guidebook, aka road map, will help readers with this goal.

Karen L. Westberg, Ph.D.
Professor Emerita
University of St. Thomas
Minnesota

PART 1

Planning Your Road Trip

1

Meet Your Tour Guide

Giftedness is defined in terms of high ability, exceptional achievement, and/or enormous potential. Gifted kids themselves tend to be intense, complicated, and fascinating. Some are driven to learn new things at an alarming pace, and some have found their niche area of focus and take a deep dive. Some are intensely empathetic humans who wear their hearts on their sleeves. Some are immersed in the arts, captivated by nature, or always with a nose in a book. Some have wildly active imaginations, and some pursue facts with determination. Some are introverted, others recharge their batteries in social settings. Some gifted kids have an additional exceptionality, or two or three, that complicate an already complex brain – these kids are "twice-exceptional (2e)," or "gifted, *and...*". Parenting gifted kids is an adventure, with surprises around every curve in the road. Advocating for these kids takes courage, kindness, and community. Thanks for joining me on this journey – I'm glad you're here.

Parents and caregivers are fortunate to find others who understand their surprise, joy, (and possibly even trepidation) upon finding out their child is gifted or twice-exceptional. Finding a community of parenting peers helps calm their utter panic about what to do next. There is nothing lonelier than working up the courage to voice your fears and struggles, only to receive the dreaded eye-roll of dismissal. On the flip side, nothing is as comforting as finding a community in which you don't have to hide

DOI: 10.4324/9781003467441-2

your family's quirky side. This book is a resource created by a fellow parent who has been down the challenging road of raising two wonderfully complex and strong-willed gifted humans and has hopefully acquired some wisdom to go with the mileage.

Meeting Fellow Travelers: Finding Your Parenting and Caregiving Peers

I remember when I first found people who were raising kids like mine. No way, they do exist! I realized they knew important stuff about how to support the intellectual and social/emotional needs of these unique kids. Such a revelation! I found our state's gifted organization and started attending everything I could – speaker events, picnics, and the annual conference. Some of the folks I met had been advocating on behalf of their gifted children for years and, wow, they knew a lot! It was a little overwhelming, a lot intimidating, and an enormous relief.

I was in awe of the parents and caregivers I met who made changes to their child's K-12 career year-to-year or sometimes more often, depending on how things were going. I was also a little skeptical, at first. As a product of public school, I had deeply ingrained training about 'how things should be done' when it came to education! That sense that I had options and a say in my kids' educational pathways was eye-opening, but I also had a new awareness of all I didn't know. I acquired a serious case of imposter syndrome (see Chapter 12 for more discussion on coping with imposter syndrome) but persevered because I knew my kids needed a strong advocate. I kept showing up (showing up is my superpower, more on this in Chapter 10) and asking questions (a hard-won skill we'll talk about in Chapter 8). On this advocacy journey for my kids, I discovered so much about myself as a gifted individual in my own right. Along the way, I found my calling – helping others become positive advocates, coura-geous caregivers, and creative educators for gifted individuals.

Landmarks: What I Learned from Going Back to School

FIGURE 1.1   This is me. A work in progress, with my work in progress.

I went back to school to get my Master's degree when our youngest started first grade. I spent 5 years taking one class at a time while working as a research assistant. My advisor/mentor/supervisor was Professor Karen Rogers, and I vividly remember the feeling of joy and amazement I had when I first saw an email from her in my inbox. Dr. Rogers authored *Re-forming Gifted Education: Matching the Program to the Child*, which was the first book on gifted education I purchased when I started advocating for my kids (Rogers, 2002). Working with her was life-changing and mind-opening. I was lucky enough to work with her directly on two Javits Grant projects, and indirectly on a third. (See Chapter 2 for more on this grant program and what you can do to make sure it continues.) My Master's program in Gifted, Creative, and Talented Education was where I finally learned to love being in school. This was where I felt successful, fully engaged, wholly invested, and absolutely appreciated. If I could have made an entire career out of being a student, I might still be there. They finally told me I needed to graduate already, so I did. Sigh.

My graduate school experience brought home to me that much of my educational history was a series of misses in the hit-or-miss systems I had participated in all those years. I experienced the joy of being in my element with people who appreciated me and worked *with* me to help me reach my goals. These same people appreciated my strengths and quirks and creativity. It was such a different atmosphere than the "play the game by our rules" situations I was familiar with as a student. All my fears of being bored or overwhelmed with busy work evaporated in this environment that played to my strengths and allowed me to personalize my learning journey. Don't get me wrong – I did plenty of data entry and microfiche printing – but being a student again helped me be a more creative advocate for change for my own kids. I've brought that insight into my work with other gifted people. How we approach our work is important, but how our work environment and our colleagues respond to our needs is equally so. We can't set kindergarteners loose on learning the way we can graduate students – kinders require a little more supervision – but there are many ways we can take lessons from graduate work norms and apply them to K-12 education.

⦿ WHAT I LEARNED IN GRADUATE SCHOOL THAT WAS ALL I NEEDED TO KNOW IN KINDERGARTEN

- ◆ Follow your interests
- ◆ Learn new skills as you need them to follow your interests
- ◆ Find mentors who can support skill-building
- ◆ Find others whose interests intersect yours and build on that connection
- ◆ Share your work with others
- ◆ Stay open to new opportunities and ideas
- ◆ Ask all the questions
- ◆ If someone doesn't like that you ask all the questions, find someone else to ask

---

Roadschooling: We Learn as We Go

I had great examples of advocacy as I was growing up. My parents were teachers – Mom was an English teacher and Dad was a Professor of Medicinal Chemistry. They both invested a great deal of time and care above and beyond their work requirements, and their students loved and respected them (in Dad's case, respect also came with a healthy dose of awe, as he was a brilliant scientist who did not suffer fools gladly). My brother was and is twice-exceptional (2e), gifted in many ways but with learning disabilities that qualified him for special education and disqualified him for gifted services (such were the 1970s in public schools). Our parents advocated for my gifted and sensitive sister and my gifted and stubborn self, too, but much time and effort was directed at making sure our brother had opportunities as well as remediation. They asked that his gifts were also addressed in a time when "gifted is as gifted does" (meaning only high-achievers could be considered gifted) was the prevailing school of thought.

⚠ A NOTE ABOUT 2E

The term, twice-exceptional, refers to gifted people who have one or more additional exceptionalities that may interfere with learning. These exceptionalities can be diagnosable, like ADHD, autism, dyslexia, etc. Or they can be more elusive, yet have an impact on a child's job of learning. A newer term, *neurodiverse*, given to us by the autism community, covers a much broader span of learning differences. The term I will use in this book, twice-exceptional (2e), was coined in the 1960s in the field of special education but did not become part of the common gifted education parlance until James J. Gallagher began using it to describe the combination of intellectual giftedness and learning challenges in one person in 1975 (Baldwin et al.).

I'll never forget my parents' wonder when I shared the term, twice-exceptional, that explained the phenomenon that is my brother. It was 2008 and I was in graduate school. I was lucky enough to be asked to be a project manager on a Javits-funded research project on twice-exceptionality led by Professor Karen Rogers. 2e (or 2x as we called it in that project) was new to me, and this project changed my entire worldview of giftedness. The complexity of the academic and social-emotional needs of twice-exceptional children can be overwhelming for educators and parents/caregivers alike. These kids need positive advocacy and self-advocacy x 100! These days, there are many opportunities for people to learn about 2e. Of course, there are now just as many models, definitions, and schools of thought as there are people studying it!

I should have taken to self-advocacy as a duck takes to water. My strong sense of justice, along with a knack for problem-solving and a gifted-kid vision of "how things could be, if only...," made me one of those kids who always had an opinion of how other people should do things. My temperamental temperament, however, meant my opinions were often stated in a confrontational (read obnoxious) manner. Even as a young adult, I was inclined to quit jobs, activities, friends, etc. when I felt disrespected or misunderstood rather than approach the problem with the idea of working for positive change.

It took me many years to learn to be a positive self-advocate, and I only really got good at that while learning how to be an effective advocate for my children, like when the gym teacher lost my kindergartener (see Chapter 7). (The example my parents set really did sink in – it just didn't emerge in my own toolkit until I was ready for it. Keep this in mind when you're modeling skills for your kids that you fear they will never learn! See Chapter 12 for a more in-depth discussion on continuing to teach and model even when it feels like you're talking to a brick wall.)

These days, friends and colleagues are amused and disbelieving when I talk about being a difficult kid to raise or a hot-headed young adult. I still have some piss and vinegar in me, but I have indeed mellowed like a fine wine, or more aptly, a hard cheese. I can sympathize with parents and caregivers who use their anger and frustration as fuel, but I hope I can help you find something to feed your efforts that is more sustainable and less of a liability to your advocacy efforts. No judgment here!

The Road Ahead: Where Do We Go From Here?

We'll talk about building relationships, picking your battles, looking for middle ground, and gathering allies. We'll look at times when creating positive relationships may lead to positive change. We'll address the quandary that if you have to fight a system (like a school district) to make change, it may very well not be a place you want to stay in the aftermath of the battle. We'll ponder the power of numbers and why it's important to never advocate alone.

♦   We'll begin Part 1 by looking at the big picture of gifted education advocacy, who we are as advocates, and what our goals (and our children's goals) are for the future.

- Part 2 is an exploration of the journey that brought you here – seeking strategies and ideas for advocating for your own child. We'll talk about changing expectations, the built-in constraints of the school systems, managing frustration, and doing the difficult work of examining how the choices we make impact others.
- In Part 3, we'll talk about collecting resources, expanding your network, collaborating with your child's teacher/coach/leader, and creating the all-important paper trail.
- Part 4 is all about modeling positive advocacy skills for your child and the process of letting them take the wheel. We'll talk about the power you have to make change, along with a look at some alternatives to the traditional K-12 pathway.
- In Appendix A and Appendix B, you'll find a list of resources. This is not a comprehensive list – you'll find many more as you continue your journey. I'm also including templates of the various organizers I talk about in the chapters. These will also be available for download on the Prufrock website.

You'll notice some special road signs indicating different voices and ideas along the way. These icons are:

◉ **Informational boxes** – expand on ideas that could use a little more explanation

⌐ **Mile Markers** – brief snippets of wisdom from experts and organizations

◉ **Author stories** – stories of my family's experiences

🚐 **Others' stories** – advocacy stories from other families, educators, administrators, and advocates

⚠ **Drive with care** – more information for families managing additional exceptionalities

🛑 **Questions to ponder** and/or discuss as you plan your advocacy road trip

"It's about building resilience, persistence, and flexibility. It's about modeling how to solve problems, fix mistakes, and give a good apology. It's understanding that there is no perfect, and that we learn the most when things are not going smoothly."

Advocacy, like any skill, takes hard work, practice, and learning from our mistakes. As you learn, you are modeling for your kids what positive advocacy looks like and what it can accomplish. Over time, the load gets lighter as your child learns and grows and eventually becomes their own best advocate. None of this is about being the perfect advocate or setting up a one-size-fits-all pathway to success for your gifted or 2e child. **It's about building resilience, persistence, and flexibility. It's about modeling how to solve problems, fix mistakes, and give a good apology. It's understanding that there is no *perfect*, and that we learn the most when things are not going smoothly.** Most of all, it's about the relationships you build and nurture along the way, especially that all-important relationship with your child.

Finding Our Way: Honoring Our Unique Journeys

Something I have learned over the years is that my experiences, many and varied as they are, do not apply to everyone. As I am writing this book, I am including stories and advice from other advocates with different experiences. Even so, there's no way I can share all the perspectives of all advocates! As you read this book, know that there is no single path to successful advocacy. Read with the intent that you will take what works for you and leave the rest. I hope that you improve upon the strategies here and personalize them to suit your needs. If this book can spark ideas and conversations, provide affirmation about what you are already doing, or give you the courage to make a change for your child, I'll consider it a success.

I know that I've had a lot of advantages in my life that have made some things easier for me. I'm incredibly grateful for that, believe me! But with every passing day, I'm more aware of how much I don't know. Part of my acquired wisdom, if I have any, is an ever-increasing awareness of my own ignorance. Happily, I love to learn, so I look at the world in the same way I look at a pile of unread books – with anticipation and glee. I welcome you to share your ideas with me and I'll share them (as I can) in my blog and in our online community.

Two more small notes before we dive in:

1. Please don't feel the need to read this book in order, from page 1 to the end. It's designed to be a take-what-you-need resource, so no guilt about putting it down partly read!
2. Also, feel free to disagree or have another opinion! Sometimes a resource that you don't agree with gives you greater enthusiasm for exploring your own opinions. Respectful disagreement is part of positive advocacy!

(STOP) SOME QUESTIONS TO PONDER AS YOU DIVE IN

- ◆ Who influenced you as a self-advocate and as an advocate for others?
- ◆ Who do you go to for advice and support?
- ◆ What kind of advocate do you hope to become?

References

Baldwin, Lois, et al. Twice-Exceptional Learners. Available at: losangeles.bridges.edu/uploads/6/3/7/5/63751333/gct_article--_history_of_the_field.pdf.

Rogers, Karen B. *Re-Forming Gifted Education: Matching the Program to the Child.* Great Potential Press, Inc., 2002.

2

The Roads We Travel

The Big Picture

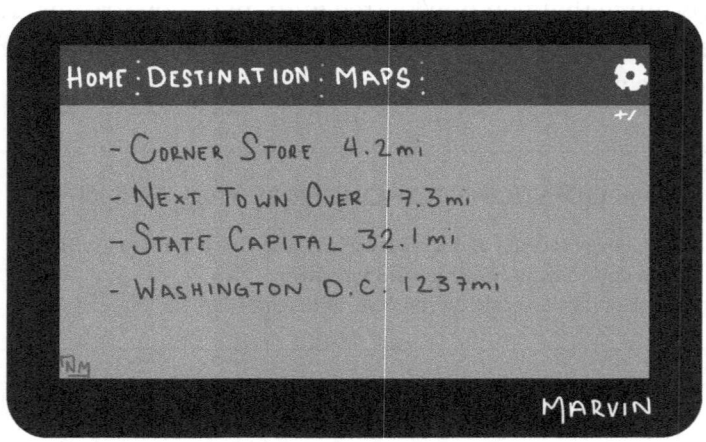

FIGURE 2.1 Technology's never failed me yet!

The Big Map: Context for Gifted and 2e Education Advocacy

Let's take a moment (or a chapter) to talk about the advocacy journey from a bird's-eye view. Advocacy has levels of complexity and commitment, kind of like our system of roads, freeways, highways, mountain passes, etc. We travel these roads with varying levels of skill and experience. Sometimes we have an empty

DOI: 10.4324/9781003467441-3

gas tank from lack of sleep, or bald tires because we haven't had a break in miles. Occasionally we slow down because we are unsure of what lies on the road ahead. And every now and then we turn around and go home, gathering our courage to set out another day.

Advocacy takes time and effort, and the more people you are advocating for, the more time and know-how it requires. It's kind of like driving through the mountains – the higher and windier the road, the more time, care, and specialized skill it takes to make it safely through, especially in less-than-optimal conditions. And the only way to become an expert mountain road driver is through driving that road, over and over again.

Most of us will become very competent drivers on our advocacy journey, but a few will decide to put the time and effort into taking that advocacy to the next level. Like long-distance trucking, it's not for everyone, nor is there room on those roads for all the potential travelers. As advocacy gets more specialized, fewer people speak on behalf of more people. While only those few people will do the heavy lifting, or expert driving, all of us can make a difference by expressing our need and adding our voices to the causes that matter to us. Supporting other advocates is advocacy in itself.

In the Garage: Advocacy at the Personal Level

Home is where all advocacy begins. We advocate for ourselves in our relationships, with colleagues, and with all the members of society we interact with on a daily basis. If you call the cable company to dispute a rate increase for your service, you are advocating on your home turf for the financial wellbeing of your family. When you talk with your child's teacher to assert, respectfully, that recess is not optional, you are advocating for the needs of your child. With every doctor or dentist appointment you make and keep, you are standing up for your own health. These personal acts of advocacy for yourself and your loved ones are essential and ongoing. They are like maintenance on your car – if you don't keep up on it, things start breaking down.

Around the Block: Advocacy that Includes Others Beyond You and Your Family

The one-to-one conversations with your child's teacher are one level of advocacy – that very personal level of what is important for your child and your family right now. This next level of advocacy involves and impacts more people.

Say your school has two first grade classrooms and each class has 28 students. That's an awful lot of first graders for one teacher to manage and a lot of desks for one room to hold! You and several other parents and caregivers talk it over and visit the principal to ask for a third first grade classroom and teacher. The administration ponders their options and creates a third cohort for first grade. If no one had said anything, that change would likely not have happened. It benefits your kid, certainly, but it also benefits the other 55 children in first grade that year and the first grade teachers.

Or perhaps your homeowner's association has decreed that no one can dry their laundry on an outside line. You may only hang a blanket outside to dry once a year or so, but you have neighbors who rely on this method of drying their clothes. Researching what rules apply to solar drying restrictions and gathering a group to talk with the HOA leaders will only benefit you a little bit, but supporting your community members is worth a lot.

Advocating beyond what's important right now for me and my loved ones started for me when I was advocating for my children. My beginning level of neighborhood advocacy was where I advocated for change that I hoped would happen in time to improve things for my child, but would benefit many kids. I talked with other parents and caregivers and learned more about what might be possible. We worked together to make a larger change than we could make on our own. My example of overloaded first grade classrooms? True story.

Heading Across Town: Advocacy on the Local Level

Local advocacy is a longer drive and requires more planning. It affects more people than you know, and will hopefully last beyond the time your child will benefit. This is advocacy on the school or district level. You might ask for teachers to receive professional development in gifted or twice-exceptional education. You might ask for funding for a gifted coordinator. You may lobby for an acceleration policy or an International Baccalaureate (IB) program. Sometimes you start the advocacy push and sometimes you have folks in the school system already working toward change. When you hear of an effort to improve identification of or services for gifted kids in your district, you can offer to add your voice in support. If you see a need and no one else is speaking up, gather your fellow advocates. Bigger changes take more time, more people, and more effort.

As Executive Director for Teaching and Learning in a large, affluent suburban school district, I could see that, generally speaking, we were close to meeting the needs of our gifted and talented students. However, there was a group that would benefit from a dramatic change in the delivery method. Rather than pull-out sessions and clustering we explored a school-within-a-school model for highly gifted students.

As we conducted our research, made site visits, established the need, and a lot more, it was clear that we could really help students in a multiage classroom in an elementary school for grades 3–5. There were obstacles like qualifications, staffing, 2e issues, finding space and more, but they were resolved through our research and understanding our own school community.

The biggest surprise was the vehemence of the opposition. Elitism, racism, haves and have-nots, and this model would not help highly gifted students to function and work in the "real world" with "regular" people. I guess the criticisms were not unexpected, but the intensity was a shock. Almost equally shocking was that there was very little in the form of advocacy for such a program. After all, many parents (and even some teachers) believe that gifted kids already have it made and highly gifted kids even more so. Therefore, they have no needs.

There were battle scars and lost collegial relationships, but when all is said and done, meeting the needs of our students is the highest value. That's for those (maybe especially those) who are unique. Doing the right thing, even with rabid opposition, is still the right thing. The program is 14 years old and simply a part of a wide variety of programming options to help our G/T students. It wasn't easy, but it was worth it.

(Mark Larson, PhD)

Road Trip: Regional or State-Level Advocacy

The regional level of advocacy is an even more complex, though less personal, proposition. In the U.S., this would be state-level advocacy. Advocating on the state level requires an even longer time commitment. Not necessarily more hours in a week, but more years on the same road. This kind of advocacy takes a lot of persistence and patience. You may think those traits are contradictory, but they are both necessary. Persistence because you may have to try for years to get the change you've been advocating for, be it funding for gifted services, a mandate for universal gifted screening, or language requiring districts to have an acceleration policy. Patience because it's easy to get frustrated with the glacial pace of this kind of advocacy and give up. State-level advocacy also requires more people. And a certain amount of credibility that goes beyond your own credentials.

State-wide non-profits are often advocacy leaders, so if your cause is supporting gifted education in your state, see what the gifted organizations are doing. Sometimes they are waiting for a volunteer to come along who has both the advocacy know-how and the determination to make things happen. Volunteer-run organizations experience turnover the way any organization does, so when their advocacy people move on, they need new people with the interest, energy, and experience.

You don't have to be an expert on state laws to work on this kind of advocacy team, but you'll probably want to have some good practice being a positive, respectful advocate on the neighborhood and local levels, so you know what you're getting into. You also don't have to already have connections with lawmakers and other stakeholder organizations, but you need to be willing to make those connections. This kind of advocacy isn't about being the expert or leading the charge – it's much more about collaboration and educating yourself and others along the way. If you're not a team player, this might not be your cup of tea, and that's okay!

Later in this chapter we'll talk about the ins and outs of state-level advocacy.

Heading to D.C.: Advocacy on the National Level

Then there is advocating for change on a federal level. This takes more elaborate planning, just like mapping out a road trip across the U.S. is more complicated than charting a trip to the corner grocery. In the case of gifted education, national organizations lead the charge in this type of advocacy. Again, if this is your passion, make those connections and become a part of the larger effort. You may wish things happened faster or in a bigger way, but the larger the mountains you are trying to move, the more patience and persistence and people you need to help budge them an inch.

This does mean that you aren't in this only for yourself or your kids anymore. At this level, it's all about the greater good. Compromise is an important part of this type of advocacy. If the group is heading in a direction you feel you want to go, hop aboard. Your voice adds power to the message as part of the larger group. Starting your own advocacy campaign running parallel to another would only dilute the energy and focus of the message as a whole. In every long-distance trip when you're traveling with others, you reap the benefits of traveling as a group, like group rates on travel and accommodations. In advocacy, traveling as a group gives you more presence and power. In all group endeavors, a few concessions go a long way. You don't want to try to change the route or halt the momentum once things get moving, even if you wish the route looked a little different.

It can be hard to let go of the steering wheel and become a passenger. You lose some autonomy and control. And you want to sign on for at least a complete stage of the larger trip, if not the whole thing. It's like if you're on a bus and realize you forgot to turn off the iron, you still need to stay put until you can exit at the next stop. If you're traveling by ferry, you find yourself on the other side of the river and now have to board the ferry going the opposite direction. Can you imagine a water bus captain turning a full boat around just to accommodate your needs? Same with most big systems – the bigger the system, the more people who are involved, the less possible it is to turn that water bus around for just one passenger, and the more disruptive it is to have someone jump overboard in the middle of the trip. With advocacy, losing a key-holding member of the team mid-stage can derail weeks, months, or even years of preparation.

Road Maintenance: Who Does the Day-to-Day Work?

Much of the time we are advocating to keep or improve what we already have in place. This kind of advocacy works against attrition by ensuring our lawmakers are aware of the continued need for things like funding, mandates, and updated language about gifted and 2e education.

In gifted education, national organizations, like the National Association for Gifted Children (NAGC) and the Council for Exceptional Children-The Association for the Gifted (CEC-TAG), keep an eye on federal legislation that may impact gifted learners in the U.S. They track potential new programs and watch out for proposed funding cuts. These organizations then put out a Call to Action to members, affiliate organizations, and the public at large to contact their legislators with a request to support programs that make a positive difference for gifted, talented, and 2e learners.

Year after year, representatives from state affiliate organizations, in my case, the Minnesota Council for the Gifted and Talented (MCGT), head to Washington, D.C., either in person or online, to advocate for the continuation or increase of funding for the Jacob K. Javits Gifted and Talented Students Education Program.[1] This program is regularly on the chopping block, and it's the continued advocacy on the part of the many stakeholders that keeps it mostly intact or brings it back after a cut.

⊓ **MILE MARKER**

The purpose of [the Jacob K. Javits Gifted and Talented Students Education] program is to carry out a coordinated program of evidence-based research, demonstration projects, innovative strategies, and similar activities designed to build and enhance the ability of elementary schools and secondary schools nationwide to identify gifted and talented students and meet their special educational needs. The major emphasis of the program is on serving students traditionally underrepresented in gifted and

talented programs (particularly economically disadvantaged, limited English proficient (LEP), and disabled students) to help reduce the serious gap in achievement
among certain groups of students at the highest levels of achievement.

(U.S. Department of Education, n.d.)

The Javits Program provides grants to educational institutions
or state departments of education for research projects that focus
on traditionally underserved populations of gifted learners. The
multi-year projects have produced more equitable identification
protocols that help schools and districts find kids who may otherwise fly under the gifted radar: twice-exceptional children,
kids who are learning English, BIPOC (Black, Indigenous, and
People of Color) students, and young people coping with food or
housing insecurity.

Javits projects have created professional development programs for educators. They have provided the foundation for
numerous high-level curricula that are designed for gifted learners. The projects also give us insight into teachers' needs, learners'
needs, and how we can involve the whole community in supporting gifted education. It's a tiny pocket of money in the overall
education budget, but it makes a big difference. The problem is
that these projects are not accomplished with publicity and fan-
fare – education researchers tend to share with other education
stakeholders, like educators, administrators, education-focused
organizations, and support professionals – so not many people
know about them.

Protecting or resurrecting things like the Javits Program
takes clear and informed leadership, a lot of people on the bus,
and a whole host of people who may not have time for the bus
trip but who can send along a message that expresses the value
they place on the program. The organizations mentioned above,
NAGC and CEC-TAG, are able to engage stakeholders across
the U.S. in advocacy efforts by sending a Call to Action with an
online form that is so simple to fill out and submit, it takes less
than two minutes. Other organizations have asked constituents
to email postcards, letters, and student work to legislators to give
the cause faces and names.

Advocacy for gifted children may be as personal as advocating for one child in a classroom or as wide-reaching as speaking for the needs of all gifted children on a national level. Many people who have tirelessly advocated for their own child are intimidated by the thought of advocating on a district, state, or federal level. It seems daunting, and long, and frustratingly incremental. Change may not happen for years, by which time the advocate's own children may already be out of school. The bigger the system, the harder and slower it is to make changes. The issues are increasingly complicated by the diverse needs and circumstances of the stakeholders. It can seem impossibly complex and we can feel unqualified to advocate on a larger stage. But as you advocate for your child, you are learning and using the same skills you will use if you decide to take your advocacy on the road. In some ways it can feel easier to manage, as having the support of a group allows for shared frustrations and successes.

Who, What, When, Where, Why, and How of Advocacy

Who

The Who is vital in advocacy. Who are we hoping to help through our advocacy? Who else will these changes affect? Who are the changemakers? Who will advocate with us? Who is our audience, and what do these people need from us to help them understand our message? We need to meet each person where they are, wherever they are. We may wish others were further along in understanding the needs of gifted or 2e kids, but we need to figure out where they are starting from and then give them what they need. That's a lot of *whos*!

Let's take the example of advocating for universal gifted screening in all public schools in a U.S. state:

◆ Whom are we hoping to serve?
  ◆ The gifted learners themselves, in particular, the gifted and 2e learners who are not being identified for gifted services. They are our reason for advocating.

♦ The educators, administrators, and staff in the schools will also be affected by our advocacy. Unless their school or district already implements a defensible universal gifted screening protocol, they will need to do a lot of work in order to prepare to screen children and then figure out how to serve them once they are identified. We need to be aware of their needs, as well as those of the gifted learners, because this impacts their jobs in a big way.

♦ The legislators are the changemakers in this case. These are the folks we need to reach and educate about the importance of universal gifted screening in our state.

♦ Who will advocate with us? Part of this initial work is gathering a group of passionate advocates who work well as a team. We each bring our knowledge, skills, and connections to the task of advocating on behalf of gifted learners. More importantly, we all understand that compromise and collaboration are essential. One or two people breaking off and pursuing their own agenda can undermine the careful work and planning of the group.

♦ Who isn't at the table yet? Keeping existing or possible inequities in mind while advocating for gifted children is essential. Advocating for some gifted children and ignoring others is how a program or service may be labeled elitist. It's not easy to keep equity top of mind when you come from a place of privilege. It takes practice and intention to think outside of your own box.

> **"** It's not easy to keep equity top of mind when you come from a place of privilege. It takes practice and intention to think outside of your own box.**"**

♦ Inviting stakeholders from diverse groups is easy, but creating a welcoming, collaborative space where everyone feels like their input is valued is more challenging. It's hard work to see things from another's perspective, but it's good work. Think of the community you are creating for your child.

◆ Who can share their story? Testimonials from constituents serve as a very powerful advocacy tool. When lawmakers hear from folks who vote in their district about the need for universal gifted screening and gifted services, it has a more powerful impact than a handful of people speaking for the entire gifted community.

◆ Who else? We hope that other stakeholders in education will see the benefits of universal gifted screening in their work and partner with us in our advocacy. We can also reach out to groups and organizations that can help in specific ways, like research, lobbying, etc.

◆ Will we step on any toes with our advocacy? How can we make sure to respect other stakeholders in gifted education? We don't want to cause harm, so we ask a lot of questions and listen to all the input. Sometimes the best we can hope for is a mutual agreement to respectfully disagree.

Gifted education has many stakeholders, all of whom have a part in your advocacy efforts. Educators and administrators, parents and caregivers, businesses and organizations, and the kids themselves. Table 2.1 is a partial list of people you might want on your advocacy team.

What: The Ask
Larger-Scale Efforts

In our example of advocating for universal gifted screening, we are asking that all districts in our state create and implement a universal gifted screening protocol with the guidance of the state department of education. We know that this is just one step of several that will help improve identification of and services for gifted learners in our state. We have a laundry list of needs and wants to achieve our ultimate goal, but we feel like this is the foundational piece that, once laid, will support the next step, and the next.

TABLE 2.1 Who's who on our advocacy team

Who	*Why*	*Where*
Parents and caregivers	Parents and caregivers can be more outspoken about what's missing or needs changing when it comes to gifted education because it won't affect their livelihood	◆ Online forums ◆ Schools with gifted services or programs ◆ After-school and Saturday programs that attract gifted kids ◆ Non-profit organizations that serve gifted families ◆ Gifted support conferences ◆ Gifted homeschool groups
Educators	Educators can speak from the school perspective but may have some restrictions about advocating for change in their own district. Many gifted educators are also parents of gifted kids, which gives them an additional layer of insight to share.	◆ Schools that offer gifted services or programs ◆ Non-profit organizations that support educators of gifted children ◆ Universities that offer gifted certifications or degrees ◆ Gifted education conferences
Administrators	Whatever level of change you are working toward, having one or more administrators working with you is very helpful. They can bring the big-picture thinking to the table.	◆ Statewide administrator groups ◆ Districts that offer gifted services or programs ◆ Gifted education conferences
Non-profit organizations	Having an organization behind your advocacy gives you: (a) more presence, (b) more resources, and (c) access to more potential volunteers and stakeholders	◆ Check with the National Association for Gifted Children to see if your area has an affiliate organization
Legal brains	Lawyers, researchers, and lobbyists bring specific and valuable skill sets to an advocacy team. Pro bono help from a lobbyist can save you a great deal of legwork and guesswork.	◆ Your State Bar Association may have leads on lawyers and lobbyists who do pro bono work in your area ◆ Other organizations that advocate for similar stakeholder groups may have legal services that they can recommend

The *ask* is just the tip of the iceberg. It needs to be backed up with current research data including state-by-state comparisons of funding, mandates, and the availability of support in the state department of education. You'll want to research the history of gifted legislation in the state. You'll need to present evidence that universal gifted screening makes a positive difference for learners. You also need a larger plan to share with those who see the implications of identifying kids for services that may not exist.

There is also the importance of understanding the ins-and-outs of a job. A teacher or administrator understands from the inside out how challenging it is to replace curriculum, rearrange schedules, or stretch a budget to another FTE (full-time employee). A seasoned legislator has a grasp on where new ideas fit into old legislation and whether there is money to fund changes. It's harder to see the constraints from the outside looking in. Think about your work – what do people never seem to understand about your job? For example, a stay-at-home caregiver has a grueling, endless, and often thankless job, but gets comments like "I'd love to stay home in my sweats all day!" or "You get to cook whatever you want whenever you want it!" or "I'd love to be able to nap when my kids nap!" Every stay-at-home caregiver ever rolls their eyes and gets on with the work.

With our ask for universal gifted screening, we are educating legislators and other stakeholders about the needs of gifted learners and the benefits of identifying and serving them. We need to make sure we can back up our ask with as much information as our audience requests, which means anticipating what they need to know. At the same time, we need to be open to learning more about the gigantic system we are trying to influence. The need for education goes both ways, and keeping an open mind helps keep communication flowing.

When
For My Child Right Now
The *when* for the personal advocacy for your child is whenever you see there is a need. You also want to keep in mind things like testing schedules, holidays, and other calendar items that take a lot of teacher time and effort. Approaching an educator right

before the winter break with a request for weekly check-ins for English assignments is likely going to get lost in the chaos of band concerts, term finals, and managing 25 kids who are *very* ready for their vacation. Instead, send a brief email (more on brevity in Chapter 10) the week after school starts up again. Then follow up the next week, if necessary.

Local Level

The *when* for asking for change on the local level has a lot to do with the school calendar, as well, but this time the administrative calendar. If you are asking for immediate change, as in the case of needing a third first grade classroom, you just go for it as soon as you can get organized and set up a meeting. If you're asking that professional development dollars be spent on awareness and strategies for gifted and 2e education, you will likely be working toward next year's calendar. If you are advocating for a new program or services, you'll want to add the school board's meeting schedule to your plan, and prepare for a longer effort.

State Level

The *when* of advocacy on the state level can feel frustratingly inconvenient. Lawmakers are in session during certain months of the year (see the *State Legislative Session Calendar*). Some of that time is intensely busy for them and some of that time is optimal for getting a meeting. There are also roadblocks like funding years or non-funding years – super important information if your ask includes funding.

Planning your advocacy road trip, especially when you have a number of people involved, can be tricky. One way is to begin at the end and work back to the present. Sometimes you'll realize there isn't enough time to get all your ducks in a row for the next legislative session, and you extend the plan to the following year. Table 2.2 is an advocacy planning calendar.

Your team will add in specifics for the projects you decide to accomplish. If you are working on capturing video testimonials from constituents, you'll add the steps into your plan. If you are building a website, put it in the plan.

TABLE 2.2 Advocacy planning calendar

Date	Proposed advocacy timeline
January	◆ Conduct initial meeting of advocates with similar goals ◆ Explore all current legislation relevant to your goals
February	◆ Invite additional team members ◆ Begin meeting with seasoned advocates for advice and guidance ◆ Develop a wish list
March	◆ Plan how you will educate others – print materials, videos, website, etc. ◆ Begin list of other education stakeholders
April	◆ Seek out legal or lobbying advice
May	◆ Assign projects to team members to begin research and development
June	◆ Work on materials ◆ Meet regularly to share progress updates
July	◆ Work on materials ◆ Meet regularly to share progress updates
August	◆ Continue inviting seasoned advocates to speak with your group ◆ Continue to develop educational materials
September	◆ Continue inviting seasoned advocates to speak with your group ◆ Continue to develop educational materials
October	◆ Meet with stakeholder groups ◆ Finalize materials for legislators
November	◆ Meet with legislators (post-election) ◆ Continue to meet with stakeholder groups
December	◆ Visit legislators at Capitol
January	◆ Meet with legislators and stakeholders ◆ Present testimony to legislative committees

Keep in mind that the timeline you create is a guide, not a set of hard deadlines. Your advocacy team most likely comprises volunteers from stakeholder non-profit organizations and community members. Everybody probably has a full-time endeavor outside of this advocacy, so timelines shift according to what your team can feasibly do without burning out and dropping out. A relentless push to make change now, now, now can alienate even your most passionate volunteers.

Where

Where Do You Need to Be?

The most important part of advocacy is showing up. You can't speak up for something when you're not there. Volunteer advocates have to prioritize family, work, and other obligations, so showing up can be really hard sometimes. Setting a pace that allows for flexibility (see *When* section above) is the key to keeping your volunteer crew intact.

A volunteer who is a 'maybe' is really as good as a 'no' when it comes to planning. It's okay to not show up everywhere all the time. Be clear with your fellow advocates about what you can and cannot do. One of the beautiful and terrible things about our gifted brains is that we can see the ideal, the best, the ultimate of what we can do. That vision of possibility can get in the way of the truly possible. If you can only show up online, be clear. You should probably not be tasked with organizing in-person visits with legislators. You could take the lead on editing filmed testimonials into bite-sized, shareable videos, or be in charge of sending Zoom® invitations, or work on the group website, etc.

"Show up where you can, and really show up."

Show up where you can, and really show up. Much of our advocacy work can be done online, but there is a certain declaration of commitment that is felt when you show up in person.

- ◆ If you are advocating on the school level, organize a meeting with the stakeholders.
- ◆ District level, show up to the school board meetings and sign up to talk.
- ◆ State level, find a day to visit the capitol when you can meet with as many legislators as possible.
- ◆ National level (in the U.S.), go to D.C., and schedule a visit with all your state offices.

You will more than likely meet with a staff member of the legislator in each Washington, D.C. office, rather than with the legislator.

The staff members specialize, so the education staffer will know the right questions to ask and be able to provide context for their boss when they give a report. So, it may feel like you are missing out by not talking with the elected legislator, but your message will be shared. Regardless, showing up in person is a powerful statement. Phone calls, emails, and online calls are all a part of your where, as well.

Where Do You Keep Your Stuff?

Each member of your team will have different constraints and preferences, and the only limit to what you can do is having someone to do it. It's okay to specialize, but be sure to leave a trail of breadcrumbs in case you need to step away from the work. When someone leaves the team and doesn't leave a way to keep and build on their contributions, it sets the entire effort back. When sharing information, share in such a way that multiple people have ownership and access. If one person holds the keys and that person gets sick or moves to Timbuktu, you've lost all that shared work. This is a key part of your Where – where do you store your Who, What, When, Why, and How? Table 2.3 depicts where, what, and how to share.

Why

The why seems obvious, doesn't it? But to people who don't know about the needs of gifted learners, our ask for funding or mandates might seem frivolous or entitled. The term gifted is problematic in that it implies "better than" thinking. In fact, gifted education does have a long and dark history of exclusion and elitism. It's not a secret, and it's not a great idea to sweep that history under the rug. Acknowledging the harm caused in the past by folks who used inclusion criteria for their gifted programs that, intentionally or through negligence, caused specific groups of gifted students to go unidentified and underserved is the only way to do better in the future.

Gifted education goes through evolutions, just as all aspects of society change as each generation reacts to the previous one's choices. Gifted education ebbs and flows in response to people seeing and saying out loud that they see the inequities that were

TABLE 2.3 Where, what, and how to share

Shared info	Where, what, and how to share
Notes	Maintain thorough notes of all meetings (you may have separate docs to share notes with individual legislators and other stakeholders, but all notes should be linked in one main notes document). You can use Google, Microsoft, Dropbox, or any other online platform that you all have access to. Avoid using personal accounts for this – create a shared account or use that of an established organization.
Contact info	Create a table with team members, legislators, experts, stakeholders, etc., and their contact information. Store this table or a link to the table in the shared notes.
Passwords	If you decide to create a website or have an email address for the team, be sure to have all the passwords and access info in the notes. Things like interactive maps and video libraries should also be shared or owned by an organization. If something lives in an account protected by a password, do your best to make sure it isn't owned by one individual.
Calendar	Advocacy involves a lot of people (and therefore a lot of schedules), from volunteers to consultants to lobbyists to the legislators themselves. Appointments with legislators can change at the drop of a hat. Their days are filled with meetings with constituents, groups, and other lawmakers, so don't be surprised if you are rescheduled a time or three. A shared calendar can help keep the team up to date on who is where and when.

built into the system. Cognitive assessments that rely on English as a first language lower the chances of English Learners (ELs) participating in gifted programs. A test with prerequisite knowledge of activities, objects, or ideas that are rooted in one culture excludes children raised in other cultures. These and many more examples have caused many schools and districts to abandon gifted programming and services entirely. This all-or-nothing attitude doesn't improve representation of the school's demographic in their gifted services – it just leaves all gifted kids without acknowledgment, challenge, and acceptance.

A great deal of work is being done to create identification protocols that find the gifted students who may have been overlooked in the past. The Javits Grant projects mentioned above are one way the field has worked to move beyond the inequities of the past. Research by foundations like the Thomas B. Fordham Institute is another way of holding education establishments accountable for their choices.

⬒ **MILE MARKER**

[T]oo many assume that advanced education is about increasing privileges for the already advantaged, rather than identifying and maximizing the strengths and potential of every student – including poor kids and kids of color with potential for high academic achievement.

This disregard has resulted in serious neglect of a vital student subgroup, with future national repercussions for weakened, less diverse leadership and less innovation, progress, and economic growth. More pragmatically, it has also resulted in a lack of informative research for the field of advanced education.

(Thomas B. Fordham Institute; https://fordhaminstitute.org/ national/research/broken-pipeline-advanced-education-policies-local-level)

The myths about gifted kids are pervasive. The National Association for Gifted Children has a good list of myths and rebuttals on their website that's worth checking out ("Myths About Gifted Students"). Your advocacy will center around educating others about the needs of gifted children in your corner of the world, but the goals are the same. Here are some talking points. What would you add?

◆ A Free Appropriate Public Education (FAPE) in the U.S. is meant to give all children access to an education that allows every child to learn something new every day. This education looks different for gifted kids because many of them start a school year with much or most of that year's content already mastered (Free Appropriate Public Education (FAPE) – Individuals with Disabilities Education Act) (Wrightslaw.Com).

◆ Gifted kids are found in all populations, but gifted kids from all populations are not identified proportionally for services.

- Gifted kids with learning disabilities or other challenges are experts of disguise. Their gifts may mask their challenges, and their challenges may mask their gifts. The most not-average kids may look absolutely average on paper.
- Gifted kids often have to wait for others to catch up. Gifted kids may demonstrate mastery more quickly with fewer repetitions and be ready to learn more. They may be frustrated with the slow pace of instruction (*A Nation Deceived*).
- Teaching multiple grade levels in one same-age classroom makes educators' jobs really hard. Math teachers may have between one-third and one-half of their classroom needing work that is outside the scope of the grade-level curriculum (Pedersen et al. 2023).
- Families experience a great deal of stress when the school they trust with their child's education is unable to meet their needs. The stress is multiplied when the family cannot afford to explore options, like moving, changing schools, or homeschooling.
- Communities suffer when families are forced to relocate to find an appropriate education for their child.

Your message may be about strategies to equitably identify and serve gifted kids in your region or state. It may be about the impossible task we set for teachers when we give them kids with a range of six or seven levels of achievement in one same-age classroom. We can all be educating others about the hidden gifted – our twice- or thrice-exceptional children who have immense strengths that may be hidden by exceptionalities that make learning in the school setting more difficult – challenges like ADHD, autism, dyslexia, depression,

"Changing people's minds can only come with their own awareness of their biases. We can't change other people. We can help people want to change, not by accusing or berating, but by educating in a positive and respectful way."

anxiety, vision or auditory issues. Some of these 2e kids may have a third e – like being a person of color or part of the LGBTQIA+ community. (These third e's are characteristics that have a long history of implicit or overt bias surrounding them.)

Changing people's minds can only come with their own awareness of their biases. We can't change other people. We can help people want to change, not by accusing or berating, but by educating in a positive and respectful way.

How

And here is where we get to the meat and potatoes of advocacy – educating others. We know what we are asking for and why. How did we get to that understanding? It certainly wasn't automatic – it took us some serious work to get where we are, and we will keep working and learning as we go.

Back to our universal gifted screening example: It takes creativity and determination to look beyond the usual assessment tools used in universal gifted screening, for instance, in order to find gifted kids from traditionally underrepresented groups. The creators of assessment tools do their best to eliminate bias, but you can only work from what you know. Include research and data to back up your ask.

> When everyone participates in the initial assessment for giftedness, issues of bias, awareness, and understanding are diminished in comparison to systems in which teachers and other school personnel are gatekeepers.
>
> (Gubbins et al.; NCRGE EL Report)

When we are advocating for funding and mandates for gifted education, we need to be very intentional about what we are asking for. If we ask for mandates that will overwhelm small rural districts, or make it impossible for a smaller school to provide gifted services at all, we are perpetuating the inequities of the past. Even the most sensible-sounding asks can have lasting repercussions we never intended.

Take, for instance, the idea of teacher training in gifted education. It sounds like a great idea to mandate that all teachers who provide gifted education services have a graduate certificate in gifted ed, right? But how about the tiny, rural school district that already has a fair bit of struggle to attract and retain educators? If we add the requirement that, in order to provide gifted services to any gifted student, they must have an educator with a certificate, we have probably just shut down all gifted services in that district.

Thinking about all the possible ramifications of the legislation you are asking for is pretty challenging. That's a big reason to invite a diverse group of stakeholders to share ideas and give feedback. If you live in a state with rural school districts and you don't have rural representation at the table, their legislators may well become your opposition. What is ideal for a large, urban district may not fit a medium-sized, suburban district or a tiny, rural district.

Whether you're advocating for your own child only, or you're involved in a larger advocacy effort, be prepared to revise, revisit, and rework your approach. Flexibility is an essential advocacy skill. We need to take into account others' perspectives and needs and wants. Our ideas will naturally change as we learn more about the constraints of the system. Our children's needs will change as they grow. We will change, too. We'll make mistakes and enjoy successes. We'll learn a lot and hopefully be able to pay forward the help we get along the way.

♦   What are your "whys" for advocating for gifted kids?
♦   What barriers do you see in your school, district, or region?
♦   Are there others who are interested in advocating for the same things you are?

Note

1 At the time of publication, this federal grant program's funding status was under administrative review. Readers should consult the program's official website or relevant government resources for current information.

References

A Nation Deceived. https://www.accelerationinstitute.org/Nation _Deceived/.

Council for Exceptional Children. The Association for the Gifted. https://cectag.com/.

Gubbins, E. J., et al. "EL Study." National Center for Research on Gifted Education, 27 May 2015. https://ncrge.uconn.edu/resources/el -study/.

National Association for Gifted Children. "Myths About Gifted Students." https://nagc.org/page/myths-about-gifted-students (accessed 1 October 2024).

National Association for Gifted Children. https://nagc.org/.

Pedersen, Blaine, et al. "Most Mathematics Classrooms Contain Wide-Ranging Achievement Levels." *SAGE*, 27 Apr. 2023. https://www .researchgate.net/publication/370347601_Most_Mathematics _Classrooms_Contain_Wide-Ranging_Achievement_Levels.

Thomas B. Fordham Institute. "The Broken Pipeline: Advanced Education Policies at the Local Level." https://fordhaminstitute.org/national/ research/broken-pipeline-advanced-education-policies-local-level.

U.S. Department of Education. "Jacob K. Javits Gifted and Talented Students Education Program." https://www.ed.gov/grants-and -programs/grants-birth-grade-12/well-rounded-education-grants/ jacob-k-javits-gifted-and-talented-students-education-program

Wrightslaw.Com. "Free Appropriate Public Education (FAPE) - Individuals with Disabilities Education Act - Wrightslaw.Com." Learn About Free Appropriate Public Education (FAPE). https://www.wrightslaw.com/ info/fape.index.htm.

3

Traveling Companions

No advocate is perfect, tireless, or always successful. All advocates need rest stops, do-overs, and roadside assistance. Whatever your advocacy role (or roles, since you probably have more than one at any given time), taking care of yourself first makes you a stronger advocate for others.

Driver's Seat: Self-Advocacy

Imagine with me that self-advocacy is the familiar network of roads you travel every day. You're comfortable navigating those roads, but every now and then you come across a construction zone or new routing and you slow down to figure out your approach. Sometimes you have new challenges – health issues, new job, new baby, a big move. Then, you have to travel well beyond your comfort zone, and hopefully you have someone who can help you navigate. Your self-advocacy will change and grow over your lifespan, from your early days of spitting out peas to your elder years when you want a say in where you live out your days.

We all advocate (I hope) for ourselves, in ways large and small. We start as babies – "No, I do not want strained peas, and because I am not yet able to tell you in words, I will make terrible faces and spit peas everywhere." And we continue to self-advocate, with varying levels of success, throughout our lives. There are

DOI: 10.4324/9781003467441-4

times when we may suffer in silence because we know the consequences of speaking up are undesirable. A child who would have to carry a giant hall pass stating "I am missing valuable learning time" may decide to hold their urine, possibly to their detriment or embarrassment. A worker whose job is on the layoff line may not report harassment to HR. A student who asks for extra help faces the choice of giving up recess, lunch, or an after-school activity to receive that help. (Ask any young person what's more meaningful to them, time with friends or more school work.)

We all need to self-advocate, to make our needs and preferences known. We can't always get our way because of the constraints of our individual situations and because the world is complicated by billions of other people with their own ideas and goals. But through self-advocacy we are more likely to get our needs met and attain or maintain some control over our own lives.

Driving Instructor: Helping Others Grow Self-Advocacy Skills

One of our most essential roles as parents and caregivers is to nurture self-advocacy skills in our children. We want them to become independent adults who, in turn, will advocate for others. This process starts when our children are small. We give them choices to make: "blue socks or green socks?" and the words to say:"yes," "no," "help," "please," and "may I?" As our kids grow, they have more complex choices to make – Girl Scout camp or language immersion camp, orchestra or band, small college or large university.

The key in the early days is to only offer choices that are acceptable. If you give an option that really isn't an option and there is only one acceptable answer, you have taken away the power of choice you just offered. "Do you want to put on your shoes?" can be answered with a "yes" or a "no." But if leaving the house without shoes is not okay with you, you've opened the door to a power struggle. Later on, they will have more say in what the options are, and eventually your job is to help them think things through and encourage them to make their own decisions. (And, wow, is that tough to do!)

🚐 When our child was in third grade we sought neuropsychological testing despite the school not noticing any issues. Results revealed giftedness and dyslexia (2e), and the tester recommended a time-intensive remediation program to close the gap between inner conceptual complexity and outward expression and achievement. In a meeting with us as a family, the principal raised the question of "What other parents/kids would think?" if they heard about this child having a modified school day to accommodate this intervention. Our 8-year-old turned to the principal and said, "What does it matter what the other parents think? If this is what I need, then that is all that matters." We proceeded, and achieved the intended progress with successful results. In 8th grade we did the same by withdrawing them from public middle school to attend an innovation school, requiring us to register this child as a "homeschooling" student. It was the best decision we ever made, and set the stage for their identity and career.

Sometimes we parents, or our children, know when something is off. We may have data or just intuit something needs to change for their education or mental health. By choosing to trust ourselves, and them, and being willing to take risks over conforming to the normative sequence or structure, we teach our children to have the courage to honor themselves. We remind them that they have the right to be different, to advocate for themselves, and are capable of charting their own paths. We model having the independence of thought, the flexibility, and responsibility to make empowered choices. By attuning to each child as an individual with unique needs, we foster the development of the very self-reflective and self-advocacy skills necessary for success in life.

(Heidi Lack, PhD, ATR-BC, parent and psychologist)

Making choices is just one part of the job. Having words to describe feelings, needs, and preferences empowers your child to speak on their own behalf. Your child needs to know that they have rights, what those rights are, and that you will back them up on exerting their rights. (We'll talk more about our children's rights in Chapter 4.) As you advocate for your child, you're showing them how to take care of themselves.

⚠️ Gifted kids with additional exceptionalities may struggle with some aspects of self-advocacy, or may take longer to develop these skills. On the other hand, having a learning disability or difference is a great reason to learn self-advocacy skills and practice them often. Sometimes our 2e kids become our most skilled and effective advocates because they need these skills more than kids who fit into systems relatively easily. A student with a 504 plan, IEP, or other individualized learning plan with the school has additional opportunities to see positive advocacy in action. When the student's voice is heard and their ideas are implemented, they are learning self-efficacy.

We'll talk more about this down the road, but it never hurts to repeat it – your child is the one who will need to access, tolerate, embrace, or accept any agreed-upon interventions, accommodations, or modifications to their job of school. If they are not involved in the process, you could be wasting your time asking for something they won't use.

Imagine putting in all the time to research an accommodation for story writing. You find that experts in the field of gifted and 2e education recommend voice-to-text, use of a scribe, or offering alternative modes of telling a story (drawing, singing, stop-action animation film, etc.). You meet with the teacher, perhaps the whole team of special education case manager, school counselor, an administrator, and perhaps your parenting partner. The accommodation you all decide on is voice-to-text. Your child will go to a quiet room during writing time so they can use voice-to-text without disturbing other kids.

Your child, presented with this fait accompli, refuses to leave the classroom, feels terrible about being singled out in front of their classmates, and decides voice-to-text is stupid and they will never use it. Ever. And now there is an even darker cloud over the topic of story writing and no forward progress. The best accommodations in the world are useless if the accommodatee refuses to be accommodated. The best intentions for supporting students backfire when they feel powerless. More on this in Chapter 4.

Travel Companions: Advocating for a Loved One

Advocating for a loved one means traveling their roads with them, sometimes as driver, other times as navigator, and occasionally simply as a companion. This can be as simple as giving feedback on an email your child will send their teacher, or as complicated as advocating for a parent with dementia. These roads will still be familiar, but it's different when your road trip is all about someone else, isn't it? It takes a new set of skills to listen instead of fix, offer suggestions instead of pronouncing solutions, and think beyond your own preferences to support ideas that wouldn't work for you, but may work for your loved one.

> ⊙ Sometimes the progression from driver to companion advocate for your child moves in a fairly linear fashion, but most often there's a lot of jumping back and forth between the roles. A young person who has become independently able to advocate for themselves in a school setting may really struggle in another environment. A school change, whether due to a transition to the next higher level or because of a move, can bring a whole new set of challenges. Young people may seem to be regressing in their advocacy skills, but those skills are still there. They simply have a new situation they need to figure out before they can begin to apply those skills again.
>
> It's okay to take a turn driving when your child is overwhelmed. Think of a time you needed or wanted someone by your side as you faced a new challenge. You have the privilege of being that person for your child. Someday, they may have the privilege of being that person for you.

We all will have advocated for another person at various times in our lives. We may have defended a sibling from a playground bully, or taken a friend's side in a disagreement. We may shield a loved one with a disability from thoughtless commenters or advocate for an elderly or ill relative at a doctor visit. I've watched in admiration as young people translate for a non-English-speaking parent or caregiver in a school meeting. We advocate for our loved ones in a thousand ways all the time.

When you become a parent or a caregiver of a child, advocacy for that small person comes with the role. We remind visitors to "hold the baby's head" when the child is a newborn. We create our own rules and guidelines for the care of our children or we adopt the rules and guidelines we knew in our own childhoods, and we use that framework in our advocacy. Have you ever asked the host of a playdate if they have guns or weapons in their home, and if so, are they safely locked away? Reminded a caregiver that your child needs reapplication of sunscreen every 2 hours during the trip to the waterpark? And if your child has food allergies, you've advocated endlessly!

With gifted education, your first advocacy will probably be for your own children. "My child has academic and social needs right now, this year, in this classroom." This is the kind of advocacy that evolves as your child grows and becomes their own advocate. These are your neighborhood streets, familiar and easy to navigate. You can see to the end of the block and you know where you're going and how long it takes to get there. You do this kind of day-to-day advocacy in the school, the pediatrician's office, the daycare, and at family reunions. You advocate with the scout troop leader, the dance teacher, and the soccer coach. It's all in a day's work.

Passers-By: Helping Others Along the Way

> **"**It's much easier, and more possible, to give someone directions to the help they need than to try to provide that intensive level of help to everyone in need.**"**

Standing up for individuals outside of your inner circle of people is like traveling in a wholly unfamiliar region with no GPS. You don't know what is around the next turn or how long the trip will take or what roadblocks you might encounter. This is a big reason people don't jump in to help others even when they want to – too much risk and uncertainty. Our time is our most valuable resource, and most of us don't promise it away to just anyone. It's why you might look the other way when approached by an unhoused person who is willing to work for food. But if you are able, you might give them some food and directions to the nearest shelter. It's why you may not be available to assist a cousin-of-a-friend-of-a-friend with their doctor visits even though their medical issues are similar to the ones you helped your mom through, but you could send them information about Visiting Angels or other in-home caregivers in their area who might be able to help. It's much easier, and more possible, to give someone directions to the help they need than to try to provide that intensive level of help to everyone in need.

There are times we don't speak up because we have other, more important needs to meet at the moment. How many times have you thought along these lines: "If I say something, I'll be involved and I truly don't have time." "If I offer to help I'll be late to my next appointment." "I can't help right now because I have young kids and they need me more."

People tend to hesitate before taking up someone else's cause, and with good reason. We can't advocate for someone else unless we know what the need is. And if we know what's going on, we would then feel the need to act. One person stepping in is often enough to get the cogs turning and engage other people in the advocacy process, but not always. So, sometimes we are left holding the advocacy bag. You know the phrase, "No good deed goes unpunished"? A lot of times, people just don't want to get involved, whether for fear of consequences to themselves, or just because it takes so much darn time.

You aren't a bad person for being unwilling to feel obligated to spend an unknown quantity of your valuable time on people you don't know. Giving the help you can feels great and makes a difference, too. As you progress on your advocacy journey, you will collect favorite articles, podcast episodes, books, and blogs. You probably already recommend favorite providers or resources to fellow parents and caregivers. Consider this a side benefit of the work you are doing for your child – you can make a bigger difference just by collecting and sharing ideas. You may even graduate to what we can call billboard advocacy, a time-effective way to share pieces of useful information with a lot of people, like a newsletter, blog, TED talk, or podcast.

Professionals in the helping fields feel this quandary keenly, as well. Therapists, coaches, tutors, occupational therapists, advocates, consultants – all of these professions are centered around one-to-one interactions. How do we reach and help more people? Some folks blog or do podcasts, others create asynchronous courses, a few teach fellow professionals how to do what they do in live or online classes, many do recorded presentations for various professional libraries, and a handful write books. We all collect our own resource libraries, whether digital or print, so that when people come to us for support, we are able to give them more than just our time.

In this, as in everything, be aware that other people have their own sets of experiences and their own preferences. So, just as when we are advocating for our child, we want to be careful not to advocate for an accommodation or modification that they will refuse, we don't want to assume that what worked for us will work for someone else. We need to honor the fact that nothing is for everyone. Even if we have the best possible experience with a provider, another person may have a wildly different take. Not because the provider has done anything differently, but because each client has their own unique history, opinions, and needs. I heartily recommend that parents and caregivers share their ideas and advice, but also that each person takes what they need and leaves the rest. We'll talk more about the benefits of respecting each person's unique needs in Chapter 8.

Carpooling: Adding Your Voice to a Larger Cause

As we talked about in Chapter 2, advocating for the greater good can happen on a local, regional, or national level. These road trips require more people, more planning, more resources, and more time. The longer the road trip, the more complex the route. If you're going cross-country, you'll want someone in charge who knows how to get the vehicle safely through the mountain passes!

We tend to get involved with causes that are close to our hearts. I advocate for gifted learners because of my experience advocating for my own gifted kids. What started as advocacy on the companion level sparked my interest in the bigger systems that provide or inhibit services for gifted learners. Now, much of my advocacy work is done in groups of like-minded advocates. We bring in all kinds of experts to support and guide our work – legal experts, lobbying experts, education experts. People join the group or drop off when life gets too busy, but as long as we have people to work together for the cause, the bus keeps going.

Trailblazers: Making Things Better for People Down the Road

We all rely on others who have traveled the road before us. The people who paved dirt roads, built bridges, and drew maps. As parents and caregivers of small children, when we are out and about we ask for highchairs, extra napkins, and kid-friendly food in restaurants, and the businesses can generally supply these items. When our kids are small, we hope someone has paved the advocacy pathway for us when it comes to having changing tables in public places. How wonderful is the family bathroom that makes it easier for caregivers of all genders to change a diaper? We take advantage of the airline's policy of allowing families with children to board early. Families with kids need extra supports and many are available for the asking because others' advocacy has smoothed the way. When we do a kind and careful job of advocacy, we leave a safer and more pleasant path behind us for others to travel.

Even bigger, systemic changes are made through advocacy – things we don't think about much. Have you ever pondered the folks who blasted the tunnel through the mountain so we could drive on a road rather than hike a treacherous trail? How about the folks who realized that letting kids rattle around in the back of a pickup truck wasn't a great idea? Car seat and car safety laws have improved dramatically from the year my older brother was brought home as a newborn, seat-belted into the back seat with only a lap belt (and that lap belt was pretty extra for the 1960s!).

FIGURE 3.4 Buckle up, baby. We've got a looong way to go.

These and more are all systemic changes brought about by advocates with children's safety at heart. This is the advocacy that goes beyond what's good for my child right now. It's about making positive changes for all the kids down the road. The journey may have begun on behalf of one child, but it takes a huge amount of work, persistence, time, and effort to make changes on a larger scale.

Advocating for gifted education may not always feel like trailblazing, but it all leaves a better path for those who follow.

Regardless of whether you are interested in advocating at other levels, your goal is to champion your child until they can be their own best advocate. You model each step of the way. You teach your child how to talk so people will be inclined to listen. You show them how to keep a record of conversations and agreements. You demonstrate how to decide when persistence is futile and it's time to make a change. This young person will talk about their teachers the way you talk about their teachers in front of them (or in the other room when you don't think they are listening). This kid will stick up for themself the way you show them you stick up for yourself and for them. Your child will have to make choices all their life, and you are modeling how to be an active and informed decision maker. Every negotiation you engage in on their behalf is part of the road map you are drawing for their own future advocacy. When you engage in larger-effort advocacy, you are empowering your child to speak up on their own behalf and for others. It's a big responsibility, but you can do this.

◆   Who do you advocate for?
◆   What are some ways you can share your knowledge with a wider audience?

4

The Long and Winding Road (Destination Goals)

Road Rules

GPS: Wherever You Are, That's Where You Start

It's easy to look at people who have been advocating for a while and think, "Why don't I know what they know?" In fact, don't we think this way about all kinds of areas of expertise, all the time? I wish I knew how to do Tai Chi, make beautiful ceramics, and speak Spanish. I could learn any of these things, but I would need to start as a beginner. Sometimes we can transfer skills from one area of our lives to another, like chemists who become bakers, and vice versa. (The most dangerous difference is that bakers need to taste everything along the way, and chemists most definitely should not!) Wherever you are starting, you have a toolkit of skills you've picked up along the way. You are not without resources. Repurpose those tools and add to your kit as you go.

Starting something new can feel intimidating. Uncertainty is uncomfortable. Asking questions is a difficult life skill for many gifted people. When your identity is tied up with being smart and knowing things, the idea of admitting you don't know something feels risky. Sometimes people struggle to admit even to themselves that they don't know something and they just

DOI: 10.4324/9781003467441-5

avoid the topic like the plague it has become. This concept is called *Imposter Syndrome*, and we'll address it in more detail in Chapter 12.

Add Coolant: Don't Panic

One best-practice in gifted education is giving the big picture first and then offering supporting information. It supports whole-to-part thinking, wherein we construct a framework for new learning, like building the chassis of a car. If you start with a radio and a steering wheel, you don't have anywhere to put them, yet. So, we start with the big idea (like we did in Chapter 2 with the overview of gifted education advocacy).

This approach helps our kids understand the purpose and goals of our advocacy. If all they see is that we worry about their math level, they won't understand that the real worry is that they may miss out on opportunities and skill-building that acceleration in math might provide. Things like math competitions, advanced coursework in high school, access to mentors, programs, and content that are only available to the kids who excel in math. Further, we worry that sliding through math and getting passing grades will become their go-to coping mechanism for things they don't find challenging and interesting. We worry they will get stuck in a job they hate because they didn't keep all their options open. We're afraid they'll get taken advantage of if they don't understand compound interest and Unit Circles. We worry. We just worry.

Our kids do plenty of this kind of thinking, themselves. Catastrophizing is a talent that many gifted people share: "If I don't get a good grade, I'll never get into college, I'll have to live in my parents' basement, I'll never get a good job, and I'll die alone like that poor guy who lived under the freeway bridge by the multiplex." Gifted kids have a knack for accelerating from 0 to doom in 3 seconds flat. So do gifted adults.

> **"Gifted kids have a knack for accelerating from 0 to doom in 3 seconds flat. So do gifted adults."**

Big picture thinking can help us see the scope of our fears in a new way and plan accordingly. If your child knows you are advocating for advanced math because you know it's good for their brain to remain challenged and engaged in learning, it takes the conversation away from math and makes it more about working those mental muscles in a way that will serve them all their life. It can also help us, as parents and caregivers, step away from the slippery-slope mentality and into life-skills thinking. I sincerely hope that no one cares what grade you got in 10th grade math at any time after your first year of college. I don't even remember what math class I took in 10th grade, but I use math daily in a dozen different ways, so I'm glad I learned it somewhere.

And that's the other side of big picture thinking – purpose. How many times has your child said, "When will I ever use this?!?" when working on a piece of school work. Take that seriously, and do a quick search for real-world applications. A Unit Circle, for instance, is used in architecture, engineering, digital imaging, geography, and astronomy. And by math educators. Who knew?

I strongly recommend leaving the closing and opening of doors conversation to the schools. They tend to be pretty relentless with that high-pressure-gets-kids-moving type of thinking. If you can counter the panic-inducing messaging that life is a series of opportunities to make doors slam in your unsuspecting face, your child will thank you someday. In reality, there are superhighways and meandering paths, one-way streets and handy alleys, front doors, side doors, back doors, loose boards, chimneys, and windows. The most important things for your child to learn are problem-solving, persistence, flexibility, critical thinking skills, frustration tolerance, a strong work ethic, and positive self-advocacy skills.

When panic is the norm rather than the exception, it's time to seek help. No one should have to live their life in a state of anxiety, and yet too many young people (people of all ages, really) do. The job of school is just a job, not the single determiner of success and happiness in life. School can grow to ominous proportions and take over the family if we don't put it into perspective. Sometimes this requires the help of an objective third party. We'll talk more about finding supporting professionals in Chapter 9.

Prioritize Relationships

A recurring theme in this book is building relationships. When it comes to our children, the first thing we want is a strong, loving relationship with our child. The second is a supportive village to help us raise them.

Your relationship with your child is the most important thing. This is the connection that you protect at all costs. If your child's job of school begins to get in the way of your relationship with your child, take a step back and remember what is most important to you. Your child's wellbeing, self-efficacy, and enjoyment of life.

Creating strong relationships with the other people in your child's life is helpful in so many ways. Having a supportive circle of trusted adults means your child has someone to turn to for help when they can't talk to you. This is especially vital for teens when they are working so hard to establish their identity and independence apart from us but still need reliable help and advice. This doesn't mean that you have to be besties with everyone. We all have relationships that are dependent on a setting or activity.

We have friends and acquaintances at work, in the neighborhood, from college, from our kids' school, etc. The groups may overlap and they may not. The key is to honor each relationship for what it is. Your relationship with your child's teacher is a combination of professional respect and shared caregiving. Your relationship with your child's therapist, physician, occupational therapist, etc. is one of shared care, but you are also in the dual role of advisor and student. You advise on what you know – your child, and they teach what you seek to learn – how to better support your child.

Very often parents and caregivers feel that they are in an oppositional role with some of the adults in their child's life. The struggle with getting your child's needs met in school may bring back some of the battles you fought with teachers when you were a student. Too often, we think in an us-versus-them mentality, especially if school was not our favorite job. In addition, if your requests for accommodations for your child's needs are met with refusals, it's easy to get angry. Or if you get a lot of negative feedback about your child's behavior at school, defensiveness is almost a given. A knee-jerk reaction can make a lasting impression and begin a spiral of negative interactions.

Don't panic if you feel like you've already set a negative tone with one or more adults in your child's life – people appreciate a good apology. I think most people are pretty surprised by a sincere apology, too, and it's a great way to break down barriers to communication. We'll talk about a good apology in Chapter 7. Saying you're sorry doesn't mean you were the only one in the wrong, and it doesn't mean that the problem is solved. It's a great way to get back to a place where communication can happen.

Avoid Power Struggles

You are the safe place for your child, so whenever outside forces begin to threaten that relationship, it's time to reevaluate. You know the phrase, "pick your battles"? This applies to so many things, including parenting. If completing schoolwork or maintaining good grades are not your child's top priority, suddenly educators who have been telling you to let your child figure things out on their own are emailing or calling to involve you. This additional pressure on you to help your child perform at school can be overwhelming and lead to power struggles. Breaking out of this cycle is really hard, so here's advice I wish I'd gotten:

- ◆ School is not the be-all-and-end-all measure of your child's success or potential for future success. Unless success in their chosen career hinges on completing predetermined assignments and scoring well on tests, their future self will likely use a different set of skills than the one they learn in school. Remind your child, and yourself, that school is their current job, not their entire future.
- ◆ Regular school for gifted kids is very much an exercise in frustration tolerance. We all need to learn some of that, for sure, but for many gifted kids, frustration tolerance is the full-time job. Find ways to keep the love of learning alive for your child, even if it doesn't happen during the school day.

◆ Keeping your kids in an educational setting that is a terrible job fit does not guarantee they will learn solid social skills. It may teach them to shut down, act out, or find other things to fill the satisfaction void. A person who hates their job may cross the line from enjoying gaming as a pastime to being addicted to the immediate feedback gaming offers. Others may self-medicate with drugs or alcohol. Still others may lose their interest in working hard toward any goal at all, even if that goal is getting out of (graduating from) their current job. Work with your child to help them make a change *they want* to the way they do school. The change can be big or small, it just has to fall within your constraints of time, money, etc. For your kid, knowing you have their back is a priceless gift.

◆ It's not unusual for kids, especially teens, to resist help from their parents or caregivers. This can turn into a power struggle of epic proportions. Find an objective third party to help out. We'll talk more about finding support in Chapter 9.

Never Advocate Alone

Lawmakers, school boards, school administrators, and educators all have constituents to answer to. Administrators and teachers are not voted into office the way school boards and lawmakers are, but they answer to the parents and caregivers of the children they educate. It's easy to dismiss a single voice asking for change, but it's impossible to ignore an organized group of advocates. This is why we never advocate alone.

In 2016, a public school district told parents and the school board that they planned to eliminate gifted services and shift to a personalized learning model that would ultimately serve the needs of all students, including gifted students. A controversial publication claiming that gifted education was the fast track to educational inequity was making the rounds of the district administration. It's a myth those of us familiar with gifted education have heard repeatedly; however, many parents and gifted educators were alarmed to hear it circulating in their district.

Two public informational meetings were held at the district headquarters, each attracting 150 to 200 parents. There was such visible consternation among parents and educator attendees that a small group of parents started an email list of concerned stakeholders. Through email connections, sign-ups at the school science fairs, and social media, the list quickly grew to approximately 250 names. Parents attended school board meetings, met with specific school board members, developed position statements, and initiated an email campaign.

Under this pressure, key administrators began meeting with parents. Involved parents approached these meetings in the spirit of collaboration, which fostered goodwill and a very productive approach. Parent volunteers, educators, and administrative volunteers were tasked with researching the history and current state of the district's gifted programs. This work resulted in a comprehensive document outlining the district's current state of gifted education and recommendations for future improvements. Any existing gifted programs and models were retained.

In 2024 this district faced serious budget deficits. A parent and an educator involved in the 2016 advocacy effort were both at a student band concert. The parent asked the educator if cutting gifted programs was ever on the list of cuts being discussed. His answer: "It was briefly brought up, but they decided they weren't going to do that again."

(Amy P.)

FIGURE 4.2 Let's Ride

📋 **MILE MARKER**

1 person = A fruitcake
2 people = A fruitcake and a friend
3 people = Troublemakers
5 people = "Let's have a meeting"
10 people = "We'd better listen"
25 people = "Our dear friends"
50 people = A powerful organization.

If you collaborate with other parents and organizations, you can make a difference. There is strength and power in numbers.
(https://www.wrightslaw.com/blog/one-person-is-a-fruitcake-50-people-are-a-powerful-organization/)

Driver Safety

Give Ownership

We all need to engage in the foundation of advocacy – self-advocacy. How did you learn this? Most likely from your parents/caregivers. Perhaps from another role model in your life. Whenever and however you learn it, self-advocacy is one of the most important life tools we have. When we don't have strong self-advocacy skills, we can fall into people-pleasing habits, passive-aggressive behavior, or situations where we might be risking our values, our reputations, or our safety.

When our children have no control over their lives, they will look for ways to exert control or find power. This may look like malicious compliance, underachievement, or rebellion. Or their feelings of powerlessness may turn inward into depression, anxiety, or self-medication. By giving our kids choices, early and often, we help them build their sense of agency and help them learn positive ways to stand up for themselves.

As parents and caregivers, we know how challenging it is to deal with a child's demands. "I want ice cream for dinner, I need a toy every time we go grocery shopping, and I do not need a nap!" These small people may have a lot of rules and requests, and we know that when we allow something once, they think it should be that way forever more. Try allowing a phone or tablet at the table once, and you'll be reminded each and every time you revert to the "no tech during dinner" rule. When it comes to self-advocacy outside the home, we want our kids to stand up for themselves in the big and small ways that matter in the long term. Whether or not you cave in to the grocery store toy demand once in a while matters a lot less than whether you respect your child's right to have some rights.

 MILE MARKER

Gifted Kid's Bill of Rights

You have a right . . .
to know about your giftedness.
to learn something new every day.
to be passionate about your talent area without apologies.
to have an identity beyond your talent area.
to feel good about your accomplishments.
to make mistakes.
to seek guidance in the development of your talent.
to have multiple peer groups and a variety of friends.
to choose which of your talent areas you wish to pursue.
not to be gifted at everything.

(Del Siegle, NAGC President, 2007–2009)

In supporting your child's self-advocacy, you are giving them the tools they need to stand up to peer pressure, report abuse, or, eventually, demand equal pay.

Have Hard Conversations

As a mom of girls, I had difficult talks with my kids about personal safety that parents of boys may not have to have, and vice versa. Parents of black children have conversations about safety that are different from the safety conversations families of white kids need to have. Young people who are LGBTQ+ are often very fearful about that first conversation with a parent or caregiver about being queer. We face different challenges in society depending on what we look like, how we dress, our gender, sexuality, age, ability, disability, economics, language, etc. These differences are more or less pronounced, depending on where we live, work, learn, worship, or socialize. Some folks have a pile of differences between themselves and their community that make their lives more challenging, and some folks have the privilege of suffering less day-to-day strife because they match their surrounding community more closely.

🚌 For 15 years, I served as the coordinator for the local gifted youth program of an international organization I belong to. Initially, I took on this role to find friends for my two profoundly gifted kids. I planned activities with other gifted families, shared resources that they could explore on their own, and provided a setting not just for the children to make friends, but also for their parents to connect with other parents. Networking in this way is very important and helpful for parents of gifted children.

There are many shared challenges faced by parents of gifted youth. But there are also additional challenges some families encounter that others do not. One of these is raising a kid who is both gifted and a member of the LGBTQ+ community. I grew up in that situation myself, and the fact that many families in my group were navigating the gifted/LGBTQ+ combination became apparent to me over the years I led the program.

As my kids' cohort entered adolescence, I felt it was essential that I would be open about my background with other parents in the group, so they would feel comfortable asking me for specific gifted/LGBTQ+ resources and advocacy tips. I had meals and conversations with a number of parents, focused not just on helping them figure out how to support their kids, but also on making sure they understood the need to guide their kids toward self-advocacy. These parents let me know that having a resource they trusted was critical to helping them become the best advocates they could be, which made me feel I was a successful advocate as well.

(Teresa Ryan Manzella)

Self-advocacy is grounded in knowing your intrinsic value as a human, feeling safe and empowered to speak on your own behalf, and understanding the systems in which you live. Sometimes self-advocacy is refusing to stay late at work because it's not safe for you to wait for the bus late at night. It might be calling a safe person and asking them to stay on the phone with you when you get pulled over by the police. A student may refuse to skip lunch to take a make-up test because they know they need to watch their blood sugar. Self-advocacy can be a young person refusing a drink or saying no to a ride with a person who has been drinking.

Self-advocacy doesn't always keep us safe and well. Life happens, and sometimes bad things happen even when we've done our best. And when we can't avoid harm, we need strong self-advocacy skills more than ever to help us recover and heal. If we can say, "I messed up and I want to make amends," that's growth. If we can admit, "I knew better but did it anyway, and now I want to use my story to help others avoid my mistakes," that's taking the step toward advocating for others. If the message is, "I was hurt through no fault of my own and I'm talking about it to help other victims find their voice," we have moved into helping others advocate for themselves. And if we are speaking up as part of a traditionally disenfranchised societal group, we are working to change the world for the better.

Talk About Gifts and Challenges

Parents and caregivers of gifted and 2e kids face the questions of how (or even if) to tell the child about their giftedness or multi-exceptionality. Will knowing they are gifted make them feel superior? Will knowing they have a learning disability make them feel defeated? In my experience, gifted and 2e kids already know they are different from most of their age peers. The asynchrony of being a gifted child is fairly obvious, especially in young kids who may not have learned the questionable art of hiding their giftedness.

> ⚠ Kids who are 2e are certainly harder to identify, since their gifts can mask their struggles and their struggles may mask their giftedness. But they feel different even if they don't look different on paper. If we don't give kids the words to understand their differences, they may just feel like there is something wrong with them, or like they will never fit in.

It is up to each family to decide for themselves how they want to address these differences with their child. I think giving a child the terminology and context of their giftedness and, when applicable, their learning challenges, is empowering. I'm not a fan of giving kids their numbers – IQ scores are a snapshot in time and have a certain amount to do with the assessment used, the experience of the practitioner administering the assessment, and how the kid was feeling on that particular day. Having a number almost screams for comparison with other kids' numbers, like the discussion of what grade you got on the spelling test. That's a slippery slope to "I'm two points smarter than you!" on the playground.

Having an understanding of what giftedness is and what it means, or twice-exceptionality and what that means, is a way for your child to know they are not alone in their experience of the world. It can explain challenges they may have finding friends, or why they prefer talking with adults. It helps make the differences they see between themselves and other students every day understandable and okay. It gives them a way to explain their needs to others.

Many gifted people, girls in particular, learn to hide their giftedness in order to fit in and get along. Many gifted people are never identified at all. Twice-exceptional kids are masters of disguise. Sometimes learning disabilities go undiagnosed until late elementary, middle school or even high school, when they are caught simply because the child's coping mechanisms can no longer keep up with the increased workload. Sometimes 2e kids aren't diagnosed until adulthood because they have mastered the art of masking.

⊟ MILE MARKER

In a desire to help a kid fit into mainstream society, sometimes a kid has been coached so thoroughly that they have successfully learned how to act "neurotypical" in many ways. However, in order to accomplish this, kids have learned to "mask" aspects of their authentic selves, which eventually becomes too heavy of a burden to bear, and can even lead to psychological distress when the teen or young adult eventually realizes the dissonance and no longer wants to pretend to be something they are not. This becomes even more problematic when gifted kids are also twice-exceptional and/or neurodivergent, and have developed many layers of masks to contend with. Our kids are often capable of masking and compensating to a great degree, much more than we realize – but just because they can doesn't mean that they should. Long term, it causes problems.

(Dr. Austina De Bonte, Ed.D.)

Destination Goals

Your Ideal Destination or Theirs?

What are your hopes and dreams for your child? Do you dream of a stellar K-12 pathway, exclusive college, eminence in their career? Or are you more in the midst of the "Let's muscle through K-12 and then see what our options are"? Or possibly survival mode, "One day, one hour, one minute at a time." Wherever you are in your parenting-hopes-and-dreams journey, you can be pretty sure it will go through all of these highs and lows over time.

If you have a child who loves school, adores ticking the boxes, dotting the i's, and planning for ever-greater academic challenges, then your concerns and challenges are different from the folks who have a kid who would rather do anything except school. If your kid loves school, you may still have other fronts on which to advocate, like family challenges, access to enrichments, financial support, health and wellness, etc. If your kid hates school, that battle can feel like it overshadows almost everything else. So let's talk about goals.

Do your goals for your child match your child's goals for themselves? Generally (and I am making a sweeping generalization here), the more invested a parent/caregiver is in a particular path for their child, the less likely it is that the child will continue to feel ownership of that path. A pageant parent, for instance, may want nothing more than the next crown for their child, while the child's priority is pleasing that parent. A student who is gifted in math may enjoy learning and performing in math until it becomes the focus and goal for the family. It can be hard to know where the line is between being encouraging and taking a supporting role, or taking the lead and driving the bus. Gifted kids who find and follow their passions need our support, certainly. No child is born knowing how to find a mentor mathematician or sign up for math competitions. Our kids need our wisdom, experience, and know-how.

Sometimes these talented kids will pursue their goals with single-minded concentration and drag you along in their wake.

Sometimes these passions can be lifelong and the basis for an enriching and eminent career. But more often, kids will change course at least once and maybe a bunch of times. What happens when they are ready to move on and pursue other interests? For parents and caregivers who are more sequential and like a clear, straight road, this can be frustrating to the extreme. You've put all your energy, time, and money into their child's efforts only for that kid to change course? At what point did your child's job become yours? How do you let go of the dream?

The Mirage of Potential

It can be hard to see a prodigious gift go untapped. This is one of the trickiest parts of parenting gifted kids. When the math kid goes to art school, or the musician decides on dentistry, our hopes and dreams need to shift, as well. Relationships can be strained by a constant refrain of "if onlys" or "might have beens." This brings us to that eternal truism of children – they are going to be their very own unique selves, no matter how many dreams and plans we have for them. For gifted people who may never have had their gifts identified or supported, a fresh chance with a child seems like the possibility of old dreams coming true. Carrying on the legacy, or correcting the past that didn't allow you to live up to your own full potential. Especially when that child exhibits gifts that remind you of your own. As hard as it was to reconcile yourself to letting go of your dreams for yourself, how much harder will it be to let them go a second time?

Many parents of bright or gifted kids get caught up in the trappings of success – the grades, the awards, the honor roll, the number of AP classes taken, test scores, etc. There is nothing wrong with celebrating your child's achievements, but be aware of your investment in them. If your child loves to push their own limits and work hard to achieve goals, great. But help them (and you) remember that no one should peak in high school. In twenty years, no one will care about the number of AP credits you had when you started college, and if they do, it's only to compare with their own success. The point of high school is to graduate to the next level. Same with college. Academic success is great, but it's not the be-all-and-end-all goal.

Parents and caregivers of 2e children may struggle with this on more than one level. A child with exceptional gifts and exceptional challenges is a bundle of contradictions. There is a grieving process that needs to happen when your child has that second (or third or fourth) "e." That tricky word, potential, is a fraught one for parents and caregivers. You see the amazing ability, and being gifted yourself, you can also see the possibilities. If only. If only they would put in the work. If only they loved it as much as they love Minecraft. If only they didn't have ADHD, autism, dyslexia, anxiety, etc. Those *if onlys* are as much a trap for you as they are a burden for your child.

If only I could find the energy to finish painting the kitchen. If only my knees didn't hurt, I could spend more time pulling weeds in the garden. If only I didn't have to go to work every day, I could pursue my passion for creating art. The "if onlys" are even worse when they come from outside. "If only you didn't read so much, your house would be tidier." or "If only you'd saved your money instead of traveling, you would be able to afford that private school." "If only you'd disciplined that child, they wouldn't be in trouble now." "If only you had listened to me…" Think about how the *if onlys* make you feel. Can you find a way to let them go for you *and* your child?

So when you talk to your child about their potential, be sure to allow for their being human and having thoughts and goals – goals that may seem silly to others but mean the world to them. Our kids need to know that they don't have to be the best just because they have an amazing ability. If they want to pursue an intense and demanding career in their area of strength, great. If they want to pursue a fulfilling career in another field and also have time to read, travel, and play Minecraft, that's actually pretty cool.

Multipotentiality

People with multipotentiality, or gifts in many areas, may seem like they've won the smarticle lottery. But all of that potential often comes with a steep price. How do you choose whether to pursue a career in physics, follow your calling of teaching high schoolers creative writing, or explore your passion for the stage?

If you can do everything, how do you decide to do anything? Some pursuits are so demanding that even relegating your other choices to hobbies isn't an option. I don't know this first hand, but I imagine eminent physicists probably don't have a ton of time to devote to community theater. Sometimes our multipotential-ites get so stuck in the choices that they can't decide on a path at all. From the outside, that looks like underachievement. On the inside, it feels overwhelming.

Sometimes, these kids leave a trail of unfinished projects in their wake. Your house can become a museum of abandoned interests. You wonder if you should invest in the next interest-du-jour, or if you need to start saying no until the last project is finished. Or your eager athlete tries out one sport after the other until your garage looks like a gear resale shop. Or you've wasted piles of money on classes that were tried once, never to be revis-ited, but your child was *so* convincing when they said they would stick with it this time! Your kid has gotten what they needed out of the experience. Their curiosity is satisfied, they see how things work, and they are ready for the next thing.

If you can change your thinking about this hobby hopping, you will be helping to remove the idea that we can only choose one path, one hobby, one career. Encouraging multipotentiality, especially when it's expressed in the concrete form of projects lit-tering every surface, can feel dangerous, like we are inviting chaos in. Well, chaos is already living in your home. Perhaps instead, you can set some kind boundaries and guidelines around it.

♦ When your child asks to explore a new hobby, see if you can find a trial version, like a free introductory class, a used art kit, a game borrowed from a friend, or a library book.

♦ Talk to your child about the skills they hope to learn from the new hobby and brainstorm ways they can gain those skills without signing up for more than they may be will-ing to do.

♦ Let them earn the money for their new project or class. Working hard for a goal makes it that much sweeter when it's achieved. And if they earn it, you don't need to feel resentment when they set it aside.

♦   Find a way of storing just enough of past hobbies that they can become components of new projects and ideas. If your child designs the system, they will be more likely to use it.

🖥 MILE MARKER

What Is Multipotentiality?

When you were 5, you were asked what you wanted to be when you grew up. You answered something like: a paleontologist-astronaut-dancer-dog trainer. And today? Not much has changed. Except now you want to be a marine biologist-organic farmer-poet-yoga instructor.

You have what is called multipotentiality. Many interests and abilities. An enormous drive to explore, to create, to gobble up new knowledge and skills. The desire to dive deeply into a new project or job, learn all about it, then move on to the next. Because this is not the norm, you may have felt like a misfit. But, in fact, multipotentiality is a strength. It is not a sign of weakness, inability to focus, or irresponsibility. It is a sign of a rainforest mind.

(Paula Prober, 2016)

Finding Their Own Path

Revisiting the parenting truism that our kids are their very own selves no matter what we want them to be – what do you do when your child sets a course that takes them beyond your comfort zone? Do you panic, rejoice, question, forbid, facilitate, or ignore? Do you cycle between these impulses and more?

When our kids are little, we have the final say. If they want to learn how to skateboard, ride a horse, play football, or rock climb, we can say no and offer an alternative. Or we can say yes and determine the safest way forward. As our kids get older, we have less say in their decisions and we need to take a deep breath and let them own their choices. This doesn't mean we aren't there as a mentor and advisor and sometimes safety net, but it does mean they need to discover their own roads.

Part of our job as parents and caregivers is to give our kids opportunities to see what's out there. What are some possible educational pathways? What are interesting jobs and careers that you don't hear about or see very often? We can do our best to give them the skills to navigate new experiences – travel, interviews, managing money, etc. And when they choose something that takes them out of our immediate orbit, we are left to manage our fears and worries. Maybe we even find ways to celebrate our child's independence – it's what we've worked so hard for, after all!

🚐 Growing up in such a creative household I had many many hobbies and special interests. Mom has about every craft in the world at our disposal, and dad fostered my love for technology and video making. When I first started pursuing a career in TV Broadcast, however, neither of them knew what that entailed or what I was getting myself into.

I started working and volunteering at a local community TV station when I was in middle school, working behind the camera. I was at almost every high school football game from 3pm to sometimes past midnight. I regularly worked concerts, graduations, and other events. This enormous time commitment concerned my parents.

I am the youngest daughter, and when I first started asking to go to all of these events the questions that would follow would generally go like this: "How long is it? Where will you be? Are there any girls going?". Let's all be real for a second. TV is a male-dominated field, and this station was no different. The hours are long and sporadic, and locations are wherever the event is. None of these questions were going to be answered in a way they liked.

Being the stubborn kid I was (and still am), I was not going to take no for an answer and so I set about convincing them. I made sure they knew how important it was to me. Gradually I convinced them to let me work more of these events, and although they didn't understand the appeal of broadcast, they understood that this was a non-negotiable for me.

Advocating for yourself can be hard, especially when it's about something other people don't share your intense interest in. It can sometimes go your way, and sometimes not, but self-advocacy is a skill that I still use today while working as a TV truck engineer, a job that I never would have known about if I hadn't advocated for myself all those years ago. My parents might not ever understand what I do, but they understand its importance to me. Trust your kids. You never know where it will lead, but at least you'll get a good story.

(Nora Malueg, TV broadcast engineer)

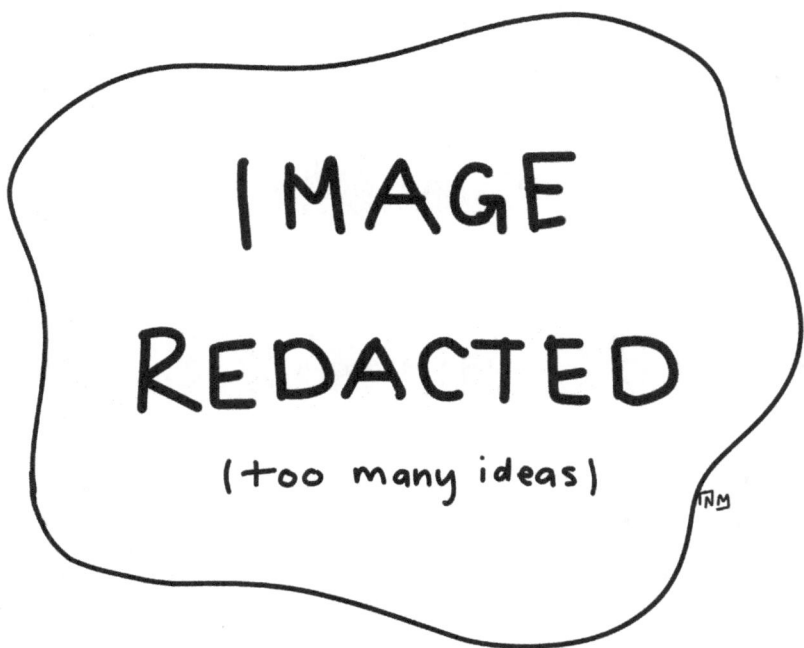

FIGURE 4.10 N/A REDACTED

The rest of this book is about advocating for your child right now. I will reference some of the other advocacy pathways we talked about in Part 1 throughout. For the most part, however, we will leave the big picture of advocacy here and move on to the immediate work of supporting your child through their educational journey – as they learn to become their own best advocate.

- ◆ Who do you envision this child to be when they are an adult?
- ◆ Who does your child want to be? Who are the people they admire, emulate, and follow?

Reference

Prober, Paula. *Your Rainforest Mind: A Guide to the Well-Being of Gifted Adults and Youth*. Editeurs divers USA, 2016.

PART 2

Hitting the Road

5

The Unexpected Fork in the Road

We all expect to advocate for our children. It's part of the job. If you're like me, though, you didn't prepare for the idea that school would not be a great fit for your child. Here are some of the obstacles in your path:

- ♦ You might have to advocate year after year.
- ♦ The traditional K-12 path would be not just a poor fit but also potentially harmful to your child's love of learning.
- ♦ Taking another route would mean encountering seemingly endless obstacles.
- ♦ Rerouting might become the norm, rather than the exception.

Learning that your child is different from their age peers – that the school doesn't have the knowledge, capacity, or willingness to meet your child where they are – comes as a shock to many parents and caregivers of gifted and 2e kids.

It's a heartbreaking realization, and one that sometimes takes years to sink in – this school isn't teaching my child anything except frustration tolerance. My kid is developing coping skills that may or may not serve them well in life. They're sliding through instead of growing a good work ethic. What happens when they encounter something difficult and they don't have the

DOI: 10.4324/9781003467441-7

skills to meet the challenge? Why isn't the system working for my child? Is this all there is? Is it worth it? What do I do now?

This is the fork in the road. The moment you realize you have a decision to make. Help your child change to fit the system or try to change the system to better fit your child? Stay and try to make things better or go somewhere else and hope it works out? Rock the boat or pray for calm waters? Work through the challenges as a family or bring in outside help? So many decisions you didn't think you'd have to make.

This looks different for every family. I've seen families make frequent changes to their child's schooling journey, tinkering endlessly hoping to get things to run more smoothly. I've seen families make a decision by not making a decision, sticking with their first choice of school, reasoning that what doesn't kill you makes you stronger. And, of course, everything in between. If you were to ask my advice (which you kind of are, since you're reading this), I would say that your family's next step depends entirely on what's best for your family right now. Sometimes that's staying put, sometimes it isn't. How was that for frustratingly vague? Don't worry – we'll talk it all through. And if staying put isn't an option for your family, we'll look at alternate routes in greater detail in Chapter 14. Meanwhile, let's think about how we got here, to the fork in the road.

When Did You Come Across Your Fork?

Stroller Days: Preschool

You send your child to the best preschool – the one other parents in your neighborhood rave about. Your child is already reading, but the teacher doesn't have another activity to replace learning all about the letter Aa. Your child creates their own replacement activity – hiding in various, and often really clever, hidey-holes around the school. The teacher is completely overwhelmed, you are called in every other day, and – finally – the director requests that you take your precious and precocious offspring elsewhere.

You wonder if there is a preschool on the planet that can challenge your child enough that they stay engaged in learning rather than exercising their newfound skill of disappearing and causing a ruckus. What if they keep this up throughout their school years?

Toy Car Days: Kindergarten

You move to the neighborhood for the schools, imagining an idyllic school career for your child – taking the bus, making friends in the neighborhood, participating in school and community events. Suddenly it's time to send them to kindergarten. Your child is so excited, ready to learn about the wonders of math, science, and literature. You have mixed feelings – they are so small and this is a big step. You both dive into the new experience.

But school is not what your child was expecting. It's not a magical place that contains all knowledge, like a library and the park and the science museum all in one. It's a lot like preschool or daycare mashed up with the waiting room at the dentist's office. They set off with visions of activity, conversation, and learning, only to find a lot more sitting and lining up and waiting around. The disillusionment is real. They come home perpetually devastated that they didn't get to learn anything new that day, week, month, or year.

> **"**It's a lot like preschool or daycare mashed up with the waiting room at the dentist's office.**"**

That first day of sending a kid off to kindergarten will stick in my head forever. Our oldest getting on the bus all by her little self. Us, racing to the car to follow and take pictures at the school. Me, waiting at home for that bus to bring my little one home. It was no easier with the second, perhaps especially because we opted for early entrance so she was a year younger than the other kids, or perhaps because I just wasn't ready for her to grow up. Fast forward a few years, and getting them out the door to go to school became a daily struggle. The exciting new landscape of learning had turned into the flat plains of boredom and ennui. By the second year of middle school, the miasma of school dread hovered over our mornings and poisoned too many of our evenings.

Bicycle Days: Late Elementary

Your child starts 4th grade and suddenly, or so it seems, things are not going well at all. The teacher is concerned about behavior and attention. Your child has transformed from a cooperative kid into the class clown. The teacher says your child is really funny and smart, but the other kids don't get their jokes. The kids do laugh at their disruptive behavior, like jumping on desks or spilling all the markers everywhere, but it's not winning your kid any friends.

Their best friend, the kid they grew up with, is in another section of 4th grade and has become part of an exclusive clique. They are no longer friends and your kid is not invited to their birthday parties or playdates. You are heartbroken for your child. Your funny, smart, sweet kid who, until this year, had a best friend and didn't need anyone else. You talk to them about showing interest in what the other kids are interested in, but they hate how shallow the other kids' conversations and activities seem. They want their kindred spirit back. They want to talk about big ideas and make up crazy games. Instead, they are acting out at school and feeling oh, so lonely.

Skateboard Days: Middle School

Middle school comes with a mixed dose of dread and hope for the whole family. The 5th-grade teacher assures you that all the kids are well prepared for the transition to middle school, but you still worry. Your child attends the orientation day and comes back with a vague idea of where they need to be and when. They don't know where the Family and Consumer Science (FACS) classroom is, yet, but surely there will be help when they need it.

The school year starts and your sunny, happy kid sullenly refuses to update you about their day, their work, their teachers, or their friends. Everything is "fine" and your child "has it under control." Mornings start really early and it's harder than ever to get out the door. Family/teacher conferences roll around and you discover that your child is consistently 5 minutes late to FACS class because it's on the opposite side of the building from the Earth Sciences classroom. Speaking of Earth Sciences, your child is missing every. single. homework. assignment. so far this year. Coincidentally, this science teacher has their own website and never posts homework or due dates on the school system.

Driver's Ed: High School

High school has loomed like the beacon of opportunity for your gifted child. Finally, finally, they will have choices about their classes, access to Advanced Placement (AP), Honors, College-in-the-schools (CIS), or even an opportunity to take a college class at the community college through the Post-secondary-enrollment-options (PSEO) program. They sign up for a set of classes that will, at long last, offer some challenge.

And then they realize they have no idea how to do this. How to study – they've never had to. How to ask for help – not a part of their toolkit. How to admit they are in over their head – just not going to happen. "Everyone will think I'm an idiot and a loser!" Evenings at home turn into a verbal boxing ring, with everyone either battling it out or retreating to their corners. The school wants you to do something, you want the school to do something, your kid wants to be left alone.

First Car: College

Your high-achieving kid is off to college! Congratulations! Oh, the freedom to be on their own, making their own decisions, do whatever they want whenever they want. They can stay up all night and binge watch shows with their friends. They can skip a class and no one is going to call home to tattle. They can eat cookies for breakfast and not hear the old "feed your brain" nutrition talk for the millionth time. They've never had so much independence and, boy, are they ready!

And then they're back home after their first semester, on probation with the school for failing two classes. With a truckload of dirty laundry. And a huge case of identity crisis. How could this happen? Everyone is surprised, including your child. You wonder if you sent them away too early, or if the school is too far away, or maybe you should have enrolled them in an adulting 101 class before moving them into the dorm. They wonder if they're really as smart as everyone thought they were, if they're just not cut out for higher ed, or if they should just get a job and an emotional support hamster.

So what do we do when school turns out to be a big disappointment or becomes what feels like a major disaster? This is a quandary faced by many families of gifted and 2e kids. So much thought, time, effort, and care goes into getting your little one ready to attend school. And with each milestone comes more expectations. We celebrate with graduation ceremonies from elementary, middle school, and high school. Emphasis is put on every academic milestone in a child's life. So much pressure to fit in and meet societal expectations is applied. The idea that it isn't working for your child can feel like the weight of the world landing squarely on your shoulders.

How the Roads Have Changed: We Managed to Get Through School, Why Can't They?

Think about your own experience of school. Were you a high achiever? If so, what was the secret to your success? If you were not a straight-A student, why do you think that was? Maybe you hated school and did the bare minimum to get by. Or maybe you weren't successful at school at all, and you're wondering if your child is doomed to struggle the way you did. It's funny how many of us forget or store away memories of our own school experiences. What are the things you recall? What are the painful memories you'd rather never think of again?

I know that my own experiences in K-12 education influenced much of my decision-making for my own kids' education. School was not my favorite job until I went to graduate school. My spouse kinda liked school and did very well all the way through, including graduate school. Could we both have benefitted from gifted services or other interventions? Probably. Did we make it through anyway? Yep. Were we pretty fortunate to have few barriers to overcome? Yes, indeed. Did we want better for our kids? Definitely.

What I'm getting at is that we did school, however we did school. Brilliantly or badly, all at once or in fits and starts, with enjoyment or with dread. Some of us had friends, some of us had one friend, and some of us struggled with the pain of isolation. Our experiences color our vision of how school should be for our kids. Your memories transposed onto the current landscape of school might lead you to try to replicate your school journey for your child, or they might influence your decision to take a sharp left and do school completely differently. So how you parent your child through their school career will look different than how I parented my kids through their K-12 and beyond. We all do our best based on what we know, and we learn along the way. What is that quote that Oprah attributes to Maya Angelou? "You did what you knew how to do, and when you knew better, you did better."

You are a big part of the equation of your child's education. Big picture, it might look like this: Parent caregiver choices and values + child's learning needs and preferences + educational options available = child's school experience. All of the factors within each of those big pots affect each other in myriad ways. It's a good reason not to compare forks – they all have a major backstory!

I think some parents spend a lot of time trying desperately to help their quirky kids fit in – buying the right shoes, wearing the right clothes, exposing them to pop culture, coaching their behavior, and so on. Parents may even go to the lengths of refusing advanced academic services at school to keep their kids in the perceived mainstream. This instinct is probably rooted in those parents' own childhood experiences of feeling like an outsider, perhaps being bullied or shunned, or just feeling different from other kids and not really knowing why. They figure if only they had known a little better how to fit in, maybe their own childhood wouldn't have been so lonely or tumultuous, and they hoped for a better outcome for their own children.

I fell victim to this thinking with my own young kids, thinking that lots of early exposure to other kids in daycare and preschool would do the trick. It did not. A much more affirming approach would have been to acknowledge from the beginning that our kids are different – they are outliers. No amount of coaching, cajoling, or buying the right sneakers was going to change that. Instead, honor who your kid is – the strengths and the challenges – and don't ask them to pretend to be something that they are not. Providing a fully safe and secure home includes allowing your kid to be exactly who they are, and providing support and understanding for their quirks and special needs, whether that's avoiding clothing with itchy tags, needing a tap on the shoulder before asking them a question, celebrating their love of bugs, connecting them with other outliers so they can experience authentic friendship, or having extra patience for a never ending stream of questions and opinions.

(Dr. Austina De Bonte, Ed.D.)

Cobblestones to Asphalt: Generational Differences in Parenting

Societal shifts in parenting styles and attitudes have a lot of influence on how we approach the job of school. When I was a kid, school was my job and mine alone. I could ask for help with math homework, but my parents were not about to stay up until 2:00 am helping me finish my diorama for history. Kids didn't change schools unless the family moved. Doing school differently was not unheard of, but certainly less talked about back then.

For my kids, school felt like the family's job. I did stay up until 2:00 am more than a few times to offer moral support and snacks for my last-minute-project-doers. We felt empowered to ask for acceleration or even to change schools. Skepticism about doing school differently still existed, but that "old-school" thinking was countered by the ever-increasing wealth of information parents and caregivers could share through the internet.

How we were raised influences how we raise our kids. It's not unheard of to hear my Mom's words come out of my mouth. Some of her phrases have become seamlessly incorporated into my vernacular, like "You decide, dear" when it came to any decision she felt we needed to take responsibility for. And some, like "smart people don't *get* bored," I carefully eliminated from my parenting toolkit. Though, truly, I can't remember the last time I was bored. That phrase may have shamed me into finding something to occupy my smart brain, but it was effective.

What has changed in the years between our own school experience and our child's? Has the system changed so much? Is our parenting different? Are our kids just more sensitive? We know the world has changed dramatically. Technology that didn't exist when I was in Junior High made the middle school experience much different for my kids. Times have certainly changed from the years my grandmother and her siblings would ride the family mule to school in the next county. You know the old boast, "When I was a kid, I walked to school barefoot. In the snow. Uphill. Both ways!" Well, the privileges and hardships our kids experience are different, but they're just as real as our experiences or those of previous generations.

Much about school feels the same, but the world has changed pretty dramatically. These changes can make for interesting conversations with our kids. Rather than proclaiming that if you could get through school, so can they, maybe examine how things have changed. A little more curiosity and a lot less judgment can open the communication pathways and help you find new ways to approach school for your child.

> "A little more curiosity and a lot less judgment can open the communication pathways and help you find new ways to approach school for your child."

Sharing your stories can help your child feel like they are not striving for a perfection they will never attain. Both of my kids were amused at my tale of Biology woe. I took a C in that high school class rather than dissect a frog. I felt like a conscientious objector in the war on helpless frogs. Looking back, I think I was a squeamish drama queen. Oh, well. I have gotten less delicate in my older age, but I would never voluntarily return to that Biology class!

FIGURE 5.4   Ah fork.

What Kind of Fork Is in Your Road?

Multiple Forks

Every conversation I've ever had with parents and caregivers about siblings includes the absolute wonderment that these kids who are being raised by the same people in the same environment are so very different. This goes for children chosen through adoption, kids with the same gene pool as their siblings, and even twins who share the same genetic code. We could get into a discussion of birth order, parenting style, sibling rivalry, and many more childrearing concerns and schools of thought. For the purposes of advocacy and self-advocacy, however, we can instead talk about how to meet the needs of each child.

- ◆ Appreciate differences and similarities. The question, "Why can't you be more like your sibling?" haunts every child who has ever heard it.
- ◆ Meet each child where they are, even if it doesn't make sense to you or you think they *should* be somewhere else.
- ◆ Don't sacrifice the family for the needs of one child. We'll talk more about this quandary in Chapter 13.
- ◆ Bring in outside help when stress is taking over the family.
- ◆ What works for one child may not work for the other(s) even if it seems like the best thing ever.

When my son was 2 years old, I was first introduced to the concept of a gifted child. I spent a few early years learning if I was an over excited parent or one that legitimately had a concern in terms of finding the right educational environment for my child. Seeking an early childhood educational experience for a gifted child was difficult. I settled on a Montessori experience at first but discovered what they could provide was not "enough." I was able to find a local gifted private school that thankfully with the help of grandparents we could not only fit into our budget but accommodate the logistics. For a few years my son attended this school which was instrumental in his development. They provided him the socialization he needed along with the academic challenges he wanted. It wasn't until 2nd grade that I had to investigate what the right thing was for his needs. I could focus on "achievement" or I could focus on providing a well-rounded education and social environment that allowed him the growth he needed. Advocating for my son was a challenge as many educators and even parents thought I was just a tiger mom, which I am, proudly! But I'm also a parent who values giving my child an educational journey that gives him the best chances to be his best self. My daughter's journey was a little easier upfront because we had a pathway. But adjusting to her educational needs was more challenging because she possessed traits that required additional intervention. Her IQ was the very same as her brother, however, how she learned was entirely different. Advocating and understanding your child's individual learning profile are something that takes patience, support, and trust in your own parenting priorities. Without the support of others we wouldn't be where we are today!

(Jinju Truong)

Comparing Forks: Validate Your Feelings

Some families have big, scary forks in their road – medical crises, mental health struggles, housing or food insecurity. Sometimes people have a forest of forks. You may feel like the difficulties you face parenting a gifted or 2e child should fade into insignificance in the face of the "real" suffering in the world. But knowing others are suffering greater hardships does not make our struggles go away. Knowing things could be worse doesn't erase what's hard right now. It's okay to acknowledge that being gifted or 2e complicates everything, and the further from the socially established norms we are, the trickier the route we travel.

I'm not advising that you sit down in the middle of the road and wallow in self-pity, but I do think that acknowledging your struggles sets a good example for your child. You're teaching them how to meet all the challenges the world will inevitably throw in their path, after all, including the internal ones. Giving some insight into how you cope with your own big emotions helps kids know how to deal with their own.

When you have additional forks, it can feel like all the pathways open to others are blocked for you. It's okay to feel envious of people who seem to have it all figured out. The dangers of social media rear their ugly heads here, though. Most people present the world with the view of open road, clear skies, no forks in sight. Unless you drove a mile on their road, you might not see the potholes and roadblocks they face. For more thoughts on finding additional help with those pesky forks, see Chapter 9.

Moving the Fork Down the Road: Every Decision Leads to More Decisions

One of the things I tell families who are just starting down the road of gifted advocacy is that you make one decision at a time, address the needs and opportunities you see in this moment, and know that next year (or month, or week) will likely bring its own set of new challenges. This is not the message families want to hear. People want a quick and permanent solution to the matter at hand. I get it. When my husband fixes the bathroom faucet, he expects it to stay fixed for a good long while. When we replaced the fridge, we did so with the expectation that we wouldn't have to think about it for years.

Advocating for your gifted child is more like chasing the squirrels out of the plant pots on my patio. It's a regular, ongoing exercise. You try new things, consult more experts. This year, I decided to try, coincidentally enough considering the title of this chapter, placing plastic forks, tines up, in all my patio pots. As far as squirrel deterrents go, this one is pretty good. At least until autumn when their determination to dig overrides their confusion about how to navigate around all the forks.

Some ideas to help you anticipate fresh forks:

◆ Treat each school year like a new project.
◆ Have family discussions about the aspects of school you have some control over and the ones you don't. (Homeschool families will have a different set of factors to take into consideration.)
◆ Plan how you'll help the teacher understand your child better.
◆ Share what works at home (more on sharing shortcuts in Chapter 10).
◆ If that teacher takes a leave of absence, you need to work with the long-term substitute to make sure the agreed-upon accommodations or modifications stay in place. Another reason for the paper trail we'll discuss in Chapter 11.
◆ Then there's next year and a new teacher. You can build on what worked last year or you may make different decisions.

Burnout is a common theme with this kind of never-ending struggle to get your child's needs met within the educational system. You want to find a school that "gets it." A place where your child thrives, feels included, learns how to work hard because they are challenged. It's so disheartening when a program your child loves is cut due to funding issues, or when the administration changes between kids and what worked so well for one kid is a nightmare for the next. We all have some periods of "getting through" in our lives. Sometimes it's because we are low on options, and other times we are simply low on fuel.

There are a number of ways to take a small step back and recharge, and what you choose depends on what your family can do. Can you unschool for a semester? Can you reduce stressors in the current educational setting by dropping a class? Can you eliminate one after-school activity? Not every decision you make needs to be about furthering your child's education. Sometimes the best move is to take something out to allow for breathing room. We'll think more about breathing room options in Chapter 14.

Sporks: When Your Child's Education Needs Its Own Section of the Utensil Drawer

When your child has additional exceptionalities, your fork in the road can be an even bigger conundrum. Like a spork. Where does it fit? How can it be a fork and a spoon? How do we combine special education services and gifted education services? Twice-exceptional kids are the most complex humans among us. They have amazing strengths and big challenges. When you are advocating for your 2e child, all of the factors you take into consideration about making a change are multiplied. What special services can this setting provide? Will we be able to find speech therapy elsewhere, and can we afford it? Will we have access to occupational therapy through the district, or will we have to go private? Can we manage the behaviors at home, or will they disappear when our child isn't so stressed out by all the sensory input of school? Is there a school that will put helping my child grow their strengths first and remediation of their areas of challenge second?

The beauty of advocating for the 2e human is that they require us to think in new ways. Their strengths are shaped by their challenges and vice versa. This makes educating them particularly perplexing. Special education (SPED) educators have a wealth of tools and strategies designed to support all kinds of learning disabilities and differences. Gifted education (GT) specialists have deep knowledge of strength-based practices and acceleration strategies. The two schools of thought have a long history of either/or. Either you are in special ed or you are in gifted ed, but you can't be in both. As we discussed in Chapter 1, times are changing with the increased awareness of 2e. Some of the best interventions, accommodations, and modifications I have seen for 2e learners have come about as a collaboration between SPED and GT experts. Getting them in a room together isn't always easy, but both belong on the 2e child's educational team.

Take advantage of all the tools and resources available to you. Your 2e child may well become an advocacy trailblazer in their own right, but your kid and your family don't need to plow through obstacles that can be removed with existing supports. We'll go into those supports in Chapter 14.

The Fork Less Traveled: Decision Paralysis or Regret Aversion

You know that wonderful poem by Robert Frost, "The Road Not Taken"? It's popularly used as an inspiring metaphor for having courage and going your own way instead of following the crowd. Turns out, this was more of a teasing jibe at Frost's good friend, poet Edward Thomas. The two would take long walks together, talking about all the things. Thomas was an inveterate waffler. He would dither over which road might take them past the unusual bird's nest he saw from a distance the other day. Or he would fret that they were missing something even more interesting if they turned right instead of left. He was this way in all aspects of his life, thinking the grass was greener somewhere, if only he could make the right choice. Frost wrote this poem with his indecisive friend in mind, and was surprised when even Thomas at first misinterpreted it as a call for bravery and independent thought. Frost was known to warn people,"you have to be careful of that one; it's a tricky poem —very tricky" (The Poetry Foundation).

Why am I sharing this story about two poets and one of the most famous poems ever? I think it's charming, first of all, that it was written to describe the feeling of wistfulness and anticipated regret one feels when faced with a choice with no clear outcome. Gifted people have the most amazing capacity to imagine that extraordinary wonders may lie down that other road, or to fear that the wrong choice of path will spell doom for all their hopes and dreams. And, like the common misconceptions about the poem's message, indecision and regret aversion are often interpreted in a variety of ways by others.

> *You:* You're so smart, why can't you get started on this essay?
>
> *Child:* Because I have the world of options open to me and if I choose one, I'm letting go of all of my other fabulous ideas. And what if I choose the wrong topic and can't find good sources and I hate what I'm writing about and I get a bad grade and have to retake 8th grade English? My entire future could be affected by this decision.
>
> *You:* Why can't you just be satisfied with your pasta? It looks delicious.
>
> *Child:* Because I saw a plate with meatballs go by and that was my other choice but I chose this because it's what I always get so it's safe and now I wonder if that dish is better than this one? But the last time I tried a new dish, I hated it and you were upset that I only ate one bite but messed it all up with my fork so no one else could eat it and I never want to go through that again.
>
> *You:* Why can't you stick it out at this college instead of putting in all the work of enrolling in and moving to another one?
>
> *Child:* Because I am struggling here and I hope that the next place will feel better. And I acted like a dweeb in front of everyone in English comp. If I move I'll have a fresh start where no one will know me and I can try to be less of a total nerd and maybe make friends.

Gifted people can see such possibility in each path that leads beyond the fork in the road that it can be utterly paralyzing. Have you ever gotten frustrated when your child/friend/partner/ colleague is struggling with indecision or feeling like they are missing out on the better thing that must have been behind door number 2? Or, like the college freshman in the last example, just wanted a way to erase a rough beginning and start fresh? Have people ever gotten frustrated with you about that same thing?

We encounter many forks in roads over the course of a lifetime. There is no perfect choice, no guarantee of success – only the best choice you know how to make with the information at your disposal. Gather as much information as you can, consult with your trusted pit crew, and then trust your gut instinct.

- How is school different now than it was when you were a kid? What challenges are the same and which are different?
- What advice would you give to a dear friend if they were facing the same fork(s) you are facing?

In Chapter 6, we'll talk about the system of school, and why it may not be flexible. An understanding of the system is helpful when determining which path to take.

Reference

The Poetry Foundation. "Robert Frost: 'The Road Not Taken.'" https://www.poetryfoundation.org/articles/89511/robert-frost-the-road-not-taken.

6

Stuck in the Roundabouts

Why can't every school meet every child's needs? Why do we, as parents and caregivers of gifted and 2e kids, have so much work to do? The difficulties schools face with funding, teacher shortages, limitations of training, archaic textbooks, not to mention the enormous divide between what we know about technology and what the students know – it's no wonder our kids' needs aren't being met. Whose needs *are* being met? Anybody's?

Adopt a Highway: The System of School Is Perpetuated by People Who Liked School

Why does school seem so much the same as when we were kids? Think about the people who do school for a living. Not professional students, like I wanted to be in graduate school – I'm talking about teachers, administrators, and school staff. Not many people go into a career because they hate the system they are returning to. In general, teachers and administrators enjoy the job of school. Most of them probably enjoyed the job of being a student. As kids, they thrived on the schedule, the setting, the satisfaction of crossing the English essay off the homework list. They enjoy people, public speaking, and a chatty break in the teacher lounge. Sure, most teachers I've talked to have stories about how they knew they could do a certain aspect of school

DOI: 10.4324/9781003467441-8

better. That's part of the appeal – make a good job even better for kids like your younger self. But by and large (and yes, I know this is another sweeping generalization), people go back to school for a career because they *like* school.

Because of this phenomenon, school stays pretty much the same over time. Technology has changed dramatically, but the general structure of school doesn't shift very much. Teachers still lecture, kids are still sorted by chronological age, loudspeaker announcements still make half the room jump, the ceiling lights flicker in any room you enter, and the chairs are the same. Exactly the same hard plastic chairs. Those chairs will last forever, apparently. Lunchrooms are noisy, gyms have a perpetual gym odor, and somehow with all the new shoe technology, the squeak of sneakers in the hallways is exactly the same as it was 40 years ago.

Rarely, someone who really hated school goes into a school career. These are our crusaders, our visionaries, our dreamers. They go back to school like they're on a mission. They have strong memories of how school was a poor fit for them and they have big ideas for how to do things differently. These dedicated folks are often welcomed into a school system with open arms. We love the idea of change! We very much want to address the needs of all students! What have you got for us? The reality is that change happens very slowly in large systems, and if everyone isn't on board with new ideas, it's much easier to squash innovation and keep the status quo. Burnout is real for these folks. It's as demoralizing to fight the system as an adult as it is for our kids.

Sometimes they can make a big difference, though, and become a trailblazer. (See Chapter 3 for more on trailblazers.) On rare occasions, these dreamers have the fortitude and wherewithal to create new programs, improve on old programs, or start their very own school. I've seen some of these new schools come and go, and I've seen a few thrive and grow. These tend to be charter schools, which are still subject to many of the guidelines that govern public schools, or private schools, where they have more leeway to do things differently. We'll talk more about school options in Chapter 14.

⊤ **MILE MARKER**

Many inventions and discoveries are derived from conditions of necessity. It was absolutely out of fundamental necessity that I had to find a way to educate my oldest son. Personal and professional exploration led me to establish a school that provides a sense of belonging and educational opportunity for twice-exceptional learners in the state of Minnesota.

Blazing any trail is no walk in the park, and the path is often lined with major resistance and challenges; however, relentless persistence is what it takes to help these students thrive. I encourage educational leaders to continue to understand these complex, gifted, and special learners and to fully embrace what it takes to meet their educational and social needs.

(Leah Brzezinski Ed. D., SLP-CCC, Founder/Executive Director Arete Academy)

What They Didn't Teach in Driver's Ed: Why Teachers May Not Be Able to Meet Our Kids' Needs

The other day one of my daughters and I were driving along and came upon a car stuck in a roundabout. It was up on the sidewalk portion in the middle of the roundabout, stopping and starting, driving around the center that was planted with flowers. The driver was obviously alarmed and confused, and we wondered if this was their first roundabout or if it had just somehow caught them by surprise. We slowed down, as did most everyone else (it was a busy day on a busy road) and eventually they saw their escape and took it without further incident. The rest of us continued on, all probably musing about how that car got stuck in the middle. I wonder how that driver felt about the whole ordeal. Did they decide to practice roundabouts at every opportunity, or were they planning to find alternate routes so as to avoid them?

I hope they decided to practice – roundabouts are popping up everywhere these days, so avoiding them would limit a lot of options for getting around. Those city planning experts have done studies and talked with other experts and think these roundabouts are the best idea. I guess they ease traffic congestion and lessen accidents. I find them hard to get used to, but I've been driving a long time and have had little experience with roundabouts until recent years. They sure were not part of my driver training. The more practice I have, though, the less thoroughly irksome they are.

Let's apply the roundabout idea to teacher training, if you'll humor me. In the U.S., teachers complete a 5-year training program at a college or university in order to earn their teacher licensure. By the time they take the final exams, they are extremely competent and ready to take the wheel. They have taken classes in child development, curriculum delivery, and classroom management. They've had hands-on training in actual classrooms, supervised by actual teachers. Many teachers also earn graduate certificates, Master's degrees, or doctorates. They have additional tools and know-how in their areas of specialty. They are ready to hit the road.

The vast majority of teacher education programs do not provide any instruction on supporting gifted learners in the classroom, though some teachers report having had one hour on gifted education in their required special education class. So when these highly educated folks encounter something out of the ordinary and outside of their training, like a 2e learner or a profoundly gifted child in their classroom, they may get stuck like the driver in the roundabout. Some teachers will see this as an opportunity to seek out information, consult experts, ask a lot of questions, and learn how to differentiate as well as possible for an outlier in the classroom, and some will just keep going around and around, trying to apply the training they have to the new problem.

They all mean well. Teaching isn't one of only two options women can choose from for their career anymore – people of all genders have a world of career and job options that include teaching. Educators have to go through years of education to even qualify for the job. It's not a default job, in other words. That means these people really want to be there, teaching your kid. They may not look as though they want to be there after 5 hours of family/teacher conferences and a long day of teaching, besides, but they had to work pretty hard to get that job. Summers off and a few good breaks in the school year are fabulous, but the sheer intensity of the work while school is in session is exhausting, and mostly thankless. It's helpful to keep the big picture of their job in mind when advocating for your child.

Back to our metaphor. Our friend in the roundabout no doubt had the necessary driver training to handle their vehicle in traffic, and they did manage to extricate themselves from their predicament, but it took them a minute. They couldn't just put the pedal to the metal and get out of there, they had to take all the surrounding factors into consideration. They needed to figure out which exit they were aiming for. They wanted to avoid signs and curbs. They did their best to avoid driving over the flowers in the middle. They had to wait for other drivers to get out of the way. Similarly, how much our teachers can do or are allowed to do within the system to differentiate for one child really depends on many things, some in their control and some not. Let's look at four important factors: time, training, money, and influence.

FIGURE 6.2 I'm tire(d). I don't get paid enough for this.

ⓥ A NOTE ON TIME, TRAINING, MONEY, AND INFLUENCE.

These are high ticket items in the education world, as they are in any large system. They are inextricably intertwined – training takes time and money. Additional time takes money and sometimes more training. Money is always tight. Who has the influence to decide how these resources are allocated?

Time, Training, Money, and Influence

Time

The time factor is a given for all teachers. The school day is scheduled to the last minute, leaving little or no time for side trips. Most of the time teachers spend on exploring new ideas is their own time. I've never met an educator who didn't put in many, many hours beyond their contracted hours. For teachers with kids, aging parents, health issues, or any of a host of other possible obligations, their outside-of-school time will necessarily be limited. Whatever your child's teacher's outside obligations are, you can help by doing a lot of the legwork for them when it comes to finding accommodations or strategies that will work for your child. In Chapter 10, we'll talk a lot about sharing your accumulated knowledge with your child's teacher and how to do that without taking up time they can't easily spare.

During the school day, the time a teacher has for any individual child depends on the composition of the classroom. A teacher with a full class and a wide range of achievement, readiness, behavior challenges, etc., has less time per kid because more time necessarily goes to the most urgent needs first. If you are asking for a 2-minute check-in for your child every day, that only adds up to 10 minutes per week. But if 5 kids need that check-in time, you've got most of an hour, or 1/35, of in-school time spent on check-ins. It's absolutely a valid request, but an overwhelmed teacher could use some additional support from the school.

> Check-ins can happen with an educational aide, the school counselor, the gifted coordinator, or, if your child is 2e and qualifies for special ed services, their case manager. It's good to have a check-in back-up plan in case your child's check-in person is absent or on leave.

There are a number of ways to ease the incredible load on our educators, many of them easy, and most of them free. All of them require buy-in from the school administrators and the other teachers involved. A few common in-school strategies:

◆ **Cluster grouping** – this is the practice of sorting kids by readiness and achievement data into groups. These groups are assigned into classrooms following whichever model the school is using (a great model came out of Purdue University as part of a Javits research project). Teachers can address the needs of their groups much more easily than they can address the full range of achievement and readiness one finds in a typical classroom. This takes more up-front work on the part of the teachers and administrators, but helps streamline instruction the rest of the year.

◆ **Flexible grouping by subject** – by grouping and regrouping according to need, teachers can address one level of readiness at a time, and the child does not have to be placed in the same level for all subjects. This can also work in collaboration with other building teachers – if you have three sections of 3rd grade, each teacher can take a math group during math time comprising kids at the same level from all three classrooms. This model is especially helpful for 2e kids who might have a strength in one subject area and challenges in another. The trick is to align schedules so that each of the 3rd grade classrooms have math, reading, science, etc., at the same time.

◆ **Subject acceleration** – a 2nd grader can go down the hall for 4th grade math, a 6th grader can join the pre-calc high school class online, or the high school junior can head down the road to the community college for advanced science. Subject acceleration works very well for kids who have mastered the content of their current grade in one subject. This takes less work than our other two strategies, but it's more fiddly because it's on a case-by-case basis. Scheduling might involve compromise, like a middle schooler giving up an elective to make time for a high school class.

◆ **Subject acceleration for a group** – like the example below, when a group of parents advocate together, novel solutions can be found.

🚗 After being a part of a new self-contained gifted academy in grades 4 and 5, my son and several other students were 2 years accelerated in math. At our district's middle schools, they did have a course offering for 1 year of accelerated math in grade 8 (Geometry instead of Algebra 1), but they did not have an option for a second year of acceleration (Algebra 2). The option offered for these four or five accelerated students was to be bussed over to the high school after the end of the middle school day to take the Algebra 2.

The main concern with this option is that it prevented these students from participating in any after-school activities, and all of these students had been involved in after-school honor band or at least one sport. The high school had recently begun offering a few zero-hour classes, mostly PE and health offerings, that began before the start of the regular school day. I and other parents were interested in pursuing a zero-hour Honors Algebra 2 offering.

We therefore arranged a meeting with the high school principal to propose this idea. He was interested in trying additional course options and was able to find a math teacher willing to teach the zero-hour Honors Alg 2, and we worked out transportation from the high school back to the middle school with the district (and no first-hour middle-school classes for our kids). We did have to drive our kids to the high school for the class, but we arranged car pools, and the zero-hour Honors Alg 2 option continued after our kids' 8th-grade year.

AH)

Training

In addition to the 5 years of pre-service education (meaning the years of college before they get their license), teachers need regular updates to their education. It's similar to how your physician needs additional education hours throughout their career in order to stay up-to-date on all things medical. Or how you have to update your smartphone every five minutes (slight exaggeration) because it needs the latest and greatest improvements. Because things change so rapidly in education, regular education for the educators is a big part of the job. New ideas about managing behaviors, citizenship, community-building, and more come about through research and design all the time. When schools need to update curriculum, teachers need training on how to use the new stuff. If schools decide on a new behavior accountability plan, teachers need training on implementation. Professional development (PD) on gifted and 2e education can be prioritized if enough stakeholders speak up.

One way to support your child's teachers is to ask that the school prioritize gifted and 2e education in their professional development calendar. Gifted and 2e education may sound like it's not for all teachers, but unless schools are universally screening all children and cluster grouping them in the classrooms, it's highly likely that every teacher will have one or more gifted or 2e students in any random same-age cohort of students. If we are identifying between 5–10% of our student population for gifted services, that's one or two out of every 20 kids.

The process of getting gifted PD on the calendar might be painless or it might be a drawn-out advocacy effort. It depends on who is in charge and how they feel about gifted and 2e education. Sometimes teachers have some say in the PD they feel they need, and sometimes it's decided only by administrators. Schools may have some professional learning topics decided by the district and others by the school, plus any mandatory training topics required by state law. The calendar can be pretty tight, and schools generally can't afford to add more time for PD because time equals money.

Time for PD is carved out of the school year in various ways. If your district has half-days from time to time, those are likely PD days for teachers. Same with short weeks that don't fall on holidays and that whole week before school starts. These professional learning workshops can include all teachers, teachers by grade level, teachers by subject, teachers by interest, etc. They can address state standards, state education laws, new district programs, current school initiatives, or special topics. One district I've worked with creates a menu of options for their teachers to further their knowledge about topics important to them.

When they can, schools will try to provide substitutes so more teachers can attend trainings offered outside of the district. This is a way for teachers to earn Continuing Education (CE) credits. These are the credits they need to renew their licenses. How many and what kind of credits they need depend on their state's Board of Teaching guidelines and their area of specialty. These trainings could be multi-day events, like conferences, or one-day workshops offered by a respected organization, institution, or other provider.

Schools very often send one teacher or staff member to an outside workshop or program to learn new content and bring it back to teach their colleagues. Depending on how your school handles their professional development calendar, you may be able to suggest topics, experts, and other resources. Here is an opportunity for you as an advocate for gifted and 2e kids in your school – find these opportunities in your region or online and let your teacher know about them. Maybe they can be the one to bring new ideas back to their school.

- ◆ Does your state gifted organization offer workshops?
- ◆ Do they host an annual conference?
- ◆ Do you have a university in your area that has a gifted certificate or Master's program, and do they offer opportunities for educators to earn CE credits?
- ◆ Are you aware of a Javits Grant research project in your area? When and where do they share what they've learned and developed?
- ◆ What online opportunities can you find and share? These may be asynchronous – content that can be accessed at any time that participants can complete at their own pace, or synchronous – where content is being delivered at a specific time.

Almost all of these things cost money, whether they are bringing an expert in or sending one or more teachers out to gather new ideas. So, let's talk about money.

Money

In this section, we're not talking about the money we pay teachers which, if you think about the time and training we just talked about, is just not enough. Well, maybe we'll talk about it just a little because, in fact, every teacher I've met spends their own money on things for their classroom, further training, or the school community. All. The. Time. Why is that? Because running a school is not cheap, so often the most basic necessities are cut from the budget with the idea that the community will step up. Have you ever gotten a back-to-school list that asks for tissue boxes, cleaning supplies, and paper in addition to the items your own child will use? Have you ever forgotten to pack a snack for your child and they were given one by the teacher anyway? I see teachers at conferences purchasing books and educational toys with their own money to bring back to their kids and colleagues. How will they access higher-level curriculum for their gifted students? Yes, there are a lot of inexpensive options, both online and in print, but if a family can't afford to provide that for their gifted child, we can't expect a teacher to afford it. This is a school- or district-level conversation about resources.

It's a good idea (but maybe not a fun one unless you are mad for numbers) to keep an eye on the school or district budget and how it is allocated. This is where you can help prioritize gifted services in your district, or perhaps keep services from being discontinued. Attending public hearings about the budget may not be your idea of an exciting night out, but knowing where the money comes from, where it goes, and what changes might be coming gives your requests greater credibility. Remember Amy P.'s story in Chapter 4? That group of parents and caregivers did a lot of work and attended a lot of meetings, and they were able to save their district's gifted services.

In the U.S., a public school's overall budget comes from things like state funding based on student population, federal funding for certain programs, and local funding from property taxes. Additional money can be raised through fundraisers, donations, and fees. If you're curious about your school district, you can find their local, state, and federal funding per student (National Center for Education Statistics) Keep in mind that reporting everything takes time, so most data you find will be a couple of years old.

How districts and schools share their budget varies, but in the U.S. all publicly funded schools are required to be transparent about how that money is spent. It's a hugely complex puzzle with moving parts like new or expired property tax levies, new or discontinued state or federal programs, etc. Schools have to factor in fluctuations in their student population, the age and condition of the buildings, and maybe a thousand other things. You can find out if your state has dedicated funding for gifted services by looking at the National Association for Gifted Children (NAGC)

"State of the States in Gifted Education" (National Association for Gifted Children).

Your funding ask might be as small as a request for supplemental curriculum that was created for gifted students in literature, math, science, philosophy, history, etc. It might be as big as the salary for a gifted coordinator for your school or district. It could be a one-time expense of professional development (PD) about the needs of gifted and 2e learners – any one of the options we talked about in the training section. Whatever you are asking for, knowing where the district stands financially and how much they spend on curriculum or PD will help you frame your request in terms of what's possible.

Another stakeholder group in your school is the parent/caregiver/guardian group that collaborates with teachers on activities, fundraisers, and special projects. Commonly known as Parent Teacher Associations (PTAs) or Parent Teacher Organizations (PTOs), these groups generally have some funds, some influence, and some energy. A request for a shareable classroom set of advanced math curriculum, either print or online, might result in success. These organizations have been known to host speaker events, too, so throw your suggestions into the hat.

If your family is able, maybe offer to give a teacher a subscription to a newsletter, a membership in a gifted organization, admission to a gifted and talented Expo, or registration for a speaker event, workshop, or conference. A great teacher gift might be books, used or new, on gifted and 2e topics (perhaps with tabs placed in relevant chapters and short notes about ideas you think they might like). If these ideas don't fit in the family budget, you can do the same thing with articles printed from the internet or a recommendation to listen to certain minutes of a podcast or TED Talk. See Appendix A for some places to look for helpful, shareable resources.

With any of these ideas, keep in mind that you are working as a collaborative team to support your child. You are offering resources to an educated professional and asking for their professional opinion and feedback. Refrain from overwhelming your child's teacher with too many ideas at once, and never tell them what they *should* be doing. We'll talk about this more in Chapter

10. Teachers know what they can and cannot do better than anyone, whether it has to do with time, money, training, or influence.

Influence

The amount of influence a teacher has over the various aspects of their job varies from school to school, district to district, region to region. Some schools are all about the collegial atmosphere, working together, learning from each other, sharing resources. Other schools are very much a collection of individuals who each have their own stuff, their own ideas, and their own way of doing things. Most fall somewhere in between. Creating a collaborative team can be tricky when there are tensions or territorial tendencies to deal with. We'll talk more in Chapter 9 about the various people you want on your child's educational team, what role they might play, and ideas for getting them on board. Getting to know the power, or influence, structure in your school will help you with this aspect of your advocacy.

An educator's influence tends to increase over time, as seniority and long hours of supporting school initiatives add up. More experienced teachers also mentor newer teachers, so their influence spreads through example as well as reputation. Some parents and caregivers worry that teachers who had their training years ago will be behind the times or slower to embrace new ideas, but I have seen long-time teachers manage the wildly different needs of the kids in their classroom with the ease of a professional juggler. Sometimes the fastest path to making change is enlisting the help of a seasoned and respected teacher who knows how to navigate the time, money, training, influence dynamic through long practice. We'll talk more about characteristics of teachers and helping the school find the best fit for your child in Chapter 10.

⊛ As a stay-at-home parent in the 2000s, I was able to spend a lot of time volunteering in the school as soon as our youngest daughter was old enough to come along with me. She wasted no time making serious headway in creating her fan club comprising every adult in that school. She very much owned the library, and the school media center specialist was her devoted minion. By the time she was 3, she was ready for 3rd grade, so the logical step was to apply for early entrance to kindergarten. I don't know how many of you have thought about sending your 4-year-old to kindergarten, but we heard every imaginable story about how awful it was for some child someone knew somewhere. Luckily, we had found our gifted community where people did things like early entrance and grade-skipping with great success, so we had plenty of positive stories, as well.

It was an amazing year for our youngest. She was placed in the classroom of an older teacher who everyone thought would have no idea what to do with a precocious 4-year-old, and, man, did she prove everyone wrong. Mrs. K was, hands-down, the most accomplished differentiator I have ever seen in action (and I spent 8 years as a researcher observing in hundreds of classrooms). My kid went to reading group with older kids while the other kinders learned their letters, was sent to small-group time with the enrichment specialist, and had all kinds of options every day in the classroom. The other kids didn't bat an eye when my kid had different work or took off for her advanced groups – differentiation was normalized in a way that put no pressure on any kid for having unique needs.

Educators walk the fine line between doing their best to meet the needs of the kids they teach and maintaining a congenial relationship with their colleagues. Making an enemy of one may irreparably damage your relationship with others. I will stress throughout this book that going over your child's teacher's head is a risky move, and one that should be given a great deal of thought and consideration. That teacher is your child's main care and education provider for whatever portion of the day they are in that classroom. Tread with care and protect that relationship. When the change you are asking for is out of your child's teacher's control, make sure they know that you are taking the next step and going to the next level of influence. Parents and caregivers may have more influence in a school or district, especially in an organized group, as we explored in Chapter 4 with Freddie the Fruitcake. Be careful not to throw your child's teacher(s) under the wheels as you go.

🚗 I was sitting at my desk, waiting for another advisory period to start. Since the official advising curriculum had been canned (and rightly so), advisory plans had been kind of a free-for-all. Sure, I had something planned to discuss, but a random adult's discussion topic wasn't topping my students' priority list. When my students walked in, I knew we were scratching today's topic. High school drama and school politics were unfolding, and my classroom had apparently become one of the places my students could talk about such things and have their feelings and concerns respected. But my heart sank when they ended the conversation with, "We know you can't do anything about it, but thank you for listening." I loved that they felt heard, but they were right – my hands were tied. Not that I had planned to rid the world of high school drama or school politics, but there was a disheartening mountain of red tape in the way of my simply advocating for students. How was I supposed to teach them to make meaningful change when we were all in a system that punished the innovation it claimed to develop? Each time my students' dreams were squashed, I understood a little better why so many students hate school.

(Eleanor K.)

Schools are communities, and like all communities, they have their own values, cultures, and hierarchies. Change happens slowly in schools because there are so many layers of decision-making and buy-in. Sudden, sweeping changes are often catastrophic because they are made without an eye to the entire ecosystem of the school. Think about times in your life when you felt the rug was pulled out from under you. As a positive advocate, keeping the whole system in mind is the key to preserving relationships with all but the most hot-headed stakeholders (who probably aren't a great asset to your advocacy efforts, anyway.)

Fixing a Flat: Improving Things for My Child Right Now

What is possible? You may have a wish list of things that could make your child's education work beautifully, but, again, the larger the system, the harder it is to make changes.

- ◆ We want the teacher, school, and/or district to be able to deliver a personalized, challenging, interesting education.
- ◆ We require that our children feel safe and cared for in the classroom and school environment.
- ◆ We hope that they are grouped with like-minded peers to work and play with every day.
- ◆ We need for them to have nutritious food and lots of time for moving their bodies.

◆ We wish for a broad assortment of extracurricular activities and clubs so our kids can have options and learn new things.

Now, imagine going into a classroom or school with that laundry list of items. What teacher or administrator in the world would look at you and say no to any of those things? Truly, their job description is to do their absolute best to provide all of the above with the resources, time, training, and personnel available. Because our kids fall outside the bubble of the bell curve, their different-than-average needs can be challenging to meet in all, or any, of those areas. Just because we see that our children don't get their needs met by what the school can offer doesn't mean the educators and administrators see that. Their focus is and has to be on the many, and often that means doing their best to fit every child into the program, rather than altering the program to fit the child.

If we're lucky, we find someone in the school setting who really sees our child. Who is able to think beyond what needs to happen for all the kids and can find time to think about new solutions for our child.

🚗 I have been an international educator for over thirty years, working with parents, teachers, students, and educational professionals. Although they are all different, they all want one thing. What is best for the children in their care. What I've discovered is that they often fail to do what's best because they fail to take the time to listen to their students to find out what they need.

When asked to remove Fred, a disruptive student from a small class working on what the teacher had identified as a high-interest, strength project, I started by kneeling so I was on his level and asking if he was physically OK, not in pain or feeling sick. He said he was fine so I enquired what the problem was and he told me the project was stupid. I asked if he would come to my office and explain why, and we could discuss what he could do instead. In my office, he shared that they couldn't do the project without an airlock. We discussed how he could create one in our school and he decided he needed the assistance of the Theatre Director, Adrian. This new project enabled Fred to learn how to use a drill, screws, measure space, etc., to build a life-sized reconstruction of an airlock.

Fred was able to explain to his original group what he was doing and a few offered suggestions and volunteered to help him. As this was a student-driven project, Fred and his fellow students often chose to work on it during their breaks and they added light and sound features which were very effective and impressed the parents who were invited to see the students' work.

> So even when you have a great idea for how your students should learn a concept, allowing them to contribute to the acquisition of their learning will extend the level of depth and complexity they will explore, as they tap into their natural curiosity and interests.
>
> (Maria Kennedy)

Change relies on the ability of the people providing education and care for our kids to make change. If the challenges your child is experiencing are systemic – meaning it's not just about the math homework taking up too much family time, but that school as a whole job is just a poor fit – you'll want to develop your vision of what an ideal educational experience might be for your child.

"Your ideal for your child and your child's version of an ideal school experience may be two very different things."

Keep in mind that achieving the *ideal* when it relies on human beings is probably not going to happen. Besides, think on this. Your ideal for your child and your child's version of an ideal school experience may be two very different things. We'll talk about this more in Chapter 12.

It's very likely that the changes you ask for require the skill, talent, time, and permission from multiple people. Implementing your full plan will take at least several steps. So, once you have this vision in mind, work backwards. Start with the first thing. What is the very first step to take in order to make improvements? If your child is learning to hate math, you start with math. If other areas are not working very well but are tolerable, they can wait a minute. Start with the most urgent thing. Really break it down to one step that is possible within the system's constraints, educate your team, make the ask, support the effort, follow up, and then give high praise. Accomplishing this first step gives you an example to stand on while working toward the next step.

If you bring your entire plan to your child's teacher, school, district, etc., they may feel overwhelmed. A simple change a classroom teacher can easily make without additional time, money, or training is one thing; a schedule change, new curriculum, or more people hours is another can of worms. Start with that first step, follow through, follow up, and be sure to express your appreciation for the effort made on your child's behalf. You now have firm footing on that first step and can move on to the next step. Table 6.1 shows a worksheet of a family's challenge and its solution.

 My style of advocacy has been a quiet yet still potent kind that sends a message that change needs to happen, while keeping the positive vibes flowing. As a former educator in the public schools myself, I have learned that the best approach to get educators to listen to your concerns is to first be their supportive ally: before, during, and after your child is their student. I try to make sure that I provide resources and offer to help in ways that the teacher feels are helpful and that might take a load of work off their hands as opposed to making more work for them. When I can't change the system, I have taken it upon myself to provide hybrid home-schooling projects, family "field trips," and activities that revolve around my children's passions and involve them with the community, without relying on the schools to provide. It makes me feel better that at least at home, they are learning at their preferred pace and they are involved in their interests. I then take what my children have accomplished at home and modestly share it with their teachers. By sharing the products that they have created from learning at home, I'm able to skip using demand phrases for the things I wish I could change. I am able to get my point across easier because I have something to show that speaks for itself. It sends the message that my children thrive when they are given opportunities to take their deep dives into their preferred topics. Any creative teacher can link a deep dive into the curriculum, but some may need your help with ideas because they have not done it before. One example: my daughter built an impressive tiny home out of recycled materials and it was accepted on display in an adult art show. I asked our town library to feature her creation in the kids' room and it was such a hit that they decided to display other children's talents as a recurring event. My point is, BE the school's inspiration for change. Show how to get it done. All the other stuff you're concerned about may end up being addressed simply by focusing heavily on their gifts and talents.

(Andrea Brucella Finnegan)

STOP

◆ What prevents your child's teacher, school, or district from providing what your child needs?
◆ What are some ways you can help make a change?

TABLE 6.1 A family challenges and solutions worksheet

The challenge	Possible solutions	Discussion	Evaluation
Em has no friends in class	◆ Move to another classroom ◆ Get Em involved in an after-school activity ◆ Find friends outside of school ◆ Change schools	Em does have a friend in the same school, but in another grade, so even if we changed classrooms, they wouldn't be in class with their friend. They don't seem unhappy having one friend right now, so this is a lower priority. We can start by looking for gifted groups outside of school.	Em attended a Saturday class and already wants to set up playdates with two kids! She likes her teacher and is comfortable in her class, so we will not make a change right now.
Em is beginning to hate math	◆ Ask the teacher is Em can do the hardest problems first and skip the rest of the homework if they score 80% or better ◆ Ask for pre-testing and offer to send in supplementary curriculum for Em to do when they test out of a unit ◆ Look into subject acceleration – send Em to the next class level during math time	Math homework is turning family time into a constant battle. Finding a solution to this is a top priority.	After trying the pre-testing idea, the teacher recommended that Em go to the next grade level for math. So far, so good, but it's still very slow-paced. I think we need to have this conversation again with the new teacher. We expressed appreciation for the flexibility of the teachers and the school. This gives us hope for more being able to make more changes.

The challenge	Possible solutions	Discussion	Evaluation
Em's social studies grade is slipping because Em loses or forgets to turn in the worksheet packet	◆ Ask the teacher if scanned and printed or emailed work is acceptable. Scan the work as each page is completed and print up a fresh packet for the due date. ◆ Ask Em what other ideas might work for their brain. New folder? Make a home copy for a backup? ◆ Ask the teacher to ask Em directly for their packet ◆ Ask if the teacher can share a calendar with due dates listed ◆ Ask if the packet can be turned in up to two days late	Em's only social studies work is giant packets of worksheets that they have to keep track of and turn in when the class is done with the unit. By that time, the packet is a disaster and missing pages, or the whole thing is missing. Everybody is frustrated and Em's grade is suffering. This is a second priority after math.	The first idea takes some commitment on our part to remind and help Em to scan and print the packet, but this might be a quick fix. If we start by making a copy of the packet to keep at home, we can try to help Em get through this next unit while we work on the math thing. We will ask the teacher to support Em with reminders and a grace period and see if Em can email the packet so they don't have to remember to have it in their backpack.
Em forgets to bring their oboe to school	◆ We deliver the oboe when it is forgotten ◆ We ask if we can store the oboe at school ◆ We get a second instrument ◆ We verify the schedule with the teacher and post a calendar with band dates on the front door each month. We can also enter the dates into the calendar app on Em's phone so it reminds them on band mornings. ◆ Em drops band and takes choir	We have been delivering the oboe when Em forgets. Band is every third day, and the schedule changes for holidays and events, so it's really hard to remember. If we store the oboe at the school, we could ask if Em can have practice time there before or after school. We can't afford a second instrument and Em really wants to stay in the band. This is a lower-level priority right now, but we'll keep thinking about it.	We decided to try the calendar option and it has helped a lot. We still deliver the oboe a couple of times a month, but that's a big improvement. Getting the calendar together is a family project, but we hope that over time Em will take over, one step at a time. 1. Put dates in Google calendar (linked to Em's phone) 2. Email teacher to verify schedule 3. Write dates on paper calendar and post on front door

(Cont.)

TABLE 6.1 (Cont.)

The challenge	Possible solutions	Discussion	Evaluation

Em procrastinates on English papers and projects	◆ Ask teacher for weekly check-ins when a larger project/paper is assigned
	◆ Ask teacher to email a rubric and timeline for papers and projects
	◆ Help Em with backwards planning and time estimation
	◆ Help Em do some detective work about English assignments:
	  ◆ email the teacher weekly to check in about current projects
	  ◆ ask a classmate what they think the current work expectations are
	  ◆ ask permission to snap pics of anything written on the board or presented in a slide about current projects.
	◆ Offer to take dictation to help Em get ideas flowing
		Em has been procrastinating on larger assignments in English, saying they don't know what the steps should be, what they should write about, or when things are due. This teacher seems more vague in their expectations and they don't share rubrics or schedules because they like to stay flexible. This makes it hard for Em to plan. The teacher also doesn't post things on the school website, so we can't see what needs to be done.
		
		This is an ongoing struggle. Em does get the work done, but it takes a lot of help from us. This is probably our third priority after math and social studies.
			We've talked with the teacher and they recommended having Em check in with classmates. They didn't really address our requests for more communication from them about assignments, so it feels like we need to do what we can at home.
			We tried scribing for Em on the last paper, and that helped them see all of their ideas typed out. That helped them choose which idea to use for the paper.
			We may do more scribing if Em asks. It's kind of fun to write things down exactly as they say them and then they're like, "I need to edit that – it looks weird!"

The challenge	Possible solutions	Discussion	Evaluation
Science is a repeat of what Em had in another school last year	◆ Ask if Em can pre-test out, unit by unit. The time they buy by testing out can be used on deeper dives into science topics Em wants to learn more about. ◆ Consider subject acceleration in science	Em tested out of the genetics unit and decided to do a deeper dive into genetic mutations. The teacher wants Em to present on this to the class, but Em doesn't have any experience creating and delivering presentations. They are dreading all science work now, and learning has come to a screeching halt.	We talked it over with the science teacher and decided, at Em's suggestion, that Em could create a PowerPoint to share with the teacher only. This will give the teacher something to grade, but not put Em on the spot in front of the whole class.

References

National Association for Gifted Children. "State of the States Report." https://nagc.org/page/state-of-the-states-report.

National Center for Education Statistics. "Public School District Finance Data." https://nces.ed.gov/edfin/search/search_intro.asp.

7

Road Rage

The only problem with knowing our schools, teachers, and administrators are doing their best is that their best isn't good enough if a child's needs aren't being met. A student can't wait for school to catch up – my child is here right now!

Hold On to Your Bridges: Managing Big Feelings

You get to feel all the feelings. The important thing in advocacy, as in life, is what you do with those feelings. If you act on your frustration, worry, or anger, you may well make mistakes and burn bridges. I understand the allure of a bridge conflagration as much as the next person, but I have been traveling these roads long enough to know that sometimes we have to backtrack, circle around, or otherwise revisit some of those bridges. It's way harder to build them anew than to simply walk away the first time.

DOI: 10.4324/9781003467441-9

FIGURE 7.1   No trolls were harmed in the burning of this bridge...

Bridge metaphor aside, we'll use this chapter to talk about how to handle our frustration. We'll talk about problems and disagreements. We'll ponder that it might be possible to leave a classroom, school, or district with relationships mostly intact. We'll keep in mind that everything we do is showing our kids how to live their lives. We'll talk about the power of a good apology. The skills we'll talk about in this chapter can apply to many aspects of life – jobs, moves, friendships, and more.

> The first time I realized I needed to be a positive, rather than confrontational, advocate is when the gym teacher lost my kindergartener. She came home that day and told us she had extra recess by accident. Turns out, the gym teacher had neglected to make sure he had all the kids in tow at the end of recess, and my kid was left outside. For an hour. Now, I could have told the teacher that when she was busy she may not pay attention to a generic whistle. She had never been summoned by a whistle during years of utterly individualized attention at home and in her small preschool. I had assumed that the educators I entrusted with her wellbeing 7 hours a day would understand this! I was ready to get that teacher fired, sue the school, and homeschool forever. My husband advised that I first call my mom and dad, both educators, who helped me cool my jets. Our kid was fine, loved having extra recess with

the big kids, and the school was taking steps to encourage teachers to be more careful about misplacing children. I swallowed my parental ire and graciously accepted a very ungracious apology from the gym teacher. It saved our good relationship with the school. Instead of being labeled "that mom," I was a welcome helper. Instead of being "that mom's kid," my child could shine as her wonderful self.

It's okay to feel your feelings. That's something we tell our kids – you get to feel how you feel, what matters is how you act upon those feelings. Like when the gym teacher lost my kindergartener – I was practically spitting fire. How dare that teacher (a) lose my child for an hour, and (b) act like it was no big deal. If I had acted without cooling down and consulting with my spouse and parents, I would have burned a bridge or three that day. Instead, I took some time, talked things over, made a plan, and then approached the principal and the teacher again. Happily, in this situation I wasn't the one who needed to apologize for my actions. The teacher was, and he sure could have used a lesson in a good apology.

Baggage on Board: Taking Responsibility for Our Words and Actions

Gifted and 2e people are generally a little (or a lot) quirky. We may have intense emotions, heightened sensory input, or a wild imagination. We're probably passionate about topics that interest us, and some of us have a really bizarre sense of humor. We know a lot of information about a lot of things and can get frustrated when others can't keep up. Many of us have been the odd egg in random groups of people our entire lives. Maybe the odd egg even still, unless you've been lucky enough to find others with whom you can be comfortable being your amazing and unusual self.

It's pretty common for gifted and 2e people to have a long track record of being misunderstood. Also not unheard of for gifted and 2e people to read far more into others' motivations than might actually be there. When you can imagine *all* the possibilities of why a person is behaving the way they are, it's sometimes hard to land on what's *most likely*. And we remember everything. So in this relatively small slice of the general population, we will certainly find a lot of folks with a lot of baggage. We'll talk about managing our feelings in this chapter, and more about handling others' feelings in Chapter 8.

Dealing with our own baggage, or our feelings about a tense situation, is our responsibility. If I have a track record of pushing folks away or zapping out an angry response to the same kinds of input, it never hurts to do a little introspection. If one or two people are hard to work with or seem to challenge me at every turn, it might be them. If one kind of setting regularly causes me anxiety or stress, the setting may be the culprit. But if the same thing happens with many people in many settings, it just may be me.

One 2e parent of a 2e child once said to me, "I am a symptom of the problem with the school/organization/program, not the problem." I thought (but did not say) that if you have difficulty everywhere you go and others are *not* having those difficulties, perhaps you *are* the problem. Maybe you're unpacking your same luggage in each new setting. Teapot goes here. Favorite pillow over there. Tendency to lash out when told "no" goes next to the bookcase. Maybe instead of placing your jumbo-size bottle of defensiveness in the middle of the kitchen table, try a different approach. Lighten your load and leave assumptions and pessimism on the side of the road. Much easier said than done, right?

The path from incident to anger gets shorter if we make that our default response in similar situations. We are leaving out that process in the middle that helps us evaluate others' intent. Are they really trying to ruin my child's love of learning math? Are they stuck in a roundabout and have no idea what to do differently, but maybe I can help? Or, do they know that it's possible to do the subject acceleration we are requesting but their plate is overloaded and this falls below 17 other things on their priority list, so it will probably not happen this year? If your default is to assume malicious intent, you lose your ability to connect, compromise, and communicate. Sometimes, a person *is* just being a jerk. But that doesn't justify leaping to that conclusion in every case.

Unfortunately (or maybe *very* fortunately) we'll never understand the inner workings of other people to the point where we can immediately see and understand their every motivation and response. We're just too complicated for that. Which brings me to one of the truisms of life that I resent with all my being – you can't change other people, even when you really, really want to. I could have talked for three days straight to that "symptom" parent and made not one iota of difference in their perception of the issues they'd been having everywhere. They needed to figure it out and do that work for themselves. Or not. It's not up to me.

As with everything, the only person we can change is us. So if family, colleagues, partners, and others push your buttons on a regular basis, how do you want to deal with it? We can have the same responses time after time, or find new ways to handle things.

How Do You Manage Your Baggage?

◆ Think about the past experiences that might be behind some of your more visceral responses.

◆ Examine the usefulness of your knee-jerk responses – have they worked in the past? Do they work now?

◆ Find new ways to handle some of your pet peeves. This takes intention and practice and maybe some help – it's not an overnight transformation.

◆ Explore the possible motivations behind another's words or actions. Could you be reading too much into things because of your own personal history? Might they have a different take?

◆ Approach with curiosity instead of getting defensive or immediately going on the offense. In calmer moments, practice possible questions you might ask.

◆ Can your default setting be changed to an expectation that most people are doing their best?

◆ Can your practice be to meet each new situation and person with fresh eyes?

> ⊙ Ponder how you react to criticism. What tone of voice really puts you on edge? What phrasing raises your blood pressure? When do you reach the point where all negotiations are off the table? Sometimes we employ these very tones and phrasings when we are pushed to the limits of our self-control. Our own hot buttons become our weapons of destruction.

Potholes: Watch Your Reactions

Why is this important in advocacy? Because, as we talked about above, feelings can rule us in the most unexpected ways. We each have a history that informs how we react in various situations. It's part of what makes all of us humans so darned unpredictable. It's like driving along and suddenly hitting a pothole disguised as a puddle. What's your first reaction? Resignation? Dismay? Anger? You might even yell a few choice words. Potholes are no fun. They can cause damage. After that first reaction, what's your next step? You might take action to protect yourself and others from the pothole by calling the city to request a work order. You might feel an obligation to publicly warn others about the dangers of potholes and write a letter to the editor of your local paper. Maybe you take your car to the neighborhood mechanic to reassure yourself there isn't lasting damage. You could simply want to vent your spleen and post a diatribe on the neighborhood conversation board. On the other hand, you might just forget about it and go on your way. Maybe mention the pothole to your family over dinner, maybe not.

Let's use potholes as our metaphor for the many real or perceived slights we encounter in our dealings with other people. Everyone has their own history with family, friends, colleagues, and acquaintances. We all remember insults and other hurts we've encountered on this bumpy road of life. Some of us are championship-worthy grudge holders, others are highly competent under-the-rug-sweepers. One person prefers talking things out directly and another prefers to talk about the situation with anyone and everyone else. We all have our preferences, habits, and styles when it comes to communicating (or not) about having our feelings hurt. A common thread is that we all have an initial reaction, like after hitting the pothole, and then we have the opportunity to take further action or no action at all.

In positive self-advocacy, we take action when

1. We've had a chance to cool down.
2. There is something constructive that can be done.
3. Speaking up will help us feel better.
4. We can help others.
5. We are not causing additional harm to ourselves or others.
6. We can approach the problem in a way that makes us feel good about ourselves and sets a good example for our kids.

Sometimes it's really hard to take action. A young woman working in a male-dominated field might worry that calling out a colleague for using disrespectful language could have repercussions that would make her job even harder. A student might worry that asking the teacher to avoid directing sarcastic comments at them could result in teasing from classmates. A younger sibling who tattles that the older sib is still teasing with that awful nickname may find themselves on the receiving end of the dreaded sibling silent treatment for a week. And there are times when it doesn't do any good to take action. An elderly person with dementia may have lost all their filters and say the darndest things about you or other people. Admonishing them isn't helpful in the least.

Find a Rest Stop: Take Some Time to Cool Down

In the heat of the moment, it can be hard to prioritize relationships, so it may help to come up with a key phrase that helps you pause and remember not to burn those bridges. I try to ask myself the question, "What is important here?"

🚗 "What would Dad say?" My Dad was a wise and patient human who always took his time before speaking or acting, especially when emotions were running high. I sometimes wonder what he was like as a young kid or a teenager – was he always so thoughtful? Were his responses always measured and fair? Certainly not. I know he was blessed with an even temperament, according to his mom, my Grammy, but I also know they had the usual power struggles. Grammy showed him how to stand up for himself and others, taught him how to consider both sides of an issue. By the time I arrived, he was in his thirties and had the dual art of ratiocination and diplomacy pretty well down. I try (and do not always succeed) to follow his example and slow down when things get stressful.

It's too easy to make an error, and maybe an enemy, when you respond too quickly to a difficult situation. There are very few things that can't wait for cooler heads to prevail.

⊚ SOME IDEAS FOR GETTING THROUGH THE DANGEROUS STRETCH OF ROAD RAGE

- ◆ Sleep on it. It'll still be there tomorrow and you can look at it with fresh eyes. Exhaustion makes everything worse, always. Take care of your basic needs before taking action.
- ◆ Talk it over with a trusted, calm, objective human. Of course, you should talk about issues that concern your child with your parenting partner(s) but you also need someone who is not in the thick of parenting with you to give you some perspective.
- ◆ Write that email, but don't send it. (And for Pete's sake, don't put their email address in the "to" line. Have you ever accidentally hit "send"?) Read it again tomorrow as though you were receiving it. Write it again. Do this several times until you have worked out all the emotions driving you. You may wind up not sending it at all!
- ◆ Trust your gut. Sometimes a friend or partner can encourage an advocacy action that seems right when they're with you but feels wrong when you reflect on it later. It's another form of peer pressure, and another reason to take your time.
- ◆ Put yourself in the other person's shoes. If you were on the receiving end of the email, voicemail, or face-to-face confrontation, how would you feel? Would you be eager for further communication with that person?

Destination Goals: Prioritize

The phrase, "What is important here?" is helpful to me because it reminds me to think about the bigger picture. Am I more concerned with being right, or with preserving the relationship? Do I want to make my feelings known more than I want to help others see a new way of approaching my child's education? It is so hard, especially in these days of speaking up and speaking out, to let a perceived insult or slight go unchallenged.

The phrase, "bite your tongue" may seem old-fashioned and against the current outspoken norm, but taking a beat before having your say gives you more control over the situation. Responding in kind to an insult or slight doesn't help your cause – just proves that you are reactive and emotional. If you react with restraint and dignity, it takes the truth and the sting out of the dismissive behavior. It's kind of a magic trick, and it takes practice.

When it comes to your kid's well-being, that's a different story. You can't politely walk away when your child is being bullied or denied recess. Firm action is needed if you think your child is in harm's way. Your approach will set the tone, however, so even when emotions are running hot, take a moment to consider your strategy.

> **Your child comes home and tells you they had an argument with a mean kid**. The teacher is keeping both kids in from recess for a week. You need to find out more. You have one person's side of things, and we know from literature and psychology that one side is not a complete picture. So instead of rushing in with judgment and anger, you try curiosity. Not that you don't believe your kid – you just need to do your detective work before leaping to conclusions.
>
> **Your teen tells you their Science teacher hates them**. They're going to get a bad grade because the teacher won't let them retake the test or make up for work they missed when they were sick. You know by now that every teacher has their own set of rules for retakes or missed work (some of them much more rigid or convoluted than seems necessary, from your perspective). But if this poor grade means your child can't participate in the university summer science program they've been looking forward to, you need to investigate a little further.

Collect your data. Study the participants. Ask all the questions. Make sure your child feels heard. Let them know you are taking them seriously. If the issue is bullying, you can keep them home while you get to the bottom of things. You are making sure they are safe while you take a minute or a day to plan your next move. If it's a grade issue, make a meeting and do *your* homework. Show up with specific questions, not accusations. Your child is learning from how you handle this. No pressure. Okay, lots of pressure, so take. your. time.

My biggest experience of advocacy regret is from my youngest's 8th grade year. Middle school is a tough time for most kids, and my kids were not exempt from that generalization. Both of my kids attended a full-time school-within-a-school gifted program, but the administration changed between kids and chose to institute new, super-strict rules about maintaining a B- or better in all classes in order to stay in the program. So, in the last year (8th grade) of the program my kid was in since 2nd grade, her grade slipped below the threshold in one class one trimester. We talked with the program's middle school admin, who assured us she would talk with the teacher and help my daughter get her grade up. I trusted that with this help the hard work my kid was doing would pay off. Two months later, we got the letter. Our daughter was being exited.

I was so conflicted. As a professional in the field of gifted education, did I want to fight this verdict and possibly ruin relationships? Yes. Yes, I did. But I took well-meaning advice from family and friends and… didn't. My kid moved to honors classes in the same school (which were honestly more interesting and fun) but lost her friend group and gained 12 bullies. It was devastating. She was unfairly judged and no longer had any kind of support system in that school. I lost my friend group of parents from that program, too. Shocking how fickle even the adults were, as though my daughter's grade of C in Social Studies could be catching! Ugh, still makes me mad. The worst part is that even though it was better my daughter didn't stay in a program that valued its kids so little, this had major lasting effects on her and impacted her high school experience, as well. I should have fought the decision. I should have spoken up.

WHAT'S IMPORTANT HERE?

◆ Is my child safe in this setting? If so, you have time to decide what changes to ask for. Take that time and consult with your parenting partner(s) and the rest of your team (teacher, support staff at the school, therapist, coach, occupational therapist, physician, etc.).

- Is my child not safe? If not, you need to pull them out immediately to keep them safe while you decide what to do. Tell the school, "We are very concerned about a particular classmate's bullying behavior toward our child. We are taking two days off of school to talk with our team of experts and as a family. Can we meet on Friday?"
- Is speaking up just my way of getting the last word in? If I want to interject my two cents just so everyone knows exactly why, in detail, I am pulling my child from a classroom or school, it might not be worth it. Ask yourself if it's helpful or spiteful. If it starts with "For the record...," consider letting it go unsaid.
- If I don't speak up, how will this affect my child's sense of safety and wellbeing? As in my example of advocacy regret, not speaking up was the easy road rather than the right road. Ask yourself who might be helped if you speak up – if it will help your child, that difficult conversation will be worth the discomfort.

🚗 To be frank, it has been arduous to advocate for my gifted son in the public school system from the very beginning. For kindergarten, I entered him into Spanish immersion, with the assumption that acquiring a new language would challenge him. He was placed in second grade math, although no other accommodations were coordinated. The second grade and kindergarten teacher were impressed by his intellect and quick language acquisition, albeit sometimes his precociousness was strenuous to accommodate. However, the administrator at this school rudely insisted we change schools because it was "a challenge to challenge him." The gifted and talented coordinator there assisted us in choosing a new school in the district in which services were more abundant. Unfortunately, the new school also did not have enough staff or resources to thoroughly nurture him. These two gifted and talented educators were exceptionally helpful and supportive, but lacked the ability to help adequately stimulate him consistently with the limited resources they were allocated by the district. While in the traditional classroom, he would be separated from his peers for not being engaged by the content which was remedial for him. He felt isolated and undesirable. It broke my heart that he was being excluded for being exceptional. Teachers would call me, frustrated, expecting his emotional and social maturity to match his intellect. When I tried to explain this common asynchronous development for children like him, they just expected me to be able to make him behave. I put him in counseling after thinking maybe I was wrong in my conclusions, to subsequently be substantiated by the counselor. As the spirited parent of a spirited and gifted child, it's been a tough and emotional journey just to provide the best education for him, which is all any parent wants and deserves.

(Kristina G.)

Turning the Car Around: Perfect a Good Apology

Sometimes, in the heat of the moment, we say the wrong thing. We hit the pothole and reacted badly. And now we need to mend that bridge. The hardest part about apologizing is recognizing and admitting your own culpability in the situation. Even if someone else is wrong and has made a mistake, you are responsible for your action or reaction. Just because someone else is more wrong, or wrong first, it doesn't mean you are suddenly right.

For instance, say a teacher made an example of your child in front of the class for not paying attention. Your child is devastated and embarrassed and doesn't want to go back to school. You visit the school and call the teacher an idiot in front of the principal and several of the teacher's colleagues (don't worry, I know you would *never* – this is just for the sake of the scenario). Are you, in your righteous indignation, justified in embarrassing another human in public? Even though they embarrassed your child in public? Of course not. Should the teacher apologize, too? Yes, indeed. But even if they never do, you can feel great about taking the high road and apologizing for what *you* did – lashing out in anger.

That teacher might have learned their unfortunate "make an example" strategy from an old-school professor or mentor teacher. They might think it's an effective, time-tested tool for classroom management. They might feel that you are questioning their professional knowledge and experience. If called out in such a way, they might never be able to see where they went wrong because they're too focused on how they were wronged by you. Communication is at a standstill. But when you apologize for your words and actions, you show them the way. You give them an opportunity to follow your lead and try to make amends. They may not take that opportunity, and that's on them. You did your part.

How will your child learn to take responsibility for themselves and their words and actions? From you and how you take responsibility for your actions and reactions. If you mess up and act rashly out of your anger or hurt, you have some uncomfortable work to do to try to set things right. If you *don't* own up to your actions and work to make amends, think about what example you are setting. Have courage and teach your kid how you do the right thing, no matter how difficult it may be to face your own mistakes.

◆ When you make a mistake, talk about how it makes you feel and what you might do to make it better. Or how you might avoid that mistake in the future.

◆ Some things in adult lives aren't meant for kids' ears, but many of our mistakes can be thought through and resolved out loud.

◆ The more you own and demonstrate how you try to live by your ethical code, the more tools you give your child to do the same.

◆ Keep the 'but' out of it. If you try to justify your actions by blaming others, it's not a true apology. Remember the old childhood excuse, "But they started it!" It still doesn't matter who started it – if you did the wrong thing, that's on you.

◆ Don't worry that you're not perfect – who is? Just show how you try to do your best. It's hard sometimes, and it will be hard for your child sometimes, too. That's life. And all we can do is our best.

A good apology is like a K turn. It's an important skill and one that deserves some practice. You've gone down the wrong road and need to turn things around. There's no easy way to turn the car around, so you engage in the always tricky and awkward-feeling K turn. You worry that other people will see you in the midst of the maneuver and judge you for getting yourself into this position. Your mistake has cost you some time and you feel a bit chagrined. But you know what to do, you're taking care of it, and you're back on track.

⦿ GIVE A GOOD APOLOGY

1. **Be specific about what you did wrong** – "I'm embarrassed that I used harsh words in my recent email. I was feeling frustrated and worried because Dee really struggles getting through their writing assignments and I took my frustration out on you."

2. **Acknowledge how it affected the other person** –"I know you have a stressful job and lots of kids in your class, and I'm sure my angry email added to your stress."

3. **Say the key words like you mean them** – "I'm sorry."

4. **State how you will handle things differently in the future** – "I'll cool down and think things through from now on before hitting *send.*"

Now, add your advocacy:

5. **Find something to admire and let them know what they're doing right** – "It's great that you post grades so quickly – it lets us know there is a problem to solve sooner than later."

6. **Ask again for what your child needs** – "Can we revisit the idea of giving Dee extra time on these writing projects? Or is it possible they can do a couple of them as oral reports? The writing really stresses them out."

7. **Ask for their professional input** – "We'd love some advice on how to better support Dee on this."

Keep it brief. Manage your expectations. Remember teachers are only human, too.

Drive On By: Walk Away When You Need To

There will be times when you just can't work with a person, school, district, job, etc., and it's okay to back away. Strategic retreat is an important skill. And even when you really, really want to throw that last, perfect barb as you walk away, remember that your history follows you, and when you're advocating on behalf of your child, it follows them, too. You are your child's first and most impactful role model. Do you want them to perfect the mic drop or the gracious exit? Envision the fierce vindication of burning that bridge, and then… let it go.

When leaving a school situation entirely is the best option for your family, it can feel like a huge relief or a major failure. You may celebrate the new possibilities or resent the wasted time and effort you put into trying to make things work. It's normal to feel all kinds of contradictory ways about deciding to make a change. You don't make these decisions lightly, and nothing about this is easy. We'll talk more about alternative pathways in Chapter 11.

Whether you are moving your child to a new school, trying an online program, or opting for homeschool, you have some choices to make:

- ◆ How will you explain your choices to others? This can be different when talking with extended family, close friends, neighbors, or acquaintances.
- ◆ How will you talk about the setting you are leaving?
- ◆ Can you let go of your resentment?
- ◆ What are the important lessons from this experience that your family can use going forward?

When things just didn't work out the way you wish they had, it can be tempting to vent your frustration and share your feelings with the wider world, thus expanding your audience. An overshare in the heat of the crisis can have serious consequences for your reputation and that of your child, and it definitely does not fall under the umbrella of positive advocacy. Negativity can close down communication pathways with people you still want to connect with, as well, and we'll talk about how that might happen and how to avoid it in Chapter 8.

8

Mind the Signals

In this chapter, we will talk about how we communicate with the other drivers and passengers on our advocacy roadways. We'll talk about how to handle interactions with other folks who don't respect the rules of the road. And, finally, we'll look at the most common roadblocks to communication in advocacy and how to get beyond them.

⌐ MILE MARKER

Children learn about communication and relationships in three primary ways: first, by how parents interact with them; second, from observing parents as they interact with others; and third, from their own interactions with others.

(Webb et al., 2007)

Positive advocates with good communication skills become trusted partners, welcome collaborators, and respected mentors for the next generation of advocates. Some communication basics of positive advocacy:

- ♦ Listening to learn, not listening to find points to argue.
- ♦ Sharing ideas in a respectful way – this sets the tone for future conversations.
- ♦ Building on others' ideas. Like the rule of improvisation, collaboration goes best with the "yes, and" approach.

DOI: 10.4324/9781003467441-10

◆ Including people with multiple points of view and respecting those points of view, even if they don't match your own.

Sharing the Road: How Do We Communicate with Others?

Horns Blaring: Aggressive Communication

Some people prepare for advocacy like they're preparing for battle. They arm themselves with knowledge and prepare to yell down their opponents. A change may well happen, but the willingness on both sides to partner in maintaining and improving upon any changes may not happen. The loudest voices may prevail, but they may leave a lasting barrier to further communication and collaboration. I recommend that you avoid this type of advocacy unless you're after a one-time change that will never have to be revisited. I can't think of an example in gifted education where yelling has been an effective tool.

Has anyone ever yelled at you at work? By yelling, I mean talking *at* you until you no longer attempted to get a word in? Browbeating you until they felt they'd won because you gave in or you walked away? Did you suddenly feel as though that person had the right idea and you wanted to do things their way? Probably not. More likely, you were hurt, angry, or afraid. Maybe you became determined not to help them, or decided to actively oppose their purpose in some way.

Using verbal force to intimidate might work in the short term. Lots of people will go out of their way to avoid being yelled at. But long term, the methods people use to avoid your yelling might mean they are working against you or avoiding working with you at all.

In its milder form, talking at you can look like someone who waits impatiently for you to be done speaking so they can continue their own train of thought. They aren't listening so they can respond to your contributions, but are instead planning their next volley. The conversation may go back and forth, but true communication is lost and compromise is impossible.

- As always, think about the modeling you are doing. Is this how you want your child to handle playground disputes or differences of opinion with siblings?
- Is this how you envision them sticking up for you when you are elderly and it's their turn to advocate for you?

Right of Way: Active Listening

You don't need me to tell you that active listening is, by far, the most effective communication style for positive advocacy. This is taking turns, listening carefully, responding to what was said, etc. and so on. Even when presenting an idea to a group or individual, leaving time and space for questions and input helps engage the listener much more than just being talked at. I think the ever-increasing number of podcasts is a wonderful illustration of this idea. People love a conversation, a give and take.

When you're talking *with* someone, instead of *at* them, you are showing respect for them as a participant in the work at hand. In an asynchronous college course, you have miles of content to read, watch or listen to, but then you have the questions. Here is where you get to participate in your learning. Hopefully (and this is for all you professors out there), you get to give and receive feedback on your thinking. A dynamic discussion board can make the difference between a lackluster credit-earning experience or a fascinating, shared learning journey.

In advocacy, we listen. A lot. We ask questions all the time. We adjust our requests as we expand our knowledge. We invite questions, and, through answering, learn more about what we still need to learn. We admit when we don't know something, and then we set out to learn more.

You know those people who, when it's their turn to respond in a group conversation or Q&A, can take you through in order, point by point, and add their ideas to the previous speaker's? I always admire people who can do this in their head. I tend to get so absorbed in each point as it comes along that I'm caught up in generating new ideas, making connections, formulating questions. When it's my turn I have to go backwards through the points, like I'm following a trail of breadcrumbs, and sometimes I'll miss one and remember my ideas long after the conversation is over. If you struggle with keeping track of what you want to say when it's your turn, try jotting down one or two-word notes as ideas and responses come into your head.

The asking questions part of advocacy is very hard for many gifted people. Admitting we don't know something feels like lighting up a sign that says, "I'm not as smart as you think I am!" More on Imposter Syndrome in Chapter 12. It's humbling to admit you don't know something, but it's also freeing. Once you start asking questions, you can ask *all* the questions. Once you let go of the feeling you *should* know a thing, you can find someone who *does* know that thing and ask them.

I've participated in many workshops, presentations, and meetings over the years. Once I decided I didn't mind showing that I don't know everything, I started to get the most interesting comments from my fellow participants. "I'm so glad you asked that question – I was feeling so stupid for not knowing the acronyms" or, "I was writing it down so I could look it up later – thanks for saving me a step." One person even told me, "I was going to go to my grave never knowing what they meant by superstimulabilities. They were just talking about Dabrowski's Overexcitabilities – why didn't they say that the first time? Thank you for asking that question!"

Indicator Lights: Non-Verbal Communication

If you've ever attended one of my workshops, you've seen my little one-woman skit. I set the scene by telling you to imagine I'm your doctor. I come into the room, holding my clipboard, looking very concerned, glancing at the clipboard, looking at you, but saying nothing. I ask, "What are you, the patient, thinking right now?" The answers range from "I'm very sick" to "I'm gonna die."

We reset the scene. I'm your teacher. I enter the same way, same clipboard, same concerned expression. I look at the clipboard, look at you. I say nothing. After a moment, I ask what you, the student, are thinking. Answers range from "I'm failing this class" to "My parents are going to kill me."

A third time with me playing your parent or caregiver. Participants worry, "Mom is so disappointed in me – what did I do?!?" or "I am going to be grounded for life."

The first response to my concerned expression is one of dread. What's wrong? What did I do? What did I not do? If you've ever been in a situation like this (and I think we all have) your imagination takes over and rational thought takes the back seat. It's super hard to hear what's coming next when you are in panic mode. Gifted people tend to catastrophize skillfully and often – leaping to the worst conclusions could be considered a common trait of giftedness.

FIGURE 8.4 Eh. What's the worst that could happen?

The moral of this story is that our non-verbal communication is incredibly impactful. If you listen with a deep frown on your face, do people tend to think you're displeased with what they are sharing? If you are looking out the window while in a face-to-face meeting, do folks wonder if you're paying attention? If your nose itches and you wrinkle it to avoid having to itch your nose in public, do people think you're sneering at their ideas?

Do all these things in the mirror or with a trusted friend and see what you think. Then practice an expression I like to call *pleasant neutral*. Pleasant neutral is a resting expression that is comfortable, sustainable, and helps you look interested and/or approachable. It takes practice, but once mastered, it can help you avoid the misunderstandings your unchecked non-verbal expressions can cause.

At the Drive-Through: Second-Hand Communication

I love an occasional fancy-schmancy coffee drink. What I struggle with are those darn speakers. I've been known to avoid coffee shops with notoriously bad speakers, because what is more frustrating than getting mocha and coconut when you want oat milk and hazelnut?

I can sense you wondering about the point of my little coffee complaint. The point is, when we have physical barriers between us and the person we are communicating with, misunderstandings can happen. Much content can be lost when people can't see us talk and monitor our non-verbal cues. This doesn't just happen with drive-throughs. It happens in virtual meetings when folks don't have their cameras on. It happens in email all the time. Any time there isn't a facial expression to go with the words.

You know those wonderful emojis we use in text messages and other messaging applications? Those were created to help bridge the divide between our words and our meaning. These tend to be frowned on in professional communications, however, so it helps to take care when sending an email to people from your collaborative team. Reread as though you were receiving the email and adjust according to how you think others might perceive your tone. It can be helpful to have someone else look over your email before you hit "send."

"Won't be at the family/teacher conferences." Can be interpreted several ways:

1. Do they think these conferences are not worth their time?
2. Do they expect me to change my schedule for them?
3. Is something going on and they need some flexibility?

You don't need to add your life story here (more on brevity in Chapter 10) but a little explanation could avoid speculation.

"We won't be at family/teacher conferences tomorrow because we have a sick dog. Can we check in another time?"

⚠ Social cues, or "signals" for the purpose of our theme, are a huge part of our lives as members of a community. Sometimes people have a neurological difference, like autism, that makes reading and responding to social cues in a "typical" way difficult or even impossible. Trying to make neurodivergent people fit into a neurotypical world only leads to frustration for everyone. It sends the harmful message that they need to change themselves in order to participate in the world. Instead, giving people with neurological differences a range of communication tools to employ in a variety of situations empowers folks to choose how they want to engage with others. It doesn't imply wrongness, it embraces differences.

Kids (and adults) have an instinctive need to belong. Being an outsider for reasons way beyond a person's control is overwhelming and can lead to additional layers of behavior that cause even more tension and ostracization. There is no easy solution here, but meeting people, especially kids, where they are is the first step. Teaching social skills in a non-judgemental way makes more sense than trying endlessly to make someone feel a way they just don't feel. And why don't we teach a more inclusive set of social rules to everyone? "Here are some useful tools to help you navigate these situations. What are some skills *others* can learn to respond to *your* preferred way of interacting?"

 WHAT KIND OF A COMMUNICATOR ARE YOU?

What are some non-verbal cues you might be giving unintentionally? (Has your child ever said "Stop yelling at me!" when you never raised your voice? Mine sure did, and, boy, were my non-verbals yelling!)

Difficult Drivers: People You Wish Would Follow the Rules

Defensive Drivers: People with Big Feelings

This is the flip side of the baggage conversation in Chapter 7. Yes, we need to deal with our own big feelings, but we also want to be aware that others have them, too. And theirs will be different from ours, so this section is about that old cliché – treat others the way you want to be treated. You're setting an example with your actions.

You have no idea that I'm a sucker for a sob story and tear up at the slightest provocation until you know. If that happens during an advocacy meeting, people tend to be pretty cool with it.

An empathetic response is much more palatable than an angry or dismissive response, but it seems like an oversized response to people who don't feel as emotionally invested in everything. You don't know what's going to turn me into a watering pot, and, honestly, I don't expect you to.

Some folks expect a lot more from others when it comes to navigating their big feelings. Trigger warnings abound, and are a nice way to help intense folks decide if they want to engage with the content. I've worked with many people over the years, in trainings, workshops, and collaborative teams, and I have learned a lot about the need to be careful with gestures, phrases, and examples. Gifted and 2e people tend to be intense, and it behooves us to take a little care. Below are just a few examples of potential problems.

We've all met people who can't stand being corrected, but we don't know that about them until we offer our knowledge. Their defensive words or actions can leave us a bit stunned at first. We can't know if we are the 10th person to correct them on something today, if they have a terrible case of Imposter Syndrome, or if this is what they consider a normal response. We might worry that we said the wrong thing or hurt their feelings. Or we might dismiss it with a throwaway comment that absolves us of any responsibility. "You must have gotten up on the wrong side of the bed" or, worse, "You must be hormonal."

The reverse is true – that some people like to offer their knowledge even when the situation doesn't call for it. One of my personal pet peeves is the phrase, "The thing you need to understand here is…" Over the years, I have learned to modulate my response to one of tolerance or humor, rather than anger at what I perceive as condescension. My knee-jerk internal reaction might be, "how dare you tell me what I need to understand!" but my outward response these days will more likely be along the lines of, "You explained that beautifully. Nice work! I would add…"

Or what about the "I know you well enough to jokingly call you out on your endearing quirks" quandary? Sometimes those seemingly humorous and caring call-outs are felt as attacks by someone who has a history of being called out for those same quirks in a negative way. We have no way of knowing what landmines we may be stepping on. This happens in families all the time. A hated nickname based on a physical characteristic, like "Short stuff" for a vertically challenged person. A characteristic or behavior named after you – "You are such a Carol for crying in that movie!" A jokey comment from a long-shared history, "That's our Carol for you! She always cries in movies!"

We may think our comments come from a place of recognition and closeness, but they may make the object of the comment feel picked on or disrespected. Think about your words, your tone, and your intention.

♦ Is there potential for misunderstanding?
♦ Is it personal, like calling out a physical or personality characteristic?
♦ Have they asked you to stop teasing?
♦ Has anyone told you they don't think it's kind or funny?

If you answer yes to any of these questions, maybe keep that comment in your head and find another way to communicate that isn't so fraught with potential harm. When you make a misstep, and we all do, remember the benefits of a good apology (see Chapter 7).

My Way or the Highway: People who Disregard Social Norms

In this day and age, we come across philosophical differences every day and everywhere. Our society comprises every kind of quirk, inclination, belief system, and bias. The very purpose and nature of American democracy are to allow for differences, as long as they don't infringe on someone else's right to life, liberty, and the pursuit of happiness. Why am I going all Hollywood (big picture) with this concept? Because it comes up in advocacy all. the. time.

A family that believes (and teaches young Bee) that there are no bad words will meet resistance when a 2nd grader comes home to their slightly more foul-language-cautious family with some impactful new expletives, courtesy of Bee. Whose "rights" are more important here? Bee's family's right to exercise their freedom of speech, or the other parents' and caregivers' expectations that a school should discourage the use of offensive language around young children?

Cee's family might disdain certain of society's mythologies, leading Cee to share the scoop on Santa and the Easter Bunny. Cee's classmates' families may well resent this. Imagine being the poor teacher who has to field the questions and tears of the students and angry emails from families! What do you tell distraught parents and caregivers who wanted to hold on to their child's suspension of disbelief a little while longer?

And let's think about the adults who never learned the fine art of filtering. Cee and Bee all grown up, perhaps. Do you know a parent who screams at the Little League coach or umpire as though their decisions were of life-or-death importance? That one who is so certain that the rules of the game are more important than letting a mistake go because the kids are just learning? How do we support their dedication and energy without allowing their unharnessed intensity ruin baseball?

Or the passionate advocate who truly believes that a voice must be raised to be heard. This person has strong convictions about how to change things for the greater good, but they have very little in the way of collaborative communication skills. How do we admire their knowledge and persistence without allowing them to undermine the larger advocacy efforts?

Some ideas for dealing with filterless folks:

◆ When it's your child's classmate that has no filter, it's best to let the teacher handle the problem. Confrontation between parents rarely goes according to plan. A teacher or administrator will have the gravity of their professional opinion to add to the conversation.
◆ As mentioned before (and I'll mention it again), we can't change other people, so helping your child learn how to cope with challenging people is your priority.
◆ Try role-playing scenarios in which your child tells the teacher, walks away, or puts on headphones and picks up a book.

◆ Find books or episodes of kid-friendly TV shows that deal with the topic of bad language/Santa/etc. and use these to help you have these conversations with your child.

◆ If you find yourself devastated that someone would allow their child to ruin a family tradition, talk with other parents and caregivers and see how they handled these things. You might find ways to help change the holiday magic from *believing* in Santa to *being* a Santa for others, for instance.

◆ While we'd prefer to avoid others' less-than-optimal behavior, you can always make it a learning moment. Have a conversation with your child from a point of curiosity rather than judgment:

◆ I wonder why they felt so strongly about the rules?

◆ What would you do if you were really mad that you thought someone would break the rules?

◆ What would you like me to say in that case?

Even more importantly, how do we change course if we are the ones behaving badly? You can cry "This is just the way I am!" until the cows come home, but it won't make anything better for anyone, including you. If your actions are consistently setting you up for conflict with others, you're putting up barriers to communication left and right.

"We all get to think our thoughts inside our heads. We can indulge in an internal eye-roll without showing any outward signs of judgment, disbelief, or outrage. We can imagine saying the most perfect set-down, or indulging in a well-timed gesture. Give yourself points every time you think it and don't say it."

We all get to think our thoughts inside our heads. We can indulge in an internal eye-roll without showing any outward signs of judgment, disbelief, or outrage. We can imagine saying the most perfect set-down, or indulging in a well-timed gesture. Give yourself points every time you think it and don't say it. Like everything, this takes practice. But imagine how much easier things will be the next time you attend a game if you don't have a reputation for being a hothead.

Teaching our kids the editing process that happens between the impulse and the action is a huge part of parenting. We work endlessly on the "no biting" and "no hitting" rules. Even Cee's and Bee's families work on those, I'm sure, because there are serious consequences to them if they don't. Wouldn't it be grand if they worked on the same process, but for speaking one's mind? Again, it's a matter of modeling. If you're a yeller, your child is learning from an expert. If you think before you speak, that's the skill your child is learning.

 I was trying to come up with a way to describe this issue of people doing what they want or taking what they need with no regard for others. The internet, in its weirdly intimate wisdom, placed a picture and a quote in my Facebook feed. The image is a neatly sliced pumpkin pie with a pie-slice-shaped hole off-centered in the middle. That missing piece took a chunk, large or small, out of all the remaining, orderly slices. The quote was something to the effect of, even though you have just as much right to your share of the pie as the next guy, the way you take it makes a difference. Or to paraphrase Wheaton's Law, don't be a jerk.

STOP

- Have you ever spoken up about a nickname or tease aimed at you? If not, what do you wish you'd said?
- How do you help your child cope with teasing?

Road Hazards: Barriers to Communication

Check Your Filter: Think About What You Put Out There
Think about what you are sharing with the world, especially when it comes to your child's life and experiences. The advent of social media makes this a bigger deal than ever, though the parental overshare has always been a thing – it just used to

happen in grocery aisles and church basements rather than on Facebook or Instagram.

When our kids are small, they don't have the means to set boundaries around parental sharing, but ponder their reaction in 10 or 15 years when the stories or photos you post now are still out there on the internet and in people's memories. Will this be a fun reminder or a big embarrassment? Will your overshare impact their lives positively or negatively? I will admit that I find internet shares of little kids doing and saying funny things entertaining, but sometimes I wonder if that cute little kid doing the Macarena for the millionth time appreciates that his parent or caregiver made him into an internet sensation? Has it impacted his life in any way, for better or worse?

Cute videos and pictures are one thing, but test scores, educational achievement data, or diagnoses of additional exceptionalities might best be kept between you and your child's educational team. You are not wrong to seek out additional input and advice. Try to find ways of asking for information without creating a different kind of data trail for your child to deal with as a teen and adult. We'll talk more about what, how, and when to share in Chapter 11.

🎡 When your child is old enough to understand the pros and cons of sharing information with others, be sure to include them in the process. When I started writing this book, I talked things over with my now-adult kids and made sure they were cool with me sharing some stories about them. Both agreed that this was fine as long as they had veto and editing power over anything about them. No problem. How can I write a book on advocacy and self-advocacy if I don't give my own children a chance to sign off on any stories that include them?

A few months later, I was ready to put out a general call to my various groups and communities for advocacy stories to include in the book. I wrote down a few stories from my days of advocating for my children that I could show as an example for anyone interested in sharing their story. I was on the verge of sending them out when it occurred to me that I had forgotten to get the kids' okay. What a close call! I immediately messaged them and sent the stories along that I was considering sharing. Both kids had great insights and wanted a few changes before the stories were shared. But if I hadn't remembered, I might have dented the trust they had in me to check with them first. I share this story because it's easy to forget that our stories don't belong only to us.

Moving Violations: Don't Make Your Problem Everyone's Problem

Social media can be a wonderful way to share resources, but it comes with some pitfalls. It can be a great place to get a lot of ideas when you're stuck, but it also opens the conversation to negativity. In the spirit of positive advocacy, here are some ideas to avoid falling into the negativity trap:

A parent posts a question about a book they are thinking of purchasing. Several people chime in with great things to say, but one or two advise against it. If you are on the "no" side of this equation, instead of "I wouldn't bother with that book," try phrasing like this: "I found these two similar resources to be very helpful, and here's why."

A caregiver asks about a type of therapy. Some are all for it, with great experiences to share. Others, not so much. It can be tempting to offer your critique of the provider or the therapy model as a whole, especially if it wasn't a great experience. But instead of "That is the worst therapy/therapist – don't do it," try, "Our family tried several things, and we found this other type of therapy to be most helpful for us. Here's how it helped in our situation."

A family is seeking advice about a school they are considering. They toured and left with a good impression, but want to hear from others. Most don't have any experience with that school, a couple have good experiences, but one has a friend of a friend who had a terrible experience. Instead of bashing the school with "Don't go there – my friend's kid hated it so much they had stomach aches every day," perhaps say, "A family I know found it a poor fit for their child's particular needs, but they found a better fit at this other school." This will be most helpful if you know (and have permission to share) what the particular needs were that were not met at that school. Better yet, instead of jumping in with the friend-of-a-friend's experience, you can offer to connect them with the friend-of-a-friend so they can get the first-hand story.

Why bother to edit your bad review? Because if the family chooses that book, that therapy, or that school, they will remember your negativity about it and maybe hesitate to share with you that they went with that option. It can block any further open communication. Or, if they take your advice to avoid a particular book, therapy, or school, they might be missing out on something that would be a wonderful fit for their family's needs.

You know when you are purchasing a new gadget online, like a food chopper, and you read all the reviews? The most useful are the ones that tell you, in detail and with pictures, how it worked for them. The reviews that say, "terrible, doesn't work right, one star" are vastly less helpful than the ones that say "chops cucumber and radishes really well, but makes a mush of berries and melon. 3 stars because I only got it for berries and melon." If you needed a food chopper for cucumber and radish but only saw the first review, you might have missed out on something great.

You know the phrase, "don't yuck my yum"? For another completely off-topic example, my husband loves broccoli and I think it's an evil alien lifeform whose sole purpose on this planet is to plague me. When our kids were small, I ate broccoli with a smile pasted on my face so I wouldn't turn the kids off a nutrient-rich veg. One kid loves the stuff and the other despises those little green trees. Now that they're adults, I never feel the need to suffer broccoli again, but I'm glad I didn't yuck that yum for my veg-loving kid.

> "Helping others through positive advocacy doesn't include bashing things that didn't work for you or someone you know. It's about helping everyone understand their options and empowering them to make their own choices."

Helping others through positive advocacy doesn't include bashing things that didn't work for you or someone you know. It's about helping everyone understand their options and empowering them to make their own choices. Your role is to educate and support. If you pass judgment or assign value, you shut down communication pathways. You get to feel however you feel, of course, but providing more neutral feedback saves hurt feelings and future recriminations.

Working well with others is the heart of positive advocacy. When we have a care for the people we interact with, they are more likely to have a care for us and our children. As Dr. Jim Webb always said, "Communication is the key to relationships" and building relationships is the key to making positive change.

♦ What are some barriers to communication you've experienced?
♦ How would you rewrite the script for the last time someone gave a negative review on something you love?

Reference

Webb, J. et al. *A Parent's Guide to Gifted Children.* Great Potential Press, 2007.

PART 3

Road Rules

9

Enlist a Good Pit Crew

The journey from preschool to college/trade school/career can present a tricky route to navigate when you are the parent of a gifted or twice-exceptional child. It can feel like a lonely, overwhelming, endless job, but you don't have to go it alone. A collaborative network including your student, parenting/caregiving peers and partners, educators, and other practicing professionals makes the journey far less treacherous and much more rewarding.

> You know your child best, and if you want your gifted child to have a successful school education, you will almost certainly need to advocate for him. One of the best approaches to advocacy is to create a collaborative education plan with the school for your gifted child that will allow him to get the best possible stimulation, curriculum enhancement, and intellectual growth possible at school.
>
> (Karen Rogers, 2002)

Don't Travel Alone: A Network of Helpers Makes Your Load Lighter

If you feel like you should be able to do it all on your own, please think again. Raising a child *should* take a village. You need people who have lived experience with all the complexities along the

DOI: 10.4324/9781003467441-12

long road of parenting, from feeding and negotiating bedtime to talking about drugs and sex. You need adults to talk with to remind you that you are still an interesting person in your own right, not just the provider of snacks and finder of socks. You need backup in case you get sick or just need a break. You need backups for your backups because life is just chaotic that way.

When your child is gifted, you also need people who understand how different your parenting journey is going to always be. When your child is 2e, you need an even more specialized group of people to support you as you raise this amazing and asynchronous human. The more complex needs your child has, the more support you need. For more discussion on *asynchrony*, see Chapter 12.

Villages are hard to find or create in these days of far-flung families, but creating this network is part of the work of caregiving. When you feel ashamed that you can't do it alone (because somehow we all have the idea we should be able to *manage* everything all by ourselves), remember what you are teaching your child. Do you want them to be able to reach out, create a support network, have a safety net? Or do you want them to put on a brave front and struggle on the inside because they don't, and never will, have all the answers all the time?

If you want your child to be able to create and nurture supportive connections with others, show them how. As you build relationships and grow your network, you will be delegating some of the work of educating and caring for your child. You'll share what you know and you'll learn from others. Your child, at the heart of it all, should be included so that they will learn how, eventually, to do this for themselves.

Who's in the Car? The People You May Want to Include in Your Collaborative Team

Your Child: It's Your Child's Journey, After All

It can be hard to include your child in the decision-making process. Many educators prefer to have parent-teacher conferences without the child present. I tend to consider that a red flag. If your child is in a traditional learning establishment, either in person or online, school is your child's full-time job. (Homeschool families have more flexibility and less time-consuming crowd management to deal with, so schooling may be a part-time job though learning is still a full-time endeavor. More on homeschooling in Chapter 14.) It follows that your child should be involved in all aspects of managing their job to the extent that they are able. I don't mean handing the reins to the kid and stepping back – I really do mean that you include them in your advocacy work, which includes teacher meetings and conferences. It's silly to meet with other adults and decide things for a child who then has only one choice – go along with it or fight against it.

> 🚌 My advocacy story holds both positive and negative elements. It's about one of my daughters. We were attempting to understand the intense and perplexing behaviors that arose when she was 10 years old (ultimately identified in relation to giftedness, Tourette's Syndrome, and autism, et al.). There is no manual for these kinds of experiences. We were relentlessly attempting to meet with a panoply of medical professionals in order to understand what our kid was experiencing so we could ultimately provide her with support.
>
> As we navigated this path, patterns emerged. When we met with these professionals (typically including our daughter), they would always address me and her mom directly. Specifically, most would speak with us using a direct, engaged body stance as well as making full eye contact. They rarely connected with our kid – physically or verbally – even though the entire point of these meetings was her experience. It felt as though she were being treated as an object to be fixed, rather than as a human being. This frustrated me profoundly.
>
> I felt it was inappropriate during these initial meetings to confront these professionals in order to express what I sensed my daughter was also feeling: objectified and an item to be processed … a checkmark on some task list. Instead, I discovered this tactic: Whenever a professional addressed her mom or me with a question, I would briefly reply (if at all) and then turn to and directly address our kid. I'd say something like: "Felicia, this is a question about what you are experiencing. Tell about what you think." I did this more times than I would have liked. Yet, I believe it gave our daughter a sense that at least someone was attempting to see and hear her.
>
> (Eric L.)

For some families, school has become such a source of anxiety that your child shuts down or acts out. In this case, it's hard for caregivers and educators to see how involving them in the meetings could be helpful. A young person who is burned out on school may not be open to much in the way of constructive criticism or additional support. Accommodations or modifications may feel like:

◆ More work (enrichment *after* regular work feels like punishment to many kids)
◆ Yucky work (remediation work is often much less suited to their strengths or interests)
◆ Boring work (imagine having to relearn content you already know, day after day)
◆ Confusing work (independent projects for gifted kids are often *too* independent. Gifted kids need scaffolding and support, too.)
◆ Missing out (missing free-reading time to do harder math doesn't feel fair)
◆ Proof that they aren't as smart as everyone thought they were (imposter syndrome is often a result of needing help)
◆ Embarrassment (anything that calls them out as different in front of their classmates)

You may have a rough time getting a burned-out student to agree to any accommodations at all. This can be incredibly frustrating for family and school alike. If you are in this spot with your child, this is the time to start asking them what changes they would like to make to their job. Nine times out of 10, you'll first get the response "let me quit." Don't panic. It's a natural response. Have you ever wanted to quit a job because it was a poor fit?

Instead, share ideas in a non-confrontational manner. Questions go over better than statements here.

You: We're wondering about asking for extended time to turn in late work. What do you think?
Child: Ugh, no way! It'll just keep piling up and I'll never be done with it!
You: What might work better?

Child: Can't I just do less? It's all the same stuff over and over again, anyway.

You: I read about a thing called "hardest first" where you can do the hardest math problems in each section. If you get 80% or better, you move on. If you get less, you want to work a little more on those concepts. Shall we ask for something like that?

Child: Yeah, okay. Maybe I won't have to do homework until midnight all the time.

- Has your child ever refused an accommodation that was decided on behind closed doors?
- Have you ever had decisions made for you this way? How did you react?

Your Parenting Partner(s): You're Both (All) in This for the Long Haul

This is a sensitive subject for many families. In cases where parenting partners are not in a relationship outside of co-parenting, tensions may be high for a host of reasons. Step-parents or additional caregivers add more opinions, and possibly more stress, to the mix. Even in families where parenting partners are in a close relationship, disagreements about educational choices are fairly common.

We all have our own history and experiences that color our view of how education should be done, and these views are not always going to be compatible. A parent who is interested in homeschooling may have a partner who is a strong public school proponent. A fan of private education may clash with a partner who wants the family to experience being a part of the neighborhood school community. People tend to have strong opinions on education, either because they hated the way they had to do school or because they loved it.

Finding a neutral way to list pros and cons of whatever educational decisions face your family can be helpful. In case of a deadlock, consult with professionals who can help guide you through the process. Table 9.1 is a pros and cons table – this is an idea of how you can lay out the options available to you and your family. For a blank template, see Appendix B.

TABLE 9.1 Pros and cons: school options

Options	Pros	Cons
Neighborhood school	◆ Walking/busing ◆ Attending school with neighbor kids	◆ Limited or no gifted services ◆ Resistant to possible modifications, like subject acceleration, curriculum compacting, or curriculum replacement
Private school	◆ Smaller class sizes ◆ Access to special courses, like Latin or orchestra	◆ Cost ◆ Transportation ◆ May not provide accommodations ◆ May foster competitiveness
Charter school	◆ May have a philosophy that feels right – classical education, naturalist education, etc.	◆ Transportation ◆ May be new with newer teachers and administrators, so will have some growing pains ◆ Requires more family involvement
Homeschool	◆ Completely individualized ◆ Frees up time for travel and deep-interest explorations ◆ Allows for real-world interactions with experts	◆ Takes parent/caregiver time to project manage ◆ Requires more transportation ◆ Feels big and scary ◆ Others might judge negatively based on what they know about homeschooling
Online school	◆ More efficient ◆ Generally includes more transparent timelines, work completion, faster or immediate feedback on progress ◆ Can work with people from all over the world	◆ Can be socially isolating ◆ Some options are expensive ◆ Asynchronous learning lacks the benefit of immediate feedback ◆ Limited availability of clubs or after-school activities

◆ Think about your educational journey – how does your experience influence what you want for your child?

◆ How does this mesh (or not) with your parenting partner's hopes and expectations for your child's education?

Your Parenting Peers: Find People Traveling the Same Road

You've experienced the eye-rolls and resentment at the neighborhood playground and the mom's or dad's club. Where do you find people who understand that parenting a gifted kid is not any easier than raising any other kid? In fact, it can be incredibly challenging. Intense brains often come with a host of other intensities that make life for your family, well, intense!

Think of the last time you met with other parents and children in a local park. Did you feel comfortable sharing stories about your child in this setting? I hear, over and over again, about how isolated parents of gifted and 2e children feel, even (or especially) in a group of geographically connected parenting peers. How do you vent about your child's obsession with the Warriors book series (which is almost infinite, as far as I can recall) when other 7-year-olds may be struggling with sight words? If your child is 2e, it's even more difficult to find your parenting peers, even though it seems like you should have double the opportunities. An autism group, for example, may offer resources and support, but most parents and caregivers will have a vastly different parenting experience if their child is not also gifted.

Many of us have different sets of peers for different activities. It's okay if your neighborhood friends are your go-to for local get-togethers, your book club friends are the people with whom you talk about books and drink wine, and your college pals are the ones you meet up with for fun travel. Finding your parenting peers is the same principle. We may wish our existing friends could also be our parenting peers, but it doesn't always happen that way. This doesn't mean you can't ever talk about your kids with your other friend groups, but you can think about *how* you talk about them.

Something like, "Em aced the math pretest but the teacher still won't let them do different, harder work!" will sound one way in a gifted parenting group, and have a very different impact in another group. Sometimes parents feel like they shouldn't have to "edit" what they say just because others don't understand how challenging it is to parent a gifted child. I think it's like all aspects of human interaction – if you care about someone's feelings, you try to meet them halfway. If I'm talking with a parent whose kid struggles in math, I may not talk about how difficult it is to schedule subject acceleration so my kid can do next-level math. I may avoid the topic of math altogether. None of my experiences as a parent of a gifted mathematician will help the parent of a child who struggles in that subject.

Many parents of gifted and 2e kids struggle with how to talk about their child's educational needs. Some are of the mindset, "We have the same answer for everyone, and who cares about their opinions?" If that's the way you roll in life, okay. But if these are people you share a community with, you might have different answers to meet their varying levels of understanding. For example, if I were talking with a neighborhood acquaintance who asks, "Why aren't your kids still in our school?" I might say, "We found a program in another district that meets their needs." If these were people I felt quite close to, I might elaborate a bit more. And those closest to us will have the full picture.

Where do you find your gifted and 2e parenting peers? Look for gifted or 2e groups in your area or online. In the U.S., many states have a statewide gifted organization, and many of these have a parent/caregiver community. Look for organizations that are dedicated to gifted education and/or support that are available online and have opportunities for parents and caregivers to connect with each other. (See Appendix A for a list of organizations that may offer or partner with parent and caregiver groups.)

◆ Have you found other parents/caregivers who understand your parenting joys and challenges?

◆ How can you help other parents and caregivers find community?

Your Child's Teacher(s): Clearing the Communication Pathways

One of the major frustrations for parents and caregivers is that you have to start over every year with a new teacher. As we talked about in Chapter 6, some teachers have had training in gifted education, but most have not. Some teachers differentiate beautifully, others believe that efficiency dictates that all children progress at the same pace on the same work. Every year, you and your child have a whole new person to connect with and learn about. It's even more complex when your child gets to middle school and has many teachers.

The conflict is this: A parent or caregiver wants a teacher to change things up to improve the school experience for their child. The educator needs to keep 25 little or big kids safe and alive day in and day out. This struggle plays out for teachers year after year – new families, same story. That's the reason so many educators build up armor and develop defensive strategies for dealing with families. That's why the scoop in the faculty lounge is whatever "that parent" demanded this week. The barrier between school and home communication can be hard to overcome.

A few educators turn the tables and send out regular news-letters, invite families to participate and volunteer, and focus on building community. They make it seem easy – make us wonder why all teachers can't do this. In reality, inviting families into the day-to-day life of the classroom isn't a big focus of teacher school. And it doesn't come naturally to all teachers. And it takes a lot of work, know-how, and time.

How do we support our educators in creating community? Offer to help. Ask how you can support the teacher's efforts to build community.

1. Make a suggestion about how you can use your skills to support them. "I have a knack for newsletters – if that's an item on your 'someday' list, I'd be happy to help." "I love organizing parties – could I help with corralling volunteers for an event you have in mind this year?" "I'd love to put together an email list of families in your class to organize a park day – can I send a note home in backpacks?"

2. Remember that the teacher is in charge here. You wouldn't want someone coming in and taking over in your place of work, so remember to defer to the teacher's preferences.

3. Change tends to happen slowly. We can learn new skills pretty quickly, but implementation can take time. Even if you have only managed to plant the seeds for a future year, you can pat yourself on the back for making a difference.

⊕ My mom was a school teacher who taught English to children whose first language was not English. Some of her kids entered her 7th grade class with a pretty good foundation in day-to-day English, and some couldn't understand a word she said. Mom's second language was Spanish, but many of her students were from Vietnam, Laos, or Cambodia, so she had no language in common from which to begin. These were countries my well-traveled parents had not visited, so Mom did not even have any experience of their cultures when she first started teaching kids from this region of the world.

What Mom had was a generous helping of curiosity and infinite kindness. And she was an utter extrovert. She just loved getting to know people. She met with families, visited their homes, helped them access the supports available for immigrants, listened to their dreams, encouraged their efforts, and became a trusted mentor. Her students recognized her everywhere we went, invited her to major life events, and remembered her so fondly when she passed. Mom loved teaching, but she was also dedicated to making sure her students (and her own kids) had a caring community and access to opportunities. She went above and beyond in ways a more introverted person would shy away from, welcoming families fully into her life and receiving welcome in return.

As parents and caregivers of gifted or twice-exceptional kids, we are likely going to suffer some stereotyping, thanks to all the intense parents of intense kids who have gone before. We may be high-maintenance, high-strung, or time-consuming in our own right, but we have years of preconceived notions to overcome, as well. It's really hard to establish new norms when the old norms are based on educators' experience with difficult parents. It takes time, patience, and persistence to dispel some of the reputation we've inherited. Think about who you want to be and do your best to live up to that, every day, every time. It's too easy to live down to expectations. You know what I mean – our kids do it, too. "If they are so sure I'm going to be obnoxious, well, then, I'm going to show them what obnoxious really means!"

Think about dealing with at least one intense, confrontational person in your place of work each year. Someone who takes up way more than their share of time. Someone whose demands for your time mean you are spending non-work hours on managing their emails, calls, or drop-ins. Someone who compares you to other professionals, to your detriment. Translate this into the job you do – how do you feel about this person? Do you look beneath the behavior and see the care and fear driving them? Or do you simply resent their determination to take up as much of your space as possible?

🚗 Have you ever tried to take over a medical appointment, telling your doctor what to do or what to prescribe? There's a saying: "when patients determine their own care; they usually get poor care." The same may hold true in education. Imagine a teacher offering services that may help a gifted child. The services may include friendship groups, ADHD coaches, an exercise club before or after school to better promote concentration, organizational tips ... but sometimes we parents think we know best.

On more than one occasion in my 30+ years as a G/T teacher, I've seen advice sometimes completely rebuffed or ignored. That may be because we as parents *know that* our gifted child would not be bored, unhappy, lonely, etc. if only the teacher were to ... fill in the blank. Too often, when people tell an expert how to do their job, they don't get the best results. When the school and teacher are trusted and advice is given to help, it's important to remember that teachers, like medical doctors, are trained professionals who have the best interests of the child in mind (and usually in their heart too).

Our best gift to our children is to give the gift of helping the whole child, meaning taking care of the intellectual needs and so much more. This isn't to unequivocally state that teachers are always right 100% of the time, but if they make a suggestion, offer a service, create a plan, their suggestions must be considered.

(Joan Larson, M.A.)

We talk more about the family-teacher relationship in many chapters of this book, but I'll keep saying this: no matter how things are going, show respect for this educated professional who is responsible for your child many hours every week. If you talk disrespectfully about your child's teacher, don't be surprised if your child does the same. If you treat the teacher with respect, this will help your cause immensely as you advocate for your child.

♦ Who was your favorite teacher (any educational setting and any grade) and why?
♦ Who has your child's favorite teacher been so far?
♦ What is one thing you can reasonably ask for to help your child feel more welcome in the classroom?

School Administrators: They Drive the School Bus

The school administrative team sets the tone for the entire building. A principal who welcomes parental input creates a warm and welcoming environment. A principal who likes to "run a tight ship" may be less willing to allow adaptations like subject acceleration or partial homeschooling. If you have options of schools for your child, meeting with the principal and finding out their attitude toward gifted education is a great first step. If you are locked into one school, developing a positive relationship with the principal and other administrators can make your advocacy journey smoother. Offer support with events, fundraising, or in any area you have skills, time, or expertise to share. Then, when you have an ask, you've built up some equity.

Other Support Staff at the School
School Psychologist or School Counselor

Find out if your school has a counselor or psychologist on site. These professionals can offer social/emotional support and guidance, but often need to be asked before they can step in. These professionals have resources and strategies that can promote communication between school and family, or special educators and gifted educators.

⊗ Our kids' elementary school had a wonderful school psychologist. Ms. Terry was there for our whole school, but one of her areas of interest was supporting the teachers and kids in the gifted program. She helped problem-solve friendship challenges and supported student-to-teacher communication. She was also incredibly helpful to families of 2e children, offering resources and guidance to families who had the added job pressure of having one foot in special education and one in gifted education.

Creating these connections between special education staff and gifted staff is a tricky job that requires tact and persistence. When it works, it can be a wonderful collaboration. Special educators have all the stuff – assistive tech, sensory supports, strategies for cooling down or focusing in, etc. Gifted educators have the strengths-based mindset that allows kids to soar in their areas of strength and find new and creative ways to approach tasks or subjects that are more challenging for them.

Gifted Specialist

Gifted coordinators, either site-based or district-based, are another wonderful source of support. They have the training and the resources to help teachers differentiate in the classroom, but, again, they may need to be invited in (like a vampire, only not). There are no universal rules for when support staff can offer help or when they need to be asked in – it depends on who makes the rules in your school or district.

Special Education Teachers and Staff

If your child has additional exceptionalities and qualifies for special education support, you have another wealth of possible helpers in the school. A special education case manager is always looking for new ways to support the children on their caseload. From them, you may get ideas of other folks who can help your child with their unique needs, both challenges and gifts.

School Nurse

The school nurse is used to having kids in and out of the nurse's office every day. This person is sometimes the safe spot for an anxious child. "I don't feel good" may mean "I need to go to my safe space in the school."

Starting Line: The Hierarchy of School

When you are advocating for your child, the teacher is always the first point of communication. A good principal will dismiss any attempts to go over the teachers' head and send you back to that first square. I know that doesn't sound good when you want that principal to intervene on your child's behalf, but a principal who doesn't send you back to the teacher would be a terrible principal to work with. Think of the ecosystem of the school. You want respected, supported educators and staff taking care of your child. The head of the school has a lot to do with keeping the school environment healthy.

So, instead of getting angry, try appreciating this respectful policy. In the next several chapters, we'll go into detail about how to create and nurture a solid working relationship with your child's teacher, even when you don't necessarily agree with their methods of teaching your child. This is your child's main person during their time in that classroom, so taking care with that relationship is essential.

When a teacher can't make a change without building approval, as in the case of subject acceleration, you then talk with the building administration. Have that conversation with your child's teacher first, though, because they will be consulted for their opinion.

When the building administration can't make a change without district buy-in, like creating a full-time gifted program, you talk with district leadership and the school board. Start, again, with your child's teacher, so they know what you are advocating for. They may have some great ideas for who to talk with and how to address concerns. Then you talk with your building administrators, who will hopefully also have insights and advice. Even if you are discouraged from pursuing your advocacy goal, you have shown the folks in your child's building the courtesy of advance notice.

Start at the beginning, ask people along the way if they want to be included, and build your network from the individual teaching your child to the person or people who make the decisions at the level of change you are asking for. You will meet resistance, as in Mark's example in Chapter 2, but you will learn a lot along the way. You might even get some new and effective ideas that will help you in your advocacy efforts.

Building relationships with teachers, staff, and administrators in your child's school is one way to ensure more eyes, ears, and hearts in your village. It's so easy to fall into the us vs. them mentality when things start to go wrong – it is MY child, after all! And MY child is my most urgent concern as a parent/caregiver. This is absolutely true and your feelings are valid. One of the sad truths of life, however, is that we can't change other people, even when we really, really want to. How we approach advocating for the most important people in our lives sets a tone for our conversations, expectations for our behavior, and how much trust we inspire in others.

Adding Experts: Other Support Professionals Outside of School

Depending on your child's needs and your family's access to additional support (constraints could be geographical, financial, etc.), you can build a comprehensive team to support your child. The following list is not complete, by any means, and this is not a recommendation to get one of each for your collaborative team. Some families will find that working with one or two experts in particular areas is enough to support their child. Other families will need specialized support in a number of areas.

Keep in mind that when finding support professionals, it is okay to shop around. A professional who worked amazingly well for one family might not be the right fit for another.

> "Keep in mind that when finding support professionals, it is okay to shop around. A professional who worked amazingly well for one family might not be the right fit for another."

Therapist

Sometimes we all need someone to talk to. For gifted and 2e kids, having a safe person who isn't a parent can be very helpful. Many, if not most, gifted and 2e kids suffer from anxiety at some point in their lives. Talking with a therapist can help kids (a) talk through possible causes for their anxiety, and (b) get some strategies for managing their anxiety. When looking for a therapist for your gifted child, check that they understand, or are open to learning more about, giftedness and twice-exceptionality. Therapists, like teachers, don't generally get training on giftedness and 2e in their many years of schooling.

> You've taken steps to find a therapist for your child, but how do you know if they will be the right fit? Basically, if your child likes them! The greatest indicator for positive change in the therapy room is the therapeutic relationship – i.e. the safety, warmth, connection, and trust your child feels with their provider. Without that, the specific interventions don't matter that much. Some questions you can ask your child's potential new therapist include:
>
> ◆ How do you help kids/teens feel comfortable in a new environment/with a new person?
> ◆ What kind of communication and involvement in my child's treatment can I expect as a parent?
> ◆ How do you measure progress, and how will we know if therapy is working?
> ◆ How will you tailor your therapeutic approach to meet the unique needs of my child?
>
> (Abby Hough, MA, LPCC)

Occupational Therapist

Occupational Therapists, or O.T.s, can help with sensory issues, motor skill difficulties, emotional regulation, social skills, or a thousand other things, depending on their area of specialty. These are the folks who can help your child find ways to manage challenges that interfere with daily life.

Pediatrician

Your pediatrician might be one of the first people to help you identify giftedness or other exceptionalities, or you may need to educate your child's doctor about the unique needs of these kids. This is another profession that doesn't get training on giftedness in school. Because a big part of advocacy is educating others, sharing information and resources with your pediatrician will benefit other families in the future.

Psychiatrist

If your child requires medication, you may be referred to a psychiatrist so they can monitor and adjust according to how your child reacts to the medication. A psychiatrist can help with diagnosis of mental health conditions, prescribe medication, and recommend accommodations or modifications to implement at home or in school.

Learning Coach

Learning Coaches and Executive Functioning (EF) Coaches work with your family to help with managing the structural or organizational components of the job of school. Some EF coaches work with families on developing organizational skills in daily life. These folks may follow a program or plan, or they may adjust according to the needs of the individual student or family.

Tutor

Tutors can support learning in a variety of ways. They can help find new ways for your child to access concepts that they are struggling to grasp, or they can work with your child to fill in gaps in learning. They might guide an independent study or extend the learning beyond what the school can offer. Many gifted kids are resistant to having a tutor because they think they should be able to do their job of school without help.

Psychological Assessment Provider

Folks who can provide psychological assessments, like an IQ test, have requirements from both the publisher of the assessment and the state in which they practice. This professional may be a psychometrician, psychologist, neuropsychologist, school psychologist, etc.

Again, not all providers have received any training on the unique needs of gifted and 2e learners, so ask your questions before making your choice. If you can find a professional who specializes in working with gifted kids, you and your child will likely get a lot more out of the experience. Your child will benefit from working with an assessor who understands their intensity and knows how to look for their strengths. You will benefit because the report you receive will have gifted-specific advice and recommendations.

Some of these folks offer packages of many tests including IQ, achievement, etc., and that can be useful if you are just not sure what's going on with your complex kid. If you are looking for an IQ test for admission to a gifted program, look for a provider who will give just the IQ test. The Davidson Institute has a map to get you started, or you can look for information on your state or regional gifted organization's webpage ("Gifted Testers and Therapists List").

Other Special Folks

If your family has a history of eyesight issues or hearing challenges, , or if you suspect your child's difficulties may be vision or hearing-related, you might consult an ophthalmologist or audiologist. You may look for a math mentor or a history buff who is happy to share their wisdom with a young, bright human who has exhausted the school curriculum. A college or graduate student might be just the person to accompany your child on a summer learning adventure in science or coding. Extended family could provide exposure to theater or music. Your collaborative team will be unique to your family.

⚠ A caveat about identifying problems and finding help: Parents and caregivers of multi-exceptional children can get lost in the weeds of the day-to-day struggle to help their child succeed. Without meaning to, these same loving folks can give the child the unspoken message that the child is broken, incomplete, and a problem to solve. This deficit-based thinking is all too easy to indulge in when all you seem to do is cope with one crisis after another. You want to "fix" things. You really want things to not be so hard.

You get to feel however you feel. We all do. It's what you communicate to your child that matters here. If someone you respect and love more than anyone tells you there is something wrong with you, you feel wrong to your bones. So be careful with your words, even (or especially) when you're talking with someone else about your child in their hearing. And I don't know about your kids, but mine could hear me say their names on the other side of the house with two closed doors between us. Like spooky-good hearing! Though for some reason that super-power failed whenever I spoke of homework or chores. Go figure.

Some Ideas for Talking with Your Kids About Their Challenges

♦ I struggle with my keys wandering off the same way your planner keeps hiding on you. I wonder if we can consult an expert on keeping track of squirrely stuff. Maybe improve on one or two of their ideas.

♦ I think it can be really hard to share big thoughts and feelings with family before having a chance to mull them over for a while. I like the idea of having a safe person who isn't invested in my life to tell things to – it's helped me when I needed an objective ear. That's a therapist's job. Would you like to talk to a safe person that isn't me?

♦ Middle school is a really hard job. I feel a little over-whelmed when I think "what if I had 9 different bosses for my one job?" Would you like to talk with someone who specializes in helping smart people manage really complicated jobs? I can find a few options and you can choose.

Roadside Assistance: Learning How to Delegate

FIGURE 9.13 Sometimes we all need a little professional help.

The fine art of delegation is often a neglected skill set in K-12. Assembling a good team is the mark of any successful CEO. The more you insist on doing yourself, the less you can get done. That is totally fine if autonomy is the career goal, but in life, many opportunities open up when people are able to play to their own strengths and work with others who have complementary strengths. Your child can learn to utilize others' strengths and choose when to exercise that option. Everyone can benefit from enlisting experts. Learning how to choose those people and how to let them go if it isn't a good fit are very valuable life skills.

⚠ People who are 2e often learn to delegate out of necessity. A person with dyslexia requires a good editor. A person with ADHD can delegate the tasks, or pieces of tasks, that are particularly challenging for them. A person who can't sit and write an essay may benefit from a scribe. Many tasks can be relegated to assistive tech devices – reminders, voice-to-text, read-aloud, etc., but you still need support learning how to best use these devices. The earlier you help your 2e child make the most of the supports available to them, the more adept they will become at finding and receiving help.

⚲ SKILLS INVOLVED IN ASKING FOR HELP

- ◆ **Courage to ask** – maybe more a trait than a skill, but it grows with practice!
- ◆ **Big picture thinking** – what am I trying to accomplish?
- ◆ **Strategizing** – who has the skills/knowledge/resources that I need?
- ◆ **Self-awareness** – what do I struggle with? What do I do well? When do I need other people? When am I the helper?
- ◆ **Clear communication** – everyone works from their own knowledge and experience – I need to be clear and check in on whether the other person understands me so I'm not surprised with their interpretation of my request.
- ◆ **Managing expectations** – even with clear communication, each person will put their own spin on their work. How do I open my mind to thinking "just as good" rather than "my way or no way"?
- ◆ **Practicing gratitude** – when I am kind and acknowledge others' work, they are more likely to help me again in the future. They also have the power of word-of-mouth, so my interactions with them should reflect how I want to be perceived in the world.

- ◆ What other skills are involved in asking for and receiving support?

The mindset that we have to know it all, do it all, and be it all is common in gifted people. We have the ability to see and understand the possibilities of what we *could* do, so we think we *should* be able to do it all. If we decide that things will only be done right if we do it all ourselves, we are only limited by our own capabilities, right? Not so much – as we talked about in Chapter 5, life throws forks in our paths at every turn.

Playing Traffic Cop: Managing Your Team

Creating a team and learning to delegate may sound complicated and overwhelming, but it's a step-by-step process. You won't be able to create a network in a day, nor would you be able to rely on said network if you did! This is a long-term project, or part of your ongoing lifelong project of building and maintaining your family's support community. And it's not new stuff. It's all about doing what you do anyway – forming and nurturing relationships with others. In this case, you have an overarching strategy – resources and champions for your child and family.

It's also not a tidy process. You won't be able to simply find and plug people in to your open spots – therapist, occupational therapist, assessment specialist, learning coach, etc. You'll do what you do – interview, ask questions, get suggestions from other families. You'll find some wonderful people. Sometimes one of your favorites will retire or move. You'll find some duds, and you'll have those hard conversations about letting them go. You'll find people you think are fabulous that your child can't stand, and vice versa. Some folks don't take insurance, some have fees outside of your budget, some want you to buy a package, some will put you on a wait list.

Enlisting the support of a collaborative team is helpful for all families, and vital for many. We all have limited time and none of us are experts in everything. The fine art of delegation is something we don't see taught in schools, and, in fact, the idea that we should be able to do it all ourselves is a common theme among gifted people. When you show your child how to access help and manage a support team, you are giving them the tools to become the CEO of their own life.

References

Davidson Institute. "Gifted Testers and Therapists List." April 26, 2023. https://www.davidsongifted.org/gifted-blog/gifted-testers-and -therapists-list/

Rogers, Karen B. *Re-Forming Gifted Education: Matching the Program to the Child.* Great Potential Press, Inc., 2002.

10

Energy Efficiency

In Chapter 6, we talked about the fact that teachers never have enough time. We can't magically put more hours in a day, but in this chapter, we will talk about ways to save your child's teacher some of that most precious commodity – time. We'll start by editing our eloquent emails, move on to sharing our shortcuts, and talk about volunteering. We'll also take a look at a few more tried-and-true methods of accelerating, compacting, or telescoping learning and ways to introduce these ideas to your child's teacher or school.

DOI: 10.4324/9781003467441-13

Avoid the Scenic Email: Brevity Is a Valuable Skill

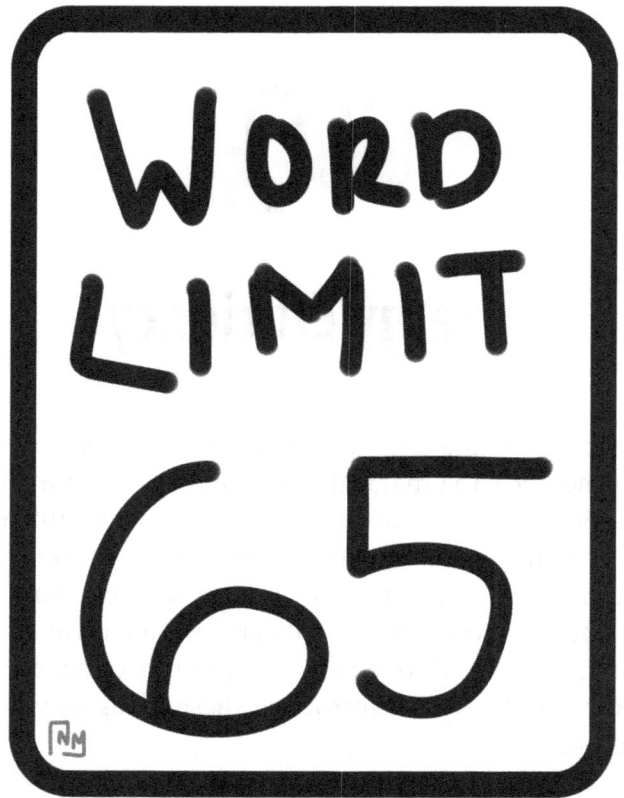

FIGURE 10.1 "You're ten paragraphs over the limit, I'll see you in court."

One of the unfortunate realizations many gifted parents and caregivers experience is that a very well-worded, elegantly stated, positively poetic 15-question email will be met with either silence or the answer to the first question or two. Sometimes the questions are so carefully couched in prose that the recipient of the email misses or misinterprets them. Parents and caregivers of gifted children are often highly verbal, complex thinkers themselves. Sometimes it's the most accomplished writer/question-asker/communicator who really needs to work on a new writing skill – brevity.

Think of the last email you received at work that would run to multiple pages if you printed it out. Was your impulse to dig right in and answer every nuance, or did you have to put it aside until you had time to look it over? Add 25 kids all needing your immediate attention into that mix. Short and sweet goes a lot further in communicating with your child's teacher.

You know the saying about endless meetings, "this could have been an email"? People in all kinds of jobs get frustrated when someone is taking up time that could be spent on more urgent tasks. I know, I know, when it's my kid, it *is* urgent. I hear you and I agree. But *your* urgency doesn't change the urgency for the professionals working with your child. Your seeming lack of respect for their time *will* impact their feelings about you. Bear with me while I do math.

One elementary teacher divided by 25 kids goes into 7 hours per day minus however much time it takes to get everyone settled in the morning, lunch, recess, all the day's transitions, and get everyone ready to go in the afternoon. Then take into account circle time, instructions for activities, and any whole-class work for that day. Teachers really have almost no time in a day for one-on-one check-ins. Many teachers find ways to seamlessly incorporate these check-ins and others struggle to make it work. See Chapter 6 for more ideas of why that is and how you can advocate with the school for additional help for your teacher.

When a teacher receives an email that requires a good scroll or two, they may need to set it aside for another day. Or they'll answer the first question or two and consider that email checked off the endless to-do list. It takes a lot of effort and time to decipher the point of some beautifully written emails. The problem isn't that you aren't clear and even eloquent, it's that it takes too much time. An inelegant email with three bullet points is more likely to receive a quick response than the very nicest 8-paragraph email. This is true for a lot of jobs, but especially in situations where one person is responsible for many people.

Here's an example:

Dear Ms. Ing,

I am writing because I am concerned that my little Em isn't getting enough of a challenge in class. They talk a lot about recess and one particular friend, El, but not about the work they are doing. I'd like to talk more about connecting with El's family, but, first, I want to address my concerns about the homework.

The worksheets coming home only take a few minutes, but Em is becoming more and more resistant to doing them. I worry they will start to tune out of school if we don't find a way to challenge them. For instance (more story here)...

Em's older sibling, for example...

(And on, and on, with stories, worries, and probably some delightful self-deprecating humor. Maybe an article or two or three, or ideas from a friend.)

...going back to the friend Em has made, we'd like to get to know the family. We're hoping to include El in Em's birthday plans. We're going to the science museum and plan to watch the documentary about Egypt. We want to make sure that El's family (more thoughts, worries, and questions that the teacher has absolutely no use for and no part in deciding)...

Thanks for any help you can give us with this!

I hope you have a happy day!

Em's Parent

Your email was friendly, interesting, thorough, humble, funny, thoughtful, and *long*. You gave background, supporting data, and your own very special insights. You asked only two very important questions in there somewhere, so you felt you were keeping it simple. You get a reply like this:

Hi, Em's Parent! I do see El and Em playing nicely at recess, but I have had to separate them in class because they talk, talk, talk! I'll send some additional worksheets home with Em from now on. Thanks for letting me know! Ms. Ing

Wait. What just happened here?!? More worksheets? What will that accomplish, except make Em feel overwhelmed with more of the same? Did the teacher not even read my email?!?

Two things happened – your email was way too long and your requests were way too vague. Pull up an old email you sent to your child's teacher that had more than three paragraphs and think about what the teacher would need to do in order to address your email carefully and thoroughly:

◆ Read the email.
◆ Find the questions.
◆ Look for the suggestions.
◆ Read the resources.
◆ Consider options.
◆ Formulate a reply that addresses each concern.
◆ Explain constraints around time, money, training, etc.
◆ Make notes about modifications or accommodations you will make based on parent/caregiver concerns.
◆ Worry that you're going to judge them for not writing back in full paragraphs.

How much time might it take? 30 minutes? An hour? Longer if they have to walk down the hall to ask another teacher or the principal about policies or possibilities.

Email is the least of the teacher's duties, so this whole process should, optimally, take about 3 minutes. Try this:

Hi, Ms. Ing,

I love hearing about the science explorations – Em is learning a lot!

I have 2 questions:

1. Em would love to stretch their brain in math. I wonder if Em could do the hardest 20% of problems on the math homework and then use the saved time for deeper work on the same concept in (alternative curriculum I will supply)? I saw this strategy in (linked article).
2. Would you please share this note with El's parents/caregivers?

"Dear El's family, I am Em's Parent. We would love to get the kids together outside of school. My number is 111-222-3333 and my email is <u>emsparent@emsfam.co</u> <u>m</u>. I look forward to hearing from you!"

Thanks for all you do!
Em's Parent

In this email, you have offered a solution to your child's homework problem that the teacher can accept, modify, or replace. The beauty of your idea is that it is specific to your child. Hardest First is a solution that means Em will still spend the same amount of time on math, but will have work that is interesting and challenging. You haven't criticized the teacher by complaining that Em is bored. You have offered to supply the replacement curriculum.

With your second request, you have given the teacher an easy copy/paste task that will help you connect with another student's family. The teacher only needs to add a few words of explanation, like "From Em's parent:" Instead of putting your effort into explaining your hopes and concerns about this new friend, you've put that time into making your request a simple thing to grant.

⦿ AN EXPLORATION OF THE WORD BORED: INSPIRING DREAD IN EDUCATORS EVERYWHERE

◆ Why do educators despise the word *bored*? A couple of reasons are:
  ◆ It implies that the teacher is boring, and
  ◆ It is a word that is used to explain away all kinds of other things.

"Bored" can mean tired, overwhelmed, distracted, worried I won't do the task well, frustrated at being constantly told what to do, resentful about the time a task will take, and so on. Gifted kids absolutely do get bored when asked to do repetitive learning tasks when they have already mastered the material. Find other ways to approach the teacher about new or more challenging work.

Instead of, "En is an expert on this historic period. This unit will be utterly boring for them." Try, "En loves the Renaissance period of history and collects lots of books and resources about it. This unit in the text has a lot of good stuff, but nothing new for En. I wonder if En could take the final test to show mastery. Maybe they can use that class time to do a deeper dive into the invention and use of the printing press, instead."

Rush Hour Traffic: Limit In-Person Conversation to the Time Allotted

Caregiver/Teacher Conferences

Conferences are generally rushed affairs for families and endless days for educators. Families are scheduled back-to-back. Teachers may have already taught the full day before they get right into conferences. They meet with a bunch of families, take a short break for dinner, and then right back to the next meeting. Educators spend hours preparing so they can share relevant information with each family. There's really nothing we can do to help make conferences easier on the teacher overall, but we can make our little pocket of time a pleasant and efficient experience.

- ◆ Look over any notes or emails the teacher has sent home about conferences.
- ◆ Spend some time with your child looking at the school's online portal. Use this as a time to ask your child questions, not to stress out over low or missing grades.
- ◆ Together, come up with a few questions for the teacher. Not 12 questions, but two or three. Things like:
  - ◆ We're not sure how En should be checking in with their social studies packet. Can you explain?
  - ◆ We've noticed some missing assignments in the online portal. We found them finished in En's backpack. Could you remind En how you tell the kids to turn in work when it's due? En will work on paying attention for that signal to turn assignments in, but could use a little help.
  - ◆ At home, we find that En works best sitting in a corner or with their back to a wall. Noises behind them are pretty distracting. Any chance of a seat change?
  - ◆ What would you like for us to know?
- ◆ Let your child lead the discussion as much as they are willing and able. This skill will grow over time.
- ◆ Redirect comments and questions back to your child if the teacher is only talking to you.

- ◆ Recap the conversation with any action items: "Sounds like En is really engaged in the hands-on labs in science, and is planning to work on getting their observations into their lab notebook. You've offered to remind them to enter their notes, and will remind them to turn in their lab book for grading each week. Thanks so much for your time."
- ◆ Send a follow-up email restating exactly what action items were decided upon during the conference. We'll go into more detail on this in Chapter 11.

Before, During, Or After School Drop-Ins

Family members who volunteer in the school or walk in at drop-off or pick-up times enjoy a feeling of belonging and the privilege of being seen and heard by teachers and staff. It's lovely to be able to stop by a classroom during a teacher's prep hour (that time set aside for all the work they can't get done with a classroom full of kids. It's never enough time, but better than nothing.) This is wonderful if you use this time to offer help, rather than as a time to vent or chat. Remember this is their work day. I would tell my kids' teachers, "Give me a job I can do to help. I'm happy to do anything that frees up your time for doing more important work – teaching my kid!"

Phone Calls/Online Calls

Phone calls or online calls are really useful for quick conversations when we need that immediate back-and-forth communication. Schedule the call ahead of time so you aren't pulling a teacher away from a busy class. Keep calls as brief as possible, using the same principle as emails. Do your homework ahead of time – jot down the one or two things you are calling about so you can get right to it.

Calls are tricky because you have an audience right there, and the topic is your child. You never have a shortage of things to say about your child! It's hard to quell the urge to share. Your child's teacher is your partner in your child's education, but they truly don't have a lot of time to hear all of your stories, fears, and concerns. If you find yourself unburdening months of worry in one call, it's okay – we've all done it. But if you do this regularly, it could get harder and harder to schedule a call with that teacher.

FIGURE 10.3 Per my last several emails...

Meetings

Scheduled meetings have an identified start and end time. Going over time means that the people who work in the school will have to leave in the middle of a thought or idea because they have to do recess duty or monitor the pick-up line. Again, prepare for meetings ahead of time so you know exactly what you need to cover in the time allotted.

Parents and caregivers of gifted and 2e kids may not have a lot of opportunities to talk with others about the joys and challenges of parenting their quirky, intense kid. Sometimes just having a table full of people who are there to talk about your child presents a huge temptation to share all the pent-up thoughts, feelings, and ideas you have. If you think this might be you, put some safeguards in place so you don't take the whole 30 minutes sharing examples and stories.

◆ Bring someone along with you. It's not your child's job to stop you mid-rant, but another adult can help you minimize your talking time. This can be a parenting partner, an advocate, a therapist, a learning coach, etc. (Be sure to let the school know who will be accompanying you.)

◆ Talk with your parenting partner or support professional ahead of time. Come up with a signal in case you start down the story-telling path.

◆ Share a list of items you want to address in the meeting. If you can, send this ahead of time.

◆ Ask for a list of items the school wants to address so you can prepare.

◆ Go in with the goal to listen more than you talk.

◆ Take notes or record the conversation (with permission from all participants).

◆ Send a follow-up email (more in this in Chapter 11).

The regular overshare is your signal to find another place where you can talk about the joys and challenges of raising your gifted or 2e kid to your heart's content. Some parents and caregivers find therapists who can listen and offer strategies. You can look for a parenting peer group, either online or in person. However you find your person or people to talk to, save your stories for them. During those meetings or calls with busy professionals, you can keep to the business at hand.

Share Your Shortcuts: What Works at Home?

Teachers graduate from teacher school after 5 years of intense work and practice. They leave school with 10,000 strategies in their toolkits to choose from in a variety of situations. When your child is unusual, quirky, intense, and asynchronous, it's way harder for a teacher to reach into that toolkit and find the strategy that will work for your child in any situation. While I'm a huge proponent of letting professionals do their job, I also think that sharing relevant information is important. When I go see my doctor about a pain in my back, I offer details about what hurts and when, what helps and what makes it worse. This helps my doc decide which of her thousands of strategies to implement in my case.

Same with our kids in the classroom. If your kid is acting out right before the bell rings every day, you might mention that loud noises really bother them at home to the point you had to disable the chime on the doorbell. If they're sitting under the bell in the classroom, they're probably preparing for the jarring noise by acting out. This information gives the teacher some specific direction in helping them. Rather than time out in the hall (where the bell might be even louder), they can put on headphones or head to the quiet corner for a few minutes.

You know your child better than anyone.

(STOP)

♦   What works at home?
♦   What has worked in other settings?
♦   What does your child want? (Voice of experience – don't advocate for something your child will reject!)
♦   What can you offer to support the work of the educators?

 I had many parenting books, but where was the book "What to Do When Your Teachers Have Never Experienced a Child Like Yours"? As a first-time parent, I had assumed that, like my parents, I would send my kid to school, maybe deal with a few issues, but all would ultimately be fine and fairly hands-off. So I was stunned when the Kindergarten teacher reached out to say that she was struggling with some of my son's behaviors she had never experienced before. How could my son's behaviors be new to a teacher of 20 years?! She must have dealt with thousands of kids while I had dealt with only one. Surely she knew more about managing my kid in the classroom than I did, right?! But she did not. Of the thousands of students she had taught, my child was unique to her. We worked together to build our understanding of when and why behaviors were showing up and to find strategies to help my kindergartener regulate. From this experience, I created a short document to share with future teachers that provided context for behaviors they might see, offered strategies for avoiding those behaviors, and provided tools to help my kid regulate when those behaviors did occur. Each year, before school started, my husband and I would connect with the teacher and share the document with them. Being open about our understanding of our child's behaviors helped to create an ongoing connection for dialogue and collaboration during the school year. I also quickly learned the importance of advocating for a good teacher match by writing the school administration not to ask for a specific teacher, but to share the type of teacher that would work well for my child. One that, like my son's K teacher, would see his strengths, have some of their own strategies for support, and be willing to listen and consider our suggestions.

(Cori Paulet)

Cori Paulet shares her regulation suggestions in Table 10.1.

Add-Ons and Features: Using Technology to Support Learning

Now, anyone who knows me will tell you that I have an optimistic internal clock (meaning I think I can get more done in the 5 minutes before I need to leave the house than I can actually get done) and no internal compass. That combo has made me late for more things than I care to recall or admit. I must say that technology has improved my ability to show up in ways I never imagined 20 years ago. For me, the advent of the portable GPS was an enormous breakthrough in my ability to get anywhere. And now it's in my phone? And my calendar not only lives in my phone but will send me reminders? Miraculous!

Look to technology to fill in where you struggle. Whether the root cause of your challenge is a diagnosable disability, an interesting quirk of your gifted brain, or simply an aversion to carrying out some essential task like note-taking, there's help. People with your same difficulties or dislikes are continually developing new ways for technology to step in and make life easier. It's not a cop-out – it's using the tools at your disposal to do your work more effectively.

Allow your child to explore and find things that work with their brain. An app that works beautifully for you to organize your schedule may not work for someone else, even your own kid. Set limits on cost and in-app purchasing ahead of time so it doesn't need to be negotiated every time a new app is downloaded.

TABLE 10.1 Regulation suggestions: early grades by Cori Paulet

Category	Description/Example
BEHAVIORS you might see	◆ Ignoring or not paying attention (e.g., covering ears, humming, focusing elsewhere) ◆ Being physically restless ("squirrely" behavior, trouble sitting still) ◆ Bothering others (e.g., getting too close, touching others' things) ◆ Defiance (e.g., saying "NO," running around, not following instructions) ◆ Not responding (you repeat multiple times with no response)
SITUATIONS where behaviors are more likely	◆ Transitions ◆ Waiting (e.g., in line, done with work, unsure what to do) ◆ Change in routine (e.g., substitute, class rearranged or shortened) ◆ A lot of activity or noise ◆ Hungry ◆ Needs to use the potty
PREVENTION of disruptive behaviors	◆ Provide a daily schedule ◆ Keep him occupied with engaging activities in his interests (dinosaurs, space, bugs, human body, earth history) ◆ Ask him what he likes to do/learn – he may have an idea for a project ◆ Give warnings about transitions (e.g., 5-minute warning before lining up) ◆ Be consistent with consequences and reward ◆ Provide warnings before negative consequences ◆ Keep him close to the teacher in class and in lines ◆ Praise good behavior as frequently as possible ◆ Set simple goals and offer immediate rewards (e.g., point system) ◆ Give him responsibilities (e.g., counting kids in line, carrying heavy books/loads) ◆ Suggest bathroom breaks, ensures he eats well, and allow chewing gum as a preventative measure ◆ Situate him with calming people – this may be people who like things he likes ◆ Give him time when possible. May take a few times before he translates what you say into action. ◆ Ask him to repeat what you said if he seems like he is not paying attention Exercise – a few minutes of running or push-ups on the wall

(Cont.)

TABLE 10.1 (Cont.)

Category	Description/Example
CALMING help regain control	ENGINE SYSTEM (from Occupational Therapist) Tell him what behaviors you notice that suggest his engine is running like a racehorse Ask him what he can do to get his engine to run like a cat Give him a suggestion if he can't come up with something. Some ideas are: ◆ Offer sensory breaks in quiet spaces (e.g. squeezing behind couch pillows at home) ◆ Encourage art or drawing ◆ Give him responsibilities requiring heavy lifting (e.g., take stack of books to library) ◆ Take a break and do push-ups on floor or wall

Free Ride: Benefits of Volunteering

Volunteering is a great way to participate in your school community. Helping out with a project, fundraiser, event, or cause helps you connect with others while you are providing a valuable contribution. Offering to help out changes how others perceive you because it goes beyond what others can do for you. Making a difference for others is a great way to make new friends, stay more active, and find a sense of purpose (Thoreson, 2023).

Parents and caregivers who work a job in addition to the job of parenting struggle with the idea of volunteering. Where is the time? Even for stay-at-home-caregivers , time is at a premium, though you may have more flexibility during the day depending on the ages and needs of your children.

The beauty of volunteering in your child's school is that it is generally optional. (Some schools have required minimums of family volunteer hours.) You can help with the carnival and leave the field day to other families. Or you can help behind the scenes by cutting out shapes for the birthday bulletin board or arranging photos into a book for a retirement celebration, but not get involved in the events themselves.

When you start out as a volunteer, you may try different tasks and decide where your interests and talents lie. Or you may know exactly what you have to offer and you can be very clear about your volunteer role. I will offer the caveat that volunteering is a lot like making a snowperson on a hill – if you don't keep careful control of that snowball, it'll roll and grow into a massive time-consumer of a snowmonster. Ask me how I know.

If you have limited hours to offer, set limits on your volunteer time in advance so people know exactly how much time you can give. This is another place where consistency is key. You know how when you extend bedtime for your child one night, they remind you of that at every bedtime forever? "But you let me stay up until 10:30 on Halloween three years ago!" It's the same idea. "But you did such an amazing job chairing the carnival last year – we can't do it without you!"

If you have flexibility, you can extend an offer of your time to the teacher, school, or district. "I can offer 3 daytime hours a week to help out – what can I do?" No daytime availability? You could volunteer to help with evening events. And some tasks can be done on your own time. If you have a particular skill set that fits in with school needs, offer that skill. Table 10.2 presents volunteering brainstorm suggestions.

Side Trips: Find Opportunities for Your Child to Volunteer

Helping to make the world a better place is an excellent value to model for your kids. Giving your child opportunities to be a helper can help them feel deeper connections with their community and a greater sense of purpose in life. If your child suffers from existential depression, making a positive difference in the world can help ground them in the here and now and help them gain perspective and feel more optimistic about the future.

Choice and ownership and understanding the impact of your effort are all important here. Your cause may be saving the whales, but your child might get more out of walking shelter dogs. Feed My Starving Children is an organization that does an excellent job at engaging communities to send aid overseas, but you might also want to help organize a backpack drive for

TABLE 10.2 What my family can offer volunteering brainstorm

If you know how to do:	Offer to help with:
Graphic design	◆ Newsletter ◆ Invitations ◆ Posters ◆ Social media posts ◆ School brochures ◆ Swag for events/teams/causes
Event planning	◆ Class parties ◆ School events ◆ District events ◆ Fundraisers ◆ Food/coat/clothing drive
Arts and crafts	◆ Art talks ◆ Museum field trip ◆ Virtual field trip ◆ Art activity ◆ Craft for fundraiser, donation, or holiday gifts, etc.
Science	◆ Lead an after-school science club ◆ Plan a field trip to a lab ◆ Give an in-class presentation ◆ Connect the teacher with a scientist who can join the class virtually for an online conversation
Math	◆ Fundraisers ◆ Donation drives ◆ Small group help ◆ Sourcing alternate curriculum for kids who pre-test out of a math unit
Theater	◆ Offer to help with the school play ◆ Be a guest judge for a competition ◆ Support small groups as a mentor in competitions like Destination Imagination and others
Engineering	◆ Lead a hands-on building activity in a classroom ◆ Mentor a robotics team ◆ Join the playground redesign committee
What you know	◆ Helping the school ◆ Teaching a group of kids ◆ Supporting the work ◆ Mentoring a group ◆ Creating a plan ◆ Lending a hand, a strong back, or a keen eye

children in foster care in your own city. Causes close to home are more visible ways of seeing your positive impact.

> 🖵 For most people, actually getting involved in causes they believe in is the best remedy to combat feelings of hopelessness and helplessness and questions of life meaning.
>
> (James T. Webb, 2013)

Shortest Road Between Two Points: Strategies for the Classroom

Schools are obligated to help students achieve mastery in a variety of grade-level standards in each core subject – in the U.S., these are English, math, science, and social studies. Because of the prevalence of standardized testing, educators work diligently to make sure all kids in their class have the tools they need to do well. Some of these tests are more to assess the teacher, rather than the student. All are a non-negotiable component of the teacher's focus. This emphasis on "teaching to the test" means newer instructional practices have a greater focus on making sure all the kids know the grade-level material so teachers know they aren't leaving anyone behind.

When you are asking for something different for your child, keeping the bigger picture of assessments (for student and teacher) in mind can help when you offer strategies. Curriculum compacting, telescoping learning, and various types of acceleration are mostly free, relatively easy, and can take minimal teacher time.

We will look at some of the many forms of acceleration in Chapter 14. For the purposes of this chapter, let's explore a few techniques and strategies that teachers can use for individuals or small groups of kids in the regular classroom. This is by no means an exhaustive list, and because this chapter is all about saving time, the strategies below are some of the less time-consuming to implement.

Curriculum Compacting

This idea is all about demonstration of mastery of a given topic. The time that is freed up for the student can now be used for learning something new or going deeper into the same topic (Vahidi, 2015). In math, for instance, a student who tests out of the factors and multiples unit can work in a more challenging curriculum on the same topic, or they can do agreed-upon math-related explorations using the principles of multiples and factors.

Alternate activities can be as simple as reading a book on a related topic or as complex as doing an independent study or small group project. Teachers can develop menus of alternate activities over time, but, to start with, it is most helpful if you can offer an idea for a supplemental curriculum. They agreement between teacher and student includes:

- ◆ the type of work the student will do (reading, researching, writing, drawing, building, work in a more challenging workbook, etc.).
- ◆ the time the student will use to do this work. Will this extend beyond the school day, or is this just for class time?
- ◆ where will the student do this work? (classroom, library, computer lab, etc.).
- ◆ the student agreement to spend the time engaged in this specific work. Behavior issues make independent work less likely to occur in future.
- ◆ the intended product (worksheets, essay, story, film, artwork, quick conversation with the teacher about their learning, etc.).

The beauty of the compacting strategies is that any student can access the options if they demonstrate mastery of the unit content. It is not a "gifted kids only" option, but available for any child ready for the next level on the topic. This can help counter the idea that gifted education is exclusionary. It's also useful for gifted kids with additional exceptionalities that make long sheets of practice homework unbearable for the whole family.

You'll see me refer to 80%, or a letter grade of B, as proficient enough to move on. This is a conversation you'll have with your teacher or educational team. A perfect, or 100% score, is setting the bar so high that a single error can prevent a child from testing out of a unit of study.

Hardest First (Aka Most Difficult First)

This technique can apply to vocabulary, grammar, and even social studies or science topics your child has already mastered beyond where the class is learning. The teacher identifies the hardest 20% of the homework for the child to complete. If they complete this work with an 80% or better, they are done with that piece of homework.

This strategy is especially helpful with kids who stall out in front of a huge assignment. If you have a child who freezes at the very sight of a packet of math problems, homework can take over family time. With hardest first, they can accomplish enough to prove mastery of the content, but don't have to sit for hours on end trying to get over their dread enough to begin the larger task.

🖳 MILE MARKER

Most Difficult First is a very effective way to ask kids who return from pull-out programs to document their mastery, without requiring them to make up all the work they missed. You get the evidence you need that the kids are competent with the materials, and they get the consideration they need that being in a pull-out class should not lead to more work for them.

(Winebrenner, 2020)

Optional Word Count

As we've talked about in this chapter, some of us gifted folk have a problem with brevity. Others of us have a problem with reaching a minimum word count. If your child is one of the latter sort, ask about having an optional word count on writing assignments.

Maybe your kid can sum up a book chapter in one concise sentence. In my world, that's a skill to be celebrated and encouraged!

If the point of the exercise is to learn about paragraphs and essay structure, one sentence will just not do. But if the point is for your child to show that they have read and understood the content, letting them do that in fewer words can help a reluctant writer to accomplish the task.

Pre-testing

We could do a whole chapter on this topic. Pre-testing is the easiest compacting solution and so rarely gets used. A student takes a unit pre-test (the standard post-test works beautifully here, so a new test does not need to be designed) and if they score 80% or better, they can skip that unit of instruction. If the test is nuanced enough, a teacher can look at components of that unit and determine if a student needs instruction in only one or two components. If they do not pass the pre-test with an 80% or better, they will do the work of the unit (or components of the unit) with the rest of the class and get that necessary knowledge.

When I mention that the teacher can use the end-of-unit test as a pre-test, some argue that the students will remember the test and have an unfair advantage. I think that if the students put in the work to study the items they know will be on the test, they have put in the work. They still have to wade through the rest of the content to get to the answers. Yes, you want the kids to have a well-rounded knowledge of the subject, but you also don't want to burn them out with needless repetition.

With these, or any, modifications to your child's job, keeping track is essential to make sure there are no misunderstandings about grading, support, or communication. In Chapter 11, we'll talk about the ins and outs of keeping records. It's not as intimidating a task as it sounds. It's all about the tools for holding yourself and the others on your child's educational team accountable and up-to-date.

References

Thoreson, Angela. "Helping People, Changing Lives: 3 Health Benefits of Volunteering." *Mayo Clinic Health System*, 1 Aug. 2023, https://www.mayoclinichealthsystem.org/hometown-health/speaking-of-health/3-health-benefits-of-volunteering.

Vahidi, Siamak. "The Eight Steps to Curriculum Compacting." The National Research Center on the Gifted and Talented (1990–2013), 23 July 2015, https://nrcgt.uconn.edu/underachievement_study/curriculum-compacting/cc_8steps/.

Webb, James T. *Searching for Meaning: Idealism, Bright Minds, Disillusionment, and Hope*. Great Potential Press, 2013.

Winebrenner, Susan. *Teaching Gifted Kids in Today's Classroom: Strategies and Techniques Every Teacher Can Use*. Free Spirit Publishing, 2020.

11

Keep a Travel Log

FIGURE 11.1 Show me your papers!

Creating a paper trail, or documenting your advocacy process, can seem overwhelming or intimidating to parents and caregivers. Very often, the very characteristics that make school a difficult job fit for your child are characteristics one or more caregivers also possess. So when the absent-minded parent of a disorganized student is told to create and maintain a paper trail, it may seem like they need an advocate for their own challenges while advocating for their child's challenges!

DOI: 10.4324/9781003467441-14

Fear not! It's not about being the most organized human on the planet. You can create a gorgeous binder with tabs with everything in plastic sleeves and organized by thread, chronological order, and people involved – or, you can pop everything into a folder or box, newest on top. If the info is online, even better. A folder for emails and a folder for all other info. We'll talk more about the how, but first, let's talk about the why.

Trail of Breadcrumbs: Why We Document Everything

We know from literature, history, science, and personal experience that people recall events differently. We recall events and conversations dissimilarly because we each have our own mental framework of experience and knowledge upon which we hang new information.

If you go into a meeting with your child's educational team hoping that you can work together to figure out how to reduce the amount of homework your child is tasked with every day, you may recall the conversation differently than the other people in the room:

- ◆ **You** – hope the sheer volume of homework can be reduced because it's taking over the family's together time in the evenings.
- ◆ **Educator** – firmly believes that completing all the assigned homework is the only way to master the material.
- ◆ **School counselor** – remembers this conversation as an opportunity to create study groups to foster friendships and encourage homework completion.
- ◆ **Case manager** – is envisioning check-ins and checklists or a supervised study hall.

All of the ideas may have actually been expressed in the meeting, but which was agreed upon as the course of action?

Or in the case of interpersonal conflict among students, everyone in the room has different experiences, ideas, and plans for helping your child:

- **You** – ask for your child to never be grouped with their nemesis.
- **Teacher** – recalls a workshop in restorative practices and is eager to give it a try in the classroom.
- **Assistant Principal** – makes a mental note to get those kids face-to-face and have a mediated conversation so they can get over it and move on.

What was decided on in that meeting, and who is responsible for holding everyone accountable?

- You ask one of your child's Scout leaders to check in regularly with your child about troop projects, and then that leader needs to take a medical leave and doesn't have a chance to communicate the details of your agreement to the other leader(s). You're now starting from square one with a different scout leader.
- You have a conversation in the school hallway with the math teacher, who agrees to try pre-testing along with the use of an alternate curriculum during in-class work time. That teacher may have a busy day/week/month and that conversation slips their mind entirely.

Verbal agreements of all kinds are subject to the memories and interpretations of all involved parties – including yours. I have caught myself, or been caught by others, in mistakes after insisting I was right. I have also narrowly escaped this fate by rereading my notes before reacting!

🗒 HOW DOES MEMORY WORK?

In its simplest form, memory refers to the continued process of information retention over time. It is an integral part of human cognition, since it allows individuals to recall and draw upon past events to frame their understanding of and behavior within the present. Memory also gives individuals a framework through which to make sense of the present and future.

(Derek Bok Center)

Documenting your advocacy is a skill that will serve you well. The record you create will serve as a collective memory keeper. After all, we are dealing with humans. You'll remember the key ideas that stood out for you. Each member of your team will recall the meeting through their own lens. The notes will help keep the plan on track.

The other side of documentation is accountability. You may have helped craft a perfectly wonderful IEP and the school still can't provide all the accommodations or modifications with consistency or fidelity. You can receive reassurance that the coach will be proactive about giving your child opportunities to participate, but other students may have more skill to lead the team to victory. There is no perfect thing, but you can improve the odds of "pretty good" by holding everyone accountable through documentation, reminders, and regular check-ins.

Now that we've talked about the why, let's dig into what we need to document and how to keep track of it all.

Traveling Down the Paper Trail: Keeping Track of All the Pieces

Taking Notes
Official Meetings with the Educational Team

Some kinds of meetings always have appointed notetakers. Anything with a legal agreement, like an IEP or 504 meeting will have someone on staff taking notes. Even so, different people will highlight and prioritize different ideas.

You should always take your own notes during meetings, or bring someone along to take notes on your behalf. If you are feeling nervous or overwhelmed or have a learning difference – anything that makes retaining information or taking notes difficult – ask the team if you can record the conversation.

If you are unable to take notes or record the meeting, take a few minutes directly following the meeting to think through the conversation and jot down what you remember as the action steps, aka the to-do list, and any questions you still have.

You can use a piece of paper, a phone app, or a computer to take notes. Be sure to get the names, job titles, and email addresses of everyone attending the meeting. Use whatever shorthand you can so you can focus on the conversations.

My notes, jotted on paper, might be "math will HF, 20% at 80%" which translates to, "Math teacher will allow Em to do Hardest First strategy. Teacher will identify 20% of homework for Em to complete. As long as Em scores 80% or better on that portion, they do not need to revisit that homework. If Em's score falls below 80%, the teacher will assign review work."

MEETING NOTES ORGANIZER

Date: (Always add the date. You are creating a timeline.)

Time: (The time of day and location of meeting can help jog your memory or someone else's.)

Place: (Phone call, hallway at school, classroom, etc.)

Reason: (Conferences, drop-in, scheduled meeting, etc.)

Attendees: (This is worth taking a few minutes to get spelling and job titles.)

    Em
    Em's Parent
    Mr. E.--Math Teacher
    Ms. Ing – English Language Arts (ELA) teacher
    etc.

Discussion item	Discussion notes	Action item
Math homework completion is a daily struggle	Tutor, Hardest First, different math class, medication	Math teacher will allow Em to do Hardest First strategy. Teacher will identify 20% of homework for Em to complete. As long as Em scores 80% or better on that portion, they do not need to revisit that homework. If Em's score falls below 80%, the teacher will assign review work.

Discussion item	Discussion notes	Action item
Participation in Language Arts discussions is low to non-existent	Discussion chips, teacher calling on Em, Em worries about having the wrong answer, discussion moves too fast, circle back	Em would like to try starting a discussion on a new topic with a question they prepare ahead of time. That way, they can listen the rest of the time and not worry about being able to break in with an idea before the discussion has moved on. Em will share their questions with the teacher before class. Em will try using "circle back" to add to the discussion on a point made earlier for which they needed time to process and formulate a response. Em will try to implement each of these strategies once per class discussion time
Writing takes a really long time and causes hand cramps	Change of keyboard, new pen, voice-to-text, scribe	Em may type (or dictate to parent) their ELA homework
Writing book reports is time-consuming and has turned into a regular power struggle	Alternatives to written report, shorter reports, oral reports	Em can choose from a teacher-provided list of options for book reports, including conversation with teacher, drawing, poem or song, or diorama

Phone Calls

Sometimes you want to schedule a call. This is helpful when you have a pretty simple question or request. Anything that requires some problem-solving or sharing student data might call for a short in-person meeting. Take notes during the call so you can email a quick follow-up and thank you.

In-Person Meetings

It's a good idea to take notes during any meeting you have on your child's behalf, but sometimes it feels awkward to whip out a notebook or open a notes app on your phone when you're having a face-to face conversation standing in a classroom or hallway. Try verbally summarizing the conversation before you part ways:

"It sounds like we decided that Kay can try dictating their answers to me for the long questions in the social studies packet. We will print those out and staple them to the packet before Kay turns it in each week. You had the idea that Kay could use a library study room to take tests that have an essay component so they can use a recording device to speak their answers instead of writing. Kay can decide on a test-by-test basis if they want to use that option. Does that sound right?"

Then, get to a device, whether it's your office computer or your phone in your parked car in the school parking lot, and make some notes. Later, you'll send that summary with a big thank you. If your child is ready for this step, they can send that email and copy you.

Online Meetings

Online meetings are great time-savers. You want to watch your non-verbal communication, even online, so think about how you take notes in this situation. If you have a doc open on your screen that you are typing madly into, let the group know you are taking notes that you will share after the meeting. Otherwise, they may get the impression you are multitasking instead of giving them your full attention.

Another way to take notes is to either share an online doc so they can see what you're typing, or use the chat feature for notes. The chat feature on online meeting platforms is wonderfully useful for this. You can suggest that everyone shares ideas and action steps in the chat. Or you can let everyone know that you will take notes in the chat so you can all refer back to them. Save this chat before leaving the call. This will serve as the outline for your follow-up summary.

Sharing Summaries

All of the careful notes you are taking during or following every meeting and conversation only go so far if they are not shared quickly and with all involved parties. As soon as possible following the meeting, share a summary with everyone at the meeting, and those who are part of the team but couldn't attend the meeting. As we talked about in Chapter 10, keep it short! Bullet points or numbered lists are effective visual tools that help people see how many items they need to think about and possibly respond to.

"All of the careful notes you are taking during or following every meeting and conversation only go so far if they are not shared quickly and with all involved parties.**"**

Reviewing your notes and creating a summary also help you process the information a second time, which will help with you keeping *your* end of the bargain. You may also think of follow-up questions for the team.

Your notes:

◆ serve as a recording of the meeting
◆ summarize the discussion and list the agreed-upon action items
◆ remind each participant of their next steps
◆ give everyone a chance to add in their perspective if it differs from yours
◆ are part of your email trail

Your summary should include the following:

1. Greeting
2. Date, time, and location of meeting
3. Participants/attendees, including noting those members of your child's educational team who could not attend but are copied on the email.
4. Thanks and expectant praise (Expectant praise is like telling your kids, "Thanks for hanging up your backpack" as you both walk in the door. In this case, you are saying "Thanks for working with us to reduce Em's stress levels." They haven't done it, yet, but you are expecting them to help.)
5. Summary and action items
6. List of action items still undecided

7. Any questions you have
8. A request for corrections, if any are needed
9. Reminder of scheduled follow-up meeting or request to schedule follow-up meeting
10. Another pat on the back

Re: Summary of October 10th, 20__ meeting with team

We met today, October 10th, 20__, from 2:30pm to a little after 3:00pm, in the school conference room. In attendance were: Em, Em's Parent A, Assistant Principal, School Counselor, ELA Teacher, and Math Teacher. Em's Parent B and Social Studies Teacher could not attend, but are copied on this email.

Dear All,

Thank you for a great conversation about helping reduce Em's stress levels and helping Em feel successful in school. Below are the changes we agreed to try:

- We agreed to the following modifications to reduce Em's homework stress and time spent:
  - Em may do Hardest First (hardest 20% of problems) in math. They agree to complete more practice problems in areas where they score less than 80% on the homework.
  - Em may type (or dictate to parent) their ELA homework.
  - Em can choose from a teacher-provided list of options for book reports, including conversation with teacher, drawing, poem or song, or diorama.
  - Em will try two strategies to increase their participation in ELA class discussions
    - Prepared questions to use when a new topic is introduced
    - "Circle back" to share ideas on something the class talked about earlier

We have one follow-up question – we discussed that it might be possible for Em to have extended time on math tests, but the team needed to find a separate space. The library was one idea. Did we find a way for that to happen?

We agreed to check in after winter break to see how things are going. That meeting is scheduled for January 15th, 20__, at 2:30pm.

Let me know if I missed anything. Thank you for your time, creativity, and dedication!

Em's Parent

If your meeting was a conversation in the hallway, you may think you don't need to follow up. "Of course, Kay's teacher will remember that they agreed to let Kay pre-test out of math units they've already mastered!" But after they talked with you, that same teacher had 100 conversations with students, colleagues, and family members, and it may have slipped their mind until they're halfway through the next math unit and you call to ask why Kay wasn't allowed to test out of the factors and multiples unit.

A short email will go a long way to keeping the agreed-upon strategy in mind. It's not fail-proof because we're human, but if it helps the teacher remember and honor the agreement, you have done them a good turn. Waiting to see if someone will forget something is just setting them up to fail – a brief follow-up can be a lifesaver.

> "Waiting to see if someone will forget something is just setting them up to fail – a brief follow-up can be a lifesaver."

Hi, Mr. E.,

Following up on our hallway conversation today, October 10th, after school. I'm copying Parenting Partner and Kay on this email.

Thank you for agreeing to allow Kay to pre-test in math and opt out of units they score 80% or higher in, starting with the new unit next week. They will use the time they earned to do the alternative math work we discussed.

My action item is purchasing the book Kay will use.
Thanks for supporting Kay!
Kay's Parent

Creating an Email Trail

An email trail is a very useful advocacy tool. With email, you have time stamps, who the email is from, the people copied on it, and the information shared. It's helpful to add these things in the body of the email, so if you're printing emails in preparation for a follow-up meeting, all the info is there.

Keep all the emails you send to and receive from the school that might be relevant down the road. An email about your contribution to the classroom winter party won't affect your work with the teacher on providing a more challenging spelling list, so delete away! Anything that has to do with your advocacy should be saved. You can pop it into a folder in your email account, save it in a folder on your computer or in the cloud, take a picture with your phone, or print it and put it in a binder of some sort. The trick is to have a way of finding a particular email again when you need it.

Many times, teachers and other school staff will delete the chain of an email and send you a stand-alone reply. If you need to reference a previous email on the same topic, you can copy the content you want to reference and include it in your reply. A few things to keep in mind:

♦ If you are referencing a previous email, include the time and date stamp if possible, as well as the names of all parties copied on that email.

♦ Don't take out anything that changes the context, tone, or meaning of the email. Sometimes you wish you could change an email to better match what you wish it said, but I know you will resist that temptation.

♦ Be aware of privacy considerations. If you had a confidential email conversation, don't paste that into a conversation with another person.

♦ It's okay to summarize points from previous emails rather than pasting the actual email in, but check your source first. Remember what we said about memory?

Another issue that comes up frequently is that one teacher or staff member will reply to only you instead of all the people copied on the original email. This makes more work for you, because you want the entire team to stay up-to-date on what the rest of the team is doing. First of all, make sure you have given the teachers and staff explicit and written permission to communicate with any non-school people on the thread, like a non-guardian parenting partner or a support professional. Sometimes the reply to only you is because they are just not certain they have the green light to share sensitive student info with everyone. Here's one possible way to get everyone on the same page:

Your follow-up email to all:

Dear Everyone,

Thank you for a productive and positive meeting on November 9th, 20__ about helping Jay manage their social studies projects.

In attendance at this meeting in the school library right after school: Jay, Jay's parent, Jay's extended family member, Social Studies Teacher, Special Education Case Manager, Gifted Coordinator, Media Specialist.

We talked about ways to support Jay as they work to complete three large social studies projects this year, including the National History Day (NHD) project. Ideas included; hiring a tutor, finding a quieter work space, reducing word count minimums, using assistive technology like voice-to-text, and replacing choir with a study hall.

We agreed to:

- Allow Jay to use the library for quiet work time during social studies class period. Media Specialist will supervise and provide assistance as time allows.
- Social Studies teacher agreed to reduce word count minimums on projects.
- Family agreed to hire a tutor to support Jay on NHD project.

Please let me know if I missed anything.

I would like to schedule a quick check-in meeting in February. Any Tuesday afternoon works for us. Can we get something on the calendar?

Thank you all for your time, and for supporting Jay in social studies!

Jay's Parent

You receive an email from the social studies teacher that is a reply only to you. It says:

Hi, Jay's Parent,

We agreed that I could reduce word count minimums on everything except for NHD project.

Thanks,

Social Studies Teacher

And an email only to you from the Media Specialist that says:

Hi, Jay's Parent,

I recall that we had a back-up plan of Jay going to the Gifted Coordinator's office for quiet work time when we had events happening in the library. I'll just plan on sending Jay there on those days.

Media Specialist

Okay, that's true on both counts, but you now need to amend the record for everyone. So, now you reply all on your original email to add:

Updates to my summary of our agreed-upon plan:

- Social Studies teacher reminded me that the NHD project has its own guidelines and they cannot reduce the minimum word count.
- Media Specialist reminded me that Jay will go to Gifted Coordinators office for quiet work time on days the library has student groups or other events.

Thanks, All!
Jay's Parent

If you don't get any more corrections, you have the entire plan in one place for easy reference.

As we talked about in Chapter 7, you don't have to make all the decisions right away. Sending summaries should not wait, however up-in-the-air the plan is. Send those summaries, any action items that have been decided upon, and any that are still undecided. Request a follow-up time or remind about the next scheduled meeting.

Your Child's Role

As your child learns more about the process of advocacy, they can begin to take on some of these tasks, like sending email follow-up and summaries. As long as they are a minor (under 18 in the U.S.), you are an essential and active part of their educational team, but your job description can change as your child is ready to do more. Some kids will take over most communications with teachers in middle school, and some will need more support all the way through graduation. Even in college and beyond, a kid might want to consult with a parent or caregiver before sending an important email, so don't fret if your child isn't on someone else's timeline. We'll talk more about the bumpy road to independence in Chapter 12.

Part of your child's job as they prepare to communicate on their own behalf is to add to the paper trail you maintain. When they send an email, they copy the team. When they have a conversation, they send a follow-up. The understanding that their job of school isn't a private journey, but is instead a group effort, can help grow the collaborative skills they need to be an effective self-advocate.

Landmarks: Saving Important Information

So, you're saving emails, what else do you need to hold on to? Things like test scores, IEP forms, notes from the doctor, etc. Save all of it, even though it feels overwhelming. It's more overwhelming to arrive at the meeting without the necessary evidence you need to support your advocacy.

What Do You Save?

- ◆ Assessment scores and reports (You don't need to share everything all the time. Feel free to redact any components of any reports you have obtained outside of the school. Save a complete copy for your records before you start making changes!)
- ◆ Any formal agreements you have with the school (we'll talk briefly about 504 plans and Individualized Education Program (IEP) plans in Chapter 14).
- ◆ Drafts of agreements you have with the school (to show changes and progress).
- ◆ All emails between you and the school.
- ◆ All emails between your child and the school (have them CC you on all communications).
- ◆ Grade reports.
- ◆ Standardized test scores.
- ◆ Doctor's notes (if applicable).
- ◆ Medication information (if applicable).
- ◆ Information, notes, recommendations, etc. from other support professionals.
- ◆ A log of meetings, phone calls, and conversation.

How Do You Save It?

Save things in whatever way works for your brain and your team. Take into account the preferences of your parenting partner(s) when you decide on your system, so you all have access when you need a document or email chain.

If you don't have a document-keeping system in place that works well for this, start with something simple. You don't need to invest in the latest and greatest filing system or software. Some things to think about:

- ◆ Storing things in an online space allows for faster sharing, when sharing is needed.
- ◆ You can use a scanning app on your phone if you don't have a working printer/scanner.

- ◆ Determine a naming convention that will help you find what you need. Something like:
  - ◆ Emschool10-24-20__ social studies
  - ◆ 20__1024EmschoolSS
  - ◆ Include the date/person/place/subject in whatever order you can remember.
  - ◆ Keep it simple, just in case someone else needs to take the lead.
- ◆ Paper is fine if you prefer. The same naming convention ideas apply.

Saving all of these things doesn't need to take up much space or time in this digital age. The trick is finding it once you've saved it!

Speaking of the digital age, your online calendar is another place to help you manage your trail of breadcrumbs. Add phone calls, conversations, and meetings to your calendar so you can look back and see when things happened. You can do this in a paper calendar, if you prefer. Just having a timeline of your advocacy is very helpful when trying to remember the who, what, and when of things.

You can find lots of ideas out there for organizing your child's records and your advocacy paper trail. There are workshops, videos, books, and online how-tos of all descriptions. I'm a firm believer in finding the way that is right for *you*, not finding *the* right way. As long as you are collecting and saving documentation along the way, keeping it in some sort of accessible order, and you're able to produce what you need when you need it, it's all good. If you are overwhelmed by the prospect and find you want more ideas, or you just want someone to teach you a good system, look to special education advocacy for ideas. Whether or not your child qualifies for special education support, these are the people who have the nuts and bolts of organizing their advocacy paper trail down pat (Wrightslaw).

Pit Stops: Take the Time You Need to Respond to the School

In advocacy, as with almost everything in life, making snap decisions is far from ideal. And if you are presented with a deadline of "right this minute," you will want to counter with a different timeline. If an offer from the school to move your child to another classroom or grade comes as a surprise and you aren't given time to do your due diligence, offer a deadline for your decision. "I can let you know in three days. I need to talk this over with the team."

"I need time" is a perfectly valid response. You need time to review your notes, look over their proposed plan, talk with your parenting partner and your child. You may want to consult others in your network, especially if something in the plan is confusing or new. You can go back to the school and ask for clarification and still take the time you requested. See Chapter 10 for more on communicating with your child's educational team.

⚠ In an IEP meeting, you don't have to consent to the plan the school is offering until you feel comfortable with it. There is almost always pressure to sign off so the educators and staff don't have an open item on their endless to-do lists, but you have every right to take time and consult your team. Sometimes you are prepared and you know exactly what you are asking for. In that case, if it's offered, go for it. Otherwise, take the time to consult with your team and get back to them as soon as you can.

- ♦ What are your organizational preferences? Are they similar to or different from your child's? Your parenting partner's?
- ♦ What tools or tricks have you found that really help you keep track of the people and plans involved in your child's education?

References

Derek Bok Center. "How Memory Works." Harvard University. https://bokcenter.harvard.edu/how-memory-works.

Wrightslaw. "Special Education Advocacy." https://www.wrightslaw.com/info/advo.index.htm

PART 4

Behind the Wheel

12

Share the Driving

Rearview Mirror: We Learn as We Go

I love remembering myself as a young adult, not yet a parent. I was so opinionated about how other people raised their children. I just knew I would do it better, do it "right." Screaming kids in the grocery store? Never. A child in public wearing dirty dinosaur pajamas? Heaven forfend! I would be organized, calm, and put together at all times. Not! I learned humility along with how to parent my kids, who persist even to this day in being their very own selves and not the paragons of my pre-parenting imagination. (Yes, they are delightful humans, but happily not obnoxiously perfect. They are waaaaay too interesting and engaged in living, growing, and learning to be perfect.) Parenting reminds me every day that I'm not even a little bit perfect, either.

Being a parent or caregiver for a child is a vast responsibility. Kids don't come with a handbook or a set of instructions. We rely on advice from family, friends, doctors, books, and, these days, the internet. Our own experiences influence our every decision. We dream of the darling child, the tidy home, the perfect report card. We find a home in the best neighborhood we can afford, we look at schools and ask about teachers, we envision finding friends. We see ourselves pursuing interesting hobbies, collecting a fascinating friend group, and making one successful decision after another.

DOI: 10.4324/9781003467441-16

This is a good thing, envisioning what we want and how to get it. People create vision boards, work on their self-talk, and set intentions all the time. The biggest barrier to becoming our most perfect selves is that we are human in a world with other humans. Keeping our own fallibility in mind even while we work toward our goals can help us meet life's challenges with greater resilience. When it comes to parenting, the same rule applies. Our kid may be the most amazing thing that's ever happened to us, but they will have to figure things out the hard way, by living one day at a time, making mistakes, and doing their best with what they've got, just like we do.

I have often wished there was some way of transferring wisdom. Wave a magic wand, and I will have the knowledge and experience of my parents to draw on when I don't know what to do. I was lucky, and had my parents around for 50 years. I could call them whenever I wanted and they would help me think through the problem at hand. But I sure didn't do that when I was a tween, teen, and young adult and already knew everything.

> **How often have you wished you could deposit your hard-won wisdom in your child's head?**

How often have you wished you could deposit your hard-won wisdom in your child's head? If you only knew what I know... And yet, you can tell them until you lose your voice and they will still insist on doing things their own way! The road has changed quite a bit over the years as well, so your wisdom may not apply to your child's situation. Trusting your child to do their best and take care of themselves is a big leap for protective parents and caregivers.

⌐ **MILE MARKER**

We give our children the tools and we teach them how to use them. We help them think things through. We make sure they know how to stand up for themselves and each other. There comes a time when you have to allow them to take care of themselves. They have good instincts and great reflexes. Trust them so they can trust themselves.

(Sarah Genereau)

Bumpy Road to Self-Advocacy: Asynchrony and the V of Love

The V of love is a parenting model created by Dr. Sylvia Rimm. The arms of the V represent your arms and the level of care your child requires. When your children are small, they are nestled in the base of the V. Babies and small kids need a lot of care and hands-on guidance – they can't be let out of sight. The arms of the V widen as they grow and they are able to have more freedom and take on more responsibility for themselves (Rimm).

Freedom and responsibility seem like they should grow concurrently, but the asynchrony of gifted kids means the journey to the top of the V (independence) may be less than smooth! Gifted and 2e kids have asynchronous skill development, meaning they can be all over the "by this age" roadmap at the pediatrician's office. Some skills are advanced, some are even with same-age peers, and some lag behind.

This looks different for every gifted child, and any additional exceptionalities make the variations on the developmental spectrum even more pronounced. The "you are so smart, you should be able to" argument is terribly unfair to gifted and 2e kids because we should not expect that their executive functioning skills are keeping up with their advanced intellect.

> Asynchrony means "out of step in time." If you envision a staircase that represents "normal" developmental ages and stages, think about where your child falls on the various categories. A child may be chronologically age 10, intellectually age 20, emotionally age 8, socially age 5, and so on. Asynchronous development is a hallmark of gifted and 2e kids. It simply means they are out of step with their typically developing age peers.

Gifted kids may be out of step intellectually, creatively, interpersonally (think about the natural leaders you know), physically (gifted athletes), etc. But gifted kids are not just two, three or ten steps ahead on everything – their patterns of asynchrony are as individual as fingerprints. They may be ahead in some ways, on track with age-peers in some ways, and at a younger-than-age level of development in other ways. And this can change in the same child from one moment to the next, depending on how they're feeling (Institute for Educational Advancement).

A 10-year-old may wax poetic about black holes and super-novas with a docent at a science museum one moment and have a screaming, flailing tantrum on the floor of the gift shop the next. A 5-year-old may be able to charm the socks off the audi-ence at the piano recital, but spent the two previous hours refus-ing to wear those blasted tights that they picked out at the store. Another child may be able to recite every line and lyric of *Hamilton* but cannot remember one word of the instructions for the history assignment. When you add additional exceptionalities into the mix, your child may be dancing all over the asynchrony staircase like Fred Astaire.

So even though your teen may be able to argue like a sea-soned lawyer, they still need your wisdom and support as they learn new skills, like self-advocacy. It's one thing to learn how to stick up for yourself at home when a sibling is taking more than their share of mashed potatoes, but something completely differ-ent to learn to speak up when a teacher is forgetting an agreed-upon accommodation for testing. Kids may advocate beautifully one day and need a hand the next. You don't have to give them the title to the car before you are sure they are ready, but give your child more time "behind the wheel" as they get older and more capable.

▽ MILE MARKER

According to the Columbus group, the very definition of giftedness is asynchronous development. This growth differential can be seen across the social, emotional, intel-lectual, and physical domains of human development. Intellectually, we can see these differences between academic areas and intra-area skill sets. It is quite common to see a gifted learner struggle in Mathematics versus English Language Arts, and vice versa. It is also quite common for a learner to struggle in either Algebra or Geometry.

Furthermore, one cannot force a gifted learner (or any other type) into a skill pro-gression for which they are not prepared. The new skills need to be within the zone of proximal development, connecting their existing knowledge schema to the new material. Otherwise, we are going to see atypical behavior such as work avoidance, dysregulation, improper decorum, and lack of conation. Although gifted learners can progress in rapid acceleration and can even appear to grow in "sling shots," they still need to be securely grounded in content to move onto the next level.

(Barry B. Gelston, Ed.D.)

Driver Education: What Is Your Child Ready To Do?

Driving Basics: Elementary

We need to include young people in the choices we make on their behalf starting at an early age. This tends to be discouraged by many educational establishments because it complicates everything, but we are doing kids a huge disservice by not modeling how to make decisions and negotiate challenges.

Yes, kids can be disruptive in caregiver-teacher conferences or meetings to discuss accommodations or learning plans. Sometimes teachers feel they can't share sensitive feedback when the child is present. Perhaps they would prefer to problem-solve with another adult because it takes much longer to help a child understand the constraints of the system in which the teacher works. Some kids have become defensive from months or years of being constantly corrected – these kids may shut down all ideas immediately.

Educators, administrators, and support staff can have many valid reasons to exclude a student from these conversations. There may be, in fact, only two good reasons to include a resistant or challenging child:

1. This is the child's job we're talking about, and
2. They need to learn how to self-advocate before we can confidently hand over the keys.

Having your child involved in caregiver-teacher conferences requires some modifications. Instead of a discussion of problems and worries, it becomes a conversation about successes and solutions. This change is good for everyone involved – approaching any job from a strengths perspective helps everyone from boss (teacher) to worker (student) feel involved and optimistic.

What if instead of:

> Em has been daydreaming when I'm trying to give directions, and I need them to pay attention. I've moved them to the front of the room but now I am not getting any work from them at all. If this keeps up, I'll have to send Em to the principal.

You heard:

> I think my approach to helping Em pay attention in class hasn't been a good fit. Em, what seating area in the classroom might be better for you? What about sitting in the corner feels like it will be better? I'd like to try it your way this time, okay?

Imagine being that empowered to speak up for your preferences and have your idea implemented! What a change!

Or instead of:

> En is currently earning an F in math. They refuse to show their work, so even if they are getting the correct answers, they are losing out on two-thirds of the possible points.

The teacher says:

> En, I know you get the math answers so quickly in your head that it's hard to know what your brain did to solve the problem. I wonder if you could try to explain how to do the math problem to an alien who has never seen the math symbols we use. They probably get the concept but need to learn how we write things out on Earth. If you tried that on 20% of the homework problems, I could give you full credit for any correct answers in the other 80%. Does that sound better than how we've been doing things?

Of course, we can't wave a magic wand and make teachers change their mindset from a deficit-remediation focus to strengths-based solution finding, but we can encourage them to problem-solve *with* their student rather than *for* their student.

For that first scenario, perhaps try this:

> Em tells me they are seated in the front of the classroom right now. They find it really hard to concentrate because they feel like they're on display. I wonder if there is another seating assignment that will help?

Or:

> Em sometimes looks as if they are daydreaming, but they often like to look at a neutral point while listening because it helps them process. At home, I check in with Em to make sure they are getting the information I need them to have.

For the second scenario, try:

> I heard about a strategy for strong math students called Hardest First (see description in Chapter 10). I wonder if something like that could work for En?

Or:

> Here's an interesting article on pre-testing – I'd love to get your thoughts.

🏅 My kids had the same homeroom teacher in 4th grade, 3 years apart. Mr. E. treated his students like colleagues, with friendly respect. His students reflected that attitude back to him. I remember being a bit taken aback in our first caregiver-teacher conference for my oldest. He asked her questions about how she thought the year was going, offered her positive feedback, and workshopped ideas for improving areas of struggle she mentioned during the initial Q&A. My husband and I were almost completely superfluous, except that this was a wonderful way of showing us that our daughter could and should take more ownership of her job. We were by no means ready to stand back and stop participating, but this was when we realized that we could ask her to take the lead in school conversations. But this was elementary school with one exceptional teacher – middle school was a bigger advocacy job for all of us.

Behind the Wheel: Middle School

Middle school, or whatever they call that space between elementary school and high school where you are, is another story altogether. This is the period in a child's school journey when they are uprooted from the relative security of having one job with one teacher as their primary supervisor to the undiluted chaos of having 7, 8, or 9 separate jobs in one. The reasoning behind the model is sound – as our kids are ready for deeper learning in a subject, they need to learn from people who specialize in a particular area. Elementary teachers are, generally, generalists and secondary teachers are, hopefully, specialists in their subject. Many kids are quick to get comfortable with this 9-in-1 job model and muddle through just fine. Other kids, particularly those who prefer a calmer or more cohesive workday or those who have lagging executive functioning skills, really struggle with this transition.

For example, if you're a gig worker and you have a dozen clients you work for, you may have enjoyed the challenge of middle and high school. You enjoy getting to know each client, figuring out their methods, expectations, and preferences. You like the demand of juggling multiple projects that may have little in common. Deadlines hold no fear for you. You have a skill-set that you get to apply to each and every job. Hopefully, it's something you feel confident about and enjoy doing.

Young people who like school and also enjoy the gig-worker aspect of middle and high school tend to do quite well. Young people who don't love it, struggle. Gifted kids who begin to struggle with school may have their entire sense of self rocked by the fact that they aren't doing well, *even though they're so smart and always did well before*. This can be a pivotal moment in their lives when they begin to question the point of school. They understand the topics and grasp the concepts but still cannot do well. Imposter syndrome settles in with its companions, stress and anxiety. How do you self-advocate when you don't understand why school is no longer easy? How do parents and caregivers help?

Remember the V of love from the beginning of this chapter? We talked about how the rise to independence is not smooth like an elevator, but a dynamic and sometimes bumpy ride. Something parents and caregivers get tripped up on is how much to help when we are encouraging independence and self-reliance. Your level of helpfulness varies according to your child's need at any given time. It's not a clean slope from total support when our children are infants to no support at all when they are adults. It's a bumpy ride because life is complex, confusing, and ever-changing, and so are we.

Learner's Permit: High School

There is a lot of pressure for high school students to manage their jobs independently. Students are expected to know how to do school, even though that job has gotten, if possible, even more complex. You hear from teachers and other parents that your child should be able to manage their work without your help. Parental involvement is kept to mentoring clubs or organizing fundraisers.

Again, give the support that your child needs right now. Let them make decisions about classes to take, clubs to join, and sports to play. Involve them in every school meeting, and ask for their input and ideas on every accommodation or modification on the table. They may be ready to take the lead in meetings, send follow-up emails, or even schedule follow-ups. Or they may not. Every kid is different, and yours is still a work in progress.

When bigger decisions come up, like orchestra trips or club retreats, your child can decide if they want to go. If they do, this is a great time for them to plan how to make it happen. Are there forms to fill out? Money to fundraise? In some cases, stepping back and saying "Convince me" gives your kid a chance to reason through the steps and make a plan. You are still there as back-up (and to sign permission slips and checks), but they have taken the wheel.

> 🚗 When I was in high school, I had the opportunity to join my Honors Orchestra on a trip to Chicago. My parents were hesitant to let me go out of state without them, but ultimately decided I could go if I could figure out the funding on my own. I sold chocolate bars, washed cars, and saved the checks I was given for my birthday and Christmas. All of my hard work paid off, and the trip was one of the most memorable, inspiring, and worthwhile experiences of my time in high school.
>
> (Mary G.)

On the other hand, withholding reminders and assistance may be setting your kids up to fail. It doesn't have to be all or nothing. "If you don't plan for your club's trip and get the forms in on time, you won't be able to go." Can instead be, "I will back off and let you handle things unless you ask for help. Let's get reminders in the calendar right now so we can check in before the due date."

Speaking of clubs, how about the pressure to participate in not one, but many extracurricular activities? "It'll look good on your college application!" is a constant refrain. I've met students who work 80+ hour weeks between classes, clubs, sports, lessons, and homework. In what world is that a good idea?

Very often, our kids are setting the pace. With so many opportunities and so much pressure to stand out on a college app, kids are burning the candle at both ends. If this is a happy, busy, enjoyable work life for your child, please ignore the next paragraph. If you and/or your child feel overwhelmed by all the expectations and obligations, read on.

It's high school. As we talked about in Chapter 5, we don't want our kids to peak in high school. It's okay to have some life-work balance, even in 12th grade. Truly. This is not the last opportunity ever to play soccer, learn Chinese, do theater, or play in an orchestra. People can and do start any of these things later, like in college or beyond. A much more important skill than managing to fit in an extra Accelerated Placement (AP) class is to be able to speak up when you need a break. To be able to say no when one more drain on your time is one too many. To have time to reflect and dream and ponder. To take care of yourself, so that when you do move out of your parent's or caregiver's home, you continue to take care of yourself.

Preventative Maintenance: Regular Check-Ins

The other side of the advice from educators to let the natural consequences play out is the moment it interferes with the educators' jobs. Then you get the emails and the phone calls asking that you step in and help your kid finish projects, turn in homework, and remember assignments. This frequently happens at the end of the quarter, trimester, or semester, depending on how your child's school schedules their academic year.

Suddenly, you're in the hot seat for making sure your kid does their job. You have to figure out the systems you've been blissfully ignoring – how work is assigned, what the rubric is, where the required resources are, what the deadline is, are there check-in points along the way?, how do you turn work in?, when can we expect feedback (grades)?, etc. Middle school is a common time for gifted and 2e kids to lose their grasp on what used to be a streamlined job and is now 7, 8, or 9 jobs in one. In this case, you now need to figure out how each of these teachers handles all of the above components. It can be daunting, difficult, and demoralizing for both you and your child.

It's kind of like making sure everyone is on the same page after a meeting. And, depending on what you do, the same kind of communication you do in your job. When people work in isolation, it's way harder to get help solving problems. If you talk about your work and share progress with others, it's easier for someone to step in and help if you need support. Our kids' job of school should never be treated like a top-secret operation. The more your child can communicate about projects, goals, and expectations, the less likely they, and you, are to be blindsided when things aren't going so well.

Do you have a person with whom you share an end-of-the-day chat? More than just, "How was work?" "Good." Instead of surface check-ins, do you get to have conversations about your job and in return ask questions about things that you remember from previous conversations? "How did your important meeting go?" "Did you manage to get so-and-so on the phone today, after all?" "Did you try answering Zee's questions with a question, like we talked about? How did that go?" "Was the presentation a hit? I know you were worried they wouldn't ask questions – how did the Q&A go?" These detail-sharing conversations help us feel seen and heard. They make our jobs feel like a worthy topic of conversation. Having someone to problem-solve with can give us a fresh perspective. Knowing someone will check in helps us get through a trying day.

For our kids, this kind of daily sharing can help prevent the protective secrecy students may develop when they want to avoid trouble. "How was your day?" "Good." That "good" may be masking a world of turmoil. "Homework done?" "Yes" (eye-roll). That "yes" may hide the worry that unfinished assignments are stacking up and your child feels too stuck and overwhelmed to even have a conversation about it. You have your own things to remember and keep track of, but remembering some specifics about your child's day-to-day work can help them see that it isn't a secret spy mission – it's a job. And you're interested. "Did Mr. E. have any comments on your presentation today?" "Did Kay want to talk all the way through math class again?" "I was thinking about what you said about your history project. So cool that you are learning about Egyptian hieroglyphs. I don't think I learned anything about that in school. What was new today?" This will also help set the tone if you have to get more involved to support your child through a rough patch.

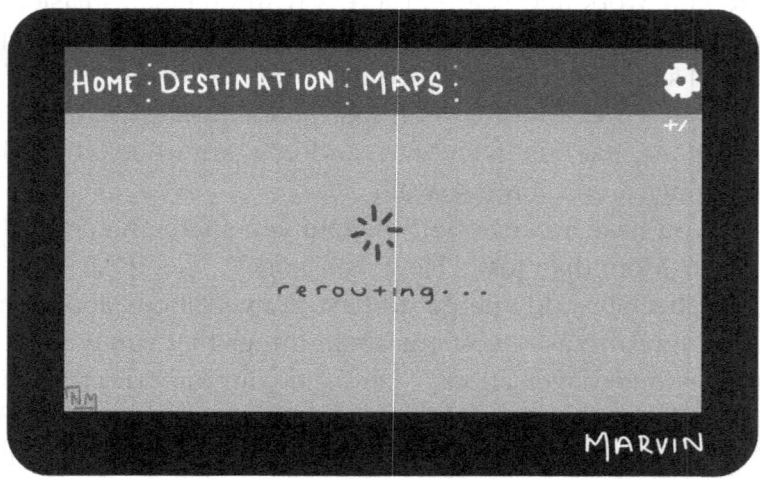

FIGURE 12.6 Rerouting...

Spare Tire: Being Your Child's Back-up

Think about the times when a task just seems like the last straw. Do you have supportive people in your life you can ask for help? I hope so. I remember when my youngest was a newborn and didn't sleep unless she was being held and I was sooooo tired. My husband had to go back to work and he was sooooo tired. My Mom had spent ten days with us helping and she'd just gotten home, suitcase not even unpacked. I called her and she could just hear that I was on the verge of tears from exhaustion, so she zipped her suitcase right back up and got on the next flight out. She stayed another ten days.

How does this relate to our kids learning self-advocacy? It's about someone having your back. I certainly didn't make my Mom come out every time I was tired or having a rough time, but the knowledge that she would be there if I really needed her gave me strength during tough times. And I knew even in those early days of parenting that I would strive to always be that person for my kids. Mom coming out to help didn't mean I wasn't a capable adult and a good mom. She just lent me her strength when mine was overtaxed. Such an amazing example she set – I am so grateful.

With my kids, I recall middle school teachers and high school teachers advising against helping my kids when they were forgetful – to let them learn from "natural consequences." And sometimes I had to let those natural consequences play out. But honestly, I would want someone to bring my lunch if I forgot it and had a long day and no other lunch options and they had time. I would be grateful if a family member showed up with my laptop, or cello, or paperwork. I've certainly had that kind of support in my life, and I readily offer a helping hand to others. I'm not going to punish my kids for being forgetful, especially when I know their absent-mindedness comes right from me!

⚠ If your child is chronically absent-minded, whether due to a diagnosable neurodivergence, like ADHD, or simply because they live in their heads and forget to manage the minutiae of life unless it really matters to them, this is a time for a different kind of intervention. To dramatically oversimplify, when someone constantly loses their keys, it's because the keys don't have a home that makes sense to that person. When a child forgets their backpack every day, it's probably because it is not a blockade in their pathway to getting out the door. I always joke that I'm terrible at keeping plants alive because they don't bark or cry. I have, during very busy periods of my life, been so bad at keeping plants alive that my children composed a song on the subject. So I may understand forgetfulness from the inside out!

My kids did not forget lunches or cellos or paperwork every day – that would have been another conversation and set of strategies all together. That's when you find an EF coach, a therapist who supports positive habit formation, etc. I won't dive into this too deeply because that is another book entirely, but I do recommend two important things:

1. Don't put strategies into place that infuriate your child or you.
2. Allow your child to develop their own strategies or modifications based on what the professionals recommend – ownership is the key to success with this type of thing!

So, no, I am not recommending that you spend your life following your child around to make sure they never forget anything. That's not good for anyone. However, if your child forgets their cello because it's only needed every 6th school day, and you have time to bring it to them, why not? If you can't, let them know you wish you could and you're sorry. Just like you would for your partner or sibling or friend. Just like you hope your partner or sibling or friend would do for you. Your child isn't learning how to be helpless, they're learning how to help. You'll appreciate this someday. Support your children the way you want them to support you in your old age. You don't want them following you around pointing at your socks, reminding you to put them in the hamper because they won't wash themselves. You do want them showing up when you're at the grocery store and forgot your wallet because you changed purses that day.

Keep Going: Your Modeling and Lessons Are Sticking

You may have many moments in your parenting journey when you wonder if your modeling, scaffolding, and reminding will ever sink in! It can feel like talking to a brick wall or screaming into the void. We have all thought, "How can they not know this by now?!?" The lovely thing about our kids growing up and becoming more independent in the world is that, eventually, those lessons we modeled, scaffolded, and reminded become useful. That's when they emerge, as if by magic, and help our kids manage their independent, young adult lives. If you can help it, never say "I told you so" about all the amazing wisdom you have imparted over the years. Let your kids own it now. They will give you all the credit you deserve eventually, especially if they decide to become parents or caregivers or educators themselves and experience the enormous challenge of imparting wisdom to a new generation.

You and your family will decide how to handle supporting each other in ways large and small. Just don't get too caught up in the "natural consequences" advice. If you can help and you would do it to help out a friend, do it to help out your kid. Don't be a martyr and sacrifice your own needs, and don't take your kid on a guilt trip. It may be mostly one-sided while they are growing up, but there comes a time when the helpers become the helped.

Bumps in the Road: Imposter Syndrome, Perfectionism, and Mindset

Imposter syndrome is that feeling that you aren't as smart as everyone thinks you are. That you don't deserve the position or award or praise you receive. That you lucked into getting the lead role in the play. That you don't deserve the recognition for your science project because you had to ask your parent for help. That being admitted to that exclusive college was a fluke and they will realize it and send you home.

⊤ **MILE MARKER**

Taking action is the biggest antidote to imposter syndrome. Imposter syndrome is anxiety and anxiety just wants us to stand still – anxiety wants us to do nothing.

That loud voice in your head may be screaming, "you're an imposter, you're an imposter, you're an imposter," but you know what? You put some paint on a canvas today. You ran today. You practiced your oboe today. You surfed today. You filled out your own application for college today. You did things today.

It doesn't make imposter syndrome go away, but every time you take a concrete action, its grip on you lessens a little bit. And that's a very cool thing.

(Dr Matt Zakreski, Elliott)

Gifted people may begin to suffer from imposter syndrome when what they can do with their gifts and talents cause a lot of comment and praise. Praise for one's abilities can set up certain expectations that can become enormous burdens over time. It's all tied up with perfectionism, which can cause us to work impossibly hard to maintain the standards we set or avoid the task altogether. You know that feeling when you enjoy a success, big or small, and you receive a lot of attention and praise? And then you are faced with a decision – do I keep going, even though I may fail miserably next time, or do I quit while I'm ahead?

The other kinds of comments that cause problems are the hurtful, critical, snarky comments that undermine your confidence. These can be from an individual, like your high school nemesis, or from a group, like the good ole boys club at work. Rather than setting high expectations you may feel you can't live up to, these comments feed your insecurities and contribute to the idea that you'll never be good enough, no matter how hard you try.

We all make choices every day about how we will handle success and failure. Our individual choices are made based on our previous experiences, whether we feel supported or discouraged by the people we live, learn, and work with, and our mindset about our abilities.

4th Grade

"Wow, you aced that test! That was such a tough one – you are so smart!" In your head, you are thinking, "That test was easy for me – I didn't work hard at all and still got 100%."

You now have some options to choose from:

◆ Sliding through – I feel great that I did well without studying and I will just see how the next test goes.
◆ Taking the easy road – I can't let anyone know how easy it is because if the teacher gives me harder work and I don't get 100% it will prove that I'm not so smart after all.
◆ Going underground – I will purposely do worse because I am uncomfortable with being the top of the class when I feel like I didn't earn it.

Middle School

You had the lead in the school musical last year and just know you'll get it again this year. You don't. It goes to another kid who is irritatingly good at hitting the high notes.

Your options:

◆ Working toward a goal – I will be the best 3rd villager ever and hope I get the lead again next year.
◆ Saving face – Pretend to be so busy you couldn't have done the lead anyway.
◆ Hiding out – Quit the play and decide theater is stupid and not for you.

High School

You have a big project due in history and you are dreading presenting it to the class. It's a song you wrote because that sounded like the most fun of the offered choices. You sing the song in front of the class and most of the kids and the teacher seem to really like it. But there are a few kids talking and laughing off to the side and you know it's about you. You hear one of them whisper, "Of course that loser did a song – they think they're soooo good. What a joke."

- ◆ Selectively ignoring – I can ignore the snarky comments and only listen to the feedback from people who liked my song.
- ◆ Going underground – I feel like a joke and a loser. I'm never singing in public again.
- ◆ Working toward revenge success – I am going to work like crazy to be a recording artist and show those jerks!

College

You've gotten into your top choice. You know other kids with better grades who didn't get their top choices. You feel lucky and terrified at the same time. What if they made a mistake? What if you get there and everyone is smarter than you? What if you fail? On the other hand:

- ◆ What if you show up and do your best?
- ◆ What if you ask questions when you don't know something?
- ◆ What if you help others when they don't know something?
- ◆ What if it's hard and you ask for help?
- ◆ What if you offer help to others who are struggling?

We talked about how hard it is for many gifted people to simply ask questions in Chapter 8. Asking questions shows that we don't know something, and that can threaten our identity as people who know stuff. I mentioned how freeing it was for me to let go of worry about what others thought and start asking all the questions. This was not a quick or total eradication of my imposter syndrome – I still get those feelings sometimes, like when I'm writing a whole entire book! I know there are many people who know more about advocacy and all the related topics in this book. You've noticed that many of these people have written works I admire and reference. Many have shared their wisdom in Mile Markers boxes throughout the book.

I've learned a lot through this process, like the fact that I still have imposter syndrome, which has reared its ugly head after some years of relative dormancy, and that I have tools to nip it in the bud. It helps when:

- ◆ I talk with people about my worries.
- ◆ I listen to others' stories about their battle with imposter syndrome.
- ◆ I keep writing anyway.
- ◆ I speak kindly to myself even when I'm stuck.
- ◆ I acknowledge my progress and growth.

⊓ MILE MARKER

Giftedness often comes with the misconception that exceptional abilities make you good at everything and less likely to fail. However, failure is a shared human experience essential for growth. While we can't control the past, how we think about it and what we do next is our choice. By embracing a growth mindset, failure becomes an opportunity. Building resilience and grit expands our comfort zones and ability to overcome failure. Understanding that no one is perfect not only allows us to feel compassion for ourselves and others but improves our overall well-being and happiness.

(Andrea L. Johnson, PsyD, LP, clinical psychologist)

- ◆ Who has your back when your road gets bumpy? Whose back do you have?
- ◆ When do you feel like an imposter? What action can you take?

References

Elliott, Sophia. "#036 Overcoming Imposter Syndrome with Dr Matt Zakreski." *OurGiftedKids*, 11 Nov. 2021. https://ourgiftedkids.com/036 -overcoming-imposter-syndrome/

Institute for Educational Advancement. "5 Definitions of Giftedness." 2 May 2012, https://educationaladvancement.org/blog-5-definitions -of-giftedness/

Rimm, Sylvia. *Foundational Principles of Parenting by Dr. Sylvia Rimm*. http://www.sylviarimm.com/article_foundprinpar.html

13

It's Not a Race to the Finish Line

On the Fast Track: What Are the Benefits?

Who says your child has to go through K-12 on the K-12 time-line? Some kids will take less time and some will take longer. This is as true with education as it is for kids to learn to walk, talk, or tie their shoes. Some kids will reach their full height at 12, and some not until they're 20. The public school system in the U.S. has the graduation "norm" set at age 18. But is that truly the optimal age?

The public education system was set up with expediency in mind. The idea of grouping children by chronological age makes sense in some regards, like physical maturation and social-emotional development (which can still be asynchronous among age peers). Because the school systems are so large and unwieldy, this dependence on sorting by age does mean that the system is likely too rigid for our unusual kids. Most kids do just fine going through school at the pace set by education experts who designed the system, run the system, create curriculum, etc. Some kids need a lot of additional educator time and support. And some kids, if given access to individualized instruction and pacing, could complete the whole 13-year she-bang in half the time.

DOI: 10.4324/9781003467441-17

⚠️ When it comes to gifted kids and school, most people think about early entrance to kindergarten or first grade, or grade-skipping, or early college. What about those gifted kids with additional exceptionalities that may take longer to get to the graduation goal post? Sometimes these kids need alternate routes (see Chapter 14).

Your goal may be for your child to be an independent self-advocate by the time they go to college, but your child may have other ideas. As we've talked about before, asynchrony is a hallmark of giftedness and twice-exceptionality. Your child may be ready for college-level material much earlier than other children, but not ready to live independently. Or your kid may want time to explore the world or possible career options before deciding on a college program. Could be that your gifted kid wants to go to trade school and dive right into their chosen career. All kinds of things are possible. Some benefits of the fast track:

◆ Accelerated learning helps prevent boredom or disengagement.
◆ Many school districts offer programs for advanced learning opportunities while your child is still enrolled in K-12.
◆ Early graduation can mean an early career start.
◆ Accelerated students can take gap years for additional explorations.

We'll talk about possible variations on the theme in Chapter 14.

Differential: Weigh Your Options

We've all heard the regrets. "My parents didn't let me..." "We couldn't afford..." "I heard about it after the deadline..." "I didn't know what I was missing out on..." "I missed the cutoff by one point..." "We moved here for the schools and they can't meet their needs...," etc. So many shoulda, woulda, couldas in the world. Is it right to move to a city you don't love for a school that *might* be great? Is it wrong to not sign your child up for a great program that will eat up all of their free time? What's right and what's wrong? That's completely up to you and your family. Even the best choices have unintended consequences. All you can do is the best you can do.

Parenting/caregiving is all about making the best decisions for the family. Sometimes this means we don't pursue an opportunity for one kid if it means someone else in the family will have negative consequences. Sometimes it means the whole family makes sacrifices in order to give one kid every chance of success in their area of passion. This happens in ways large and small all the time. We hear about siblings of elite athletes who spend life being dragged from practice to game. We know families who have moved across the city, state, country, or world to give a child access to resources – schools, coaches, programs. Sometimes families live apart so more family members can access what they need.

FIGURE 13.2 Sidequest?

When pondering life-changing moves to support one member of the family, weigh the known pros and cons and then explore the possibilities. I know we try to keep our kids from catastrophizing – "I got a B on the test, which will ruin my grade and lower my GPA and I'll never get into my top college and I'll struggle to get a job in my field and I'll have to move home and live in my parents' basement FOREVER!" And I don't recommend it here, either. But do travel down the proverbial rabbit hole a little bit and think about that gifted school you found and are moving across town, country, or globe so your kid can attend.

♦ What if it's great the first year and then the administration changes, funding is lost, there is a new teacher with no G/T training yet?
♦ What if the focus is solely on output and not process and your all-about-the-process kid hates it?
♦ What if elementary is great but middle school is the abyss?

Sometimes our sensitive young people struggle with the move from being a smart fish in a typical pond to being an average fish in a gifted pond. The later this shift happens, the more jarring it can be. What if your kid experiences imposter syndrome and anxiety to the point of not being able to attend school at all for a while? What then? You moved so your child could attend this school. That's an enormous sacrifice and an equally huge burden on your child to make this school a success.

What if the climate in your new location exacerbates your allergies, you can't find a job you love, or you all feel like fish out of water because your new town-mates hold different values dear? What then? If the school is working for your child but the rest of you hate it there, do you stay? How much of a sacrifice? How much of a burden?

(STOP) So here's the challenge. Can you think about the best-case scenarios and plan for the more challenging possibilities? If you make a huge move and it doesn't pan out the way you wish it had, can you accept and move on to solutions? Can your child?

⊕ I remember the first time I heard about a residential high school/college program for profoundly gifted kids. A parenting team who have since become dear friends had enrolled their child in this program, and when they described it to me I just panicked a bit about the idea of sending one of my kids off to college at 13 or 14. Rather than opening my mind and asking all the questions, I pretended this program did not exist. And when we got invitations from the school in the mail to learn more, I recycled them immediately. I could not bring myself to ponder that option. A few years later, I had the opportunity to work with this young person when they interned on a research project I was managing. I asked them if they would do it all again, given the chance. They said it was the best thing their parents could have done for them. I'm still grateful every day that I had my kids home during their high school years, but I'm pretty sure they, too, would have loved learning in an environment that met their intellectual needs alongside their same-age gifted peers. And while I endlessly admire my friends' courage for sending their young kid to college, and their kid absolutely thrived, I'm okay that I took the selfish route.

It's Okay to Ask for Directions: We Learn from Wrong Turns and Mistakes

Even the most well-meaning, educated, dedicated parents and caregivers have regrets. Parental guilt is built into the job. We do our absolute best to make sure our kids have the best opportunities we can provide, and we work so hard to help them find success.

Sometimes we do the wrong thing. That's because we're human. It's so awful to know you messed up on something that affects your most precious human, but all parents and caregivers make mistakes. We hope they are the kind that increase resilience and determination, rather than resentment and despair. Sometimes we don't know we even made a mistake until years later, when it has become a looming roadblock in our child's life. We stay up nights worrying, replaying, wishing we could undo or redo.

Here's an example that seems like a small mistake, but it feels huge to me right this minute because it's fresh. Just the other day, my youngest and I were going through boxes of photos and she brought up that we are missing two years of her school pictures because she didn't get the order form turned in on time. I thought, and said, "That was my responsibility. You were a kid. I shouldn't have put the burden entirely on you. I'm sorry."

All these years, she had thought it was her fault. That she hadn't done her job. But by being hands-off and letting her sink or swim, I was setting her up for failure. It was, in retrospect, not a teaching moment but an unkindness, and one I needed to apologize for. I can't go back in time and get the school pictures, but by talking about it, I hope I've taken an unfair burden off her shoulders. I'm an occasionally forgetful adult. She was an occasionally forgetful kid. Why would I place expectations on her that I, the adult, might not be able to live up to?

A reminder is a wonderful thing. Have you ever missed out on an opportunity or deadline because you were busy with other things and forgot? Have you ever not missed out because someone took a minute to send you a reminder? If a one-minute or less conversation, email, text, backpack check, or phone call means the difference between success and failure for your child, choose success.

Sometimes we ignore past mistakes because it feels bad to admit we were wrong. Or we don't bring things up because what if they have forgotten about it? Will we open old wounds? And many times, like with the pictures, we forget until it comes up again, maybe years later. And sometimes, we just did the very best, most thoughtful parenting we knew how to do, and it still didn't work out the way we hoped it would.

STOP

◆ How do you handle things when you've made a mistake? Do you talk about it or ignore it and pretend it will go away?
◆ How do you wish you could handle talking about your mistakes?

Reasons for Rerouting: Why Can't School Be More Like Video Games?

You know in video games where you must complete a level to advance to the next one, and if you mess up you have to do that easy level all over again? In the early days of video games, you had to start from the very first level every time you failed, no matter how far you had proceeded on your previous play. Are there any games like that anymore? The joy of a game having memory – when you can drop down to a lower level to try again (assuming you had another life to use), but not the lowest – what an innovation! Now, games save everything along the way so you don't ever have to start from the absolute beginning unless some catastrophe resets your device and it loses your progress.

Technology has advanced remarkably, but schools have gotten less user-friendly over the years. Our kids' brains are wired for progress, but many of our schools still embrace the one-size-fits-all, practice and repeat (aka drill-and-kill) methods of teaching. In some ways, the individualized progress feature has become even more rare in schools because of the large class sizes and the demands on teachers to teach to the next standardized, grade/age-based test. The ease of compacting and subject acceleration in the old one-room schoolhouse model has become instead an obstacle course worthy of an Indiana Jones movie.

It's no wonder that kids (and adults) become addicted to video games. That immediate reinforcement, both positive and negative, is what our brains crave (University of California, 2024). When your full-time job is filled with repetition and review, it makes sense that you'll crave some activity or interaction that actually works with your brain in the way your brain is made to work – "Let's think, let's act, interact, and do something new, novel, interesting! I want to do something that I'm good at! Work on a task in which I can see my own skill development." But what if your full-time work was engaging, dynamic, and interactive?

So, when people criticize you for making different educational choices on behalf of, and hopefully with, your child, know that you are doing your part to provide them access to a job of school that provides feedback, some challenge, lots of interest, and more opportunities for engagement. Stop listening to naysayers who say you need to do school "by the book." Ask instead who wrote that book, in what educational era, and with what audience in mind.

Roadblocks: Siblings, Elderly Parents, Health Issues, and Other Detours

Advocacy rarely exists as the sole purpose and work in anyone's life, even in short bursts. There is always something (or a lot of things) clamoring for attention. For families advocating for their gifted and 2e children, distractions on the advocacy road can be as minor as having overlapping schedules for kids' activities, to something as major as being the primary caregiver for an elderly parent dealing with health issues or dementia. Most often, the distractions are numerous and, in concert, overwhelming. Like driving on a winding mountain road in a rainstorm at night with fighting children in the backseat and one headlight out, advocacy requires determination, focus, and steadiness. On the up side, your advocacy efforts aren't generally as dangerous as the mountain road in the rain. On the down side, they require longer-term effort and a lot of persistence.

Siblings
A tricky thing to navigate is when you have more than one child and one of those kids needs more of you. Families with kids with varying needs struggle with the division of their most scarce resource – time. In some families, kids seem to take turns demanding more time, attention, and resources. In other families, one child needs more care and effort all the time. This can add fuel to the flames of parental guilt in a particularly poignant way. We, as parents and caregivers, feel the strain of the imbalance keenly, but we likely have no choice. This is especially difficult for single parents of multiple children, but also a challenge for families with present and involved parenting partners. Our

kids, on the other hand, have no basis for comparison and may feel an increased sense of sibling rivalry. Even if a situation in which one child requires the elephant's share of attention and resources is temporary, it leaves a set of lasting memories.

James Webb et al. recommend special time – uninterrupted time with each child, every day if possible. It doesn't need to be a lot of time – "Five special times of two to five minutes each will be far more powerful than one special time of an hour" (Webb, 2007). Even if you've got a baseball team at home, two minutes per kid still seems like it should be doable most days, right? Who is rolling their eyes at me right now?

♦   How do you cope when one child needs much more of your time?
♦   What are some ways you help your other child(ren) feel connected and loved?

Elders

In Chapter 12, I shared the story of my Mom coming out to help when my child-who-wouldn't-sleep was born, and how she came back at the drop of a hat when that darling baby still wasn't sleeping and I was at my wits' end. This wasn't the first time she dropped everything to help one of us. She was there for my sister and her kids, and my grandmother, and her own sister, and so many others. I had the example of care all my life. So when it was her turn to need care, my sister and I were all in. Well, my sis was all in for years and years, being our parents' primary caregiver in their old age.

In my family, we planned and pondered and talked about end-of-life stuff fairly frequently, so we had some idea of what our plan would be when the various times came – giving up driving, moving to assisted living, or hiring in-home care. Even so, and even though we were part of the care our parents gave their elders in their last years, it was still a new and difficult advocacy road to travel. All the practice and work we had done over the years of raising our kids helped immensely when advocating for our parents. We were still not perfect at it – never that – but at least we had some solid skills. Negotiating accommodations, finding outside support, documenting, following up, giving reminders, and educating new people about existing needs. The big difference was that we were reversing our roles with this beloved elder, and that felt strange as can be.

This book doesn't stretch to the nuances and challenges of caring for a loved parent or caregiver, but I include this to remind you that, if all goes well and you live to a ripe old age, you will at some point likely rely on your child or children to advocate for you. And I want to acknowledge that if you are still in the process of helping your child become a strong self-advocate and you need to also become an advocate for another loved one or loved ones, it's a lot. It's hard. You need help. Help exists. Part of your job is to find help and welcome it in.

 MILE MARKER

Having an aging parent while still raising or supporting one's own children presents certain challenges not faced by other adults – caregiving and financial and emotional support to name just a few.

(Kim Parker, Pew Research Center, 2013)

(STOP)

◆ Are you part of the "sandwich generation," caught between the needs of your growing kids and your aging parents?
◆ When was the last time you asked for help with either role?

Personal or Health Struggles

Life is messy, and sometimes really unfair. Health issues can derail our momentum faster than anything. Relationship problems can upend all plans. Financial woes pose real concerns that take a great deal of time and problem-solving bandwidth. When life throws you lemons and you don't have the strength, stamina, or time to make lemonade, it can feel like your kids are really missing out. When you have gifted kids with special interests, you may feel you are depriving them of opportunities to practice and shine. If your child is 2e and struggling with school, your inability to advocate for them at the level you feel you ought can seem like a major failure in your parenting journey.

These speed bumps on your road of life may be small and easily overcome, or they may be enormous and life-altering. Whatever life rolls your way, your kids are learning how to deal with adversity because you are showing them how. We hope beyond hope that our kids' lives will be smooth and happy roads to success and fulfillment, but everyone has bumps in the road, large and small. When you're overwhelmed with parental guilt, remember that the very most important thing you will ever teach your child is how to live life in all its pain and joy. You do that every day. I wish you courage on those rough patches of road.

References

Parker, Kim. "The Sandwich Generation." Pew Research Center, 30 Jan. 2013. https://www.pewresearch.org/social-trends/2013/01/30/the -sandwich-generation/

University of California. "Can't Stop Worrying? Why Video Games Help." 21 Mar. 2024. https://www.universityofcalifornia.edu/news/cant-stop -worrying-why-video-games-help

Webb, James T. A Parent's Guide to Gifted Children. Great Potential Press, Inc., 2007.

14

Look for Alternate Routes

Rerouting: Taking the Non-Traditional Route to School

Partial or full homeschool, subject or grade acceleration, micro, private, charter schools – there is a world of possible options for your family to explore. Access to these options varies by location, cost, eligibility requirements, and laws in your region. There are entire books and websites devoted to exploring these educational alternatives, so when you know what kind of avenue you are considering taking, you can focus in and gather all the information you need to make an informed choice. In this chapter, we'll explore some of the most commonly talked-about ideas for tailoring K-12 education to better suit the needs of gifted and 2e learners. This is by no means a complete overview, but I hope you can find some useful ideas for further inquiry.

FIGURE 14.1 Ooooooh a garage sale?

DOI: 10.4324/9781003467441-18

Changing Lanes: Looking for a New Way to Do School

When you advocate in a positive, respectful manner with your educational establishment, you increase your chances of success when asking for something new or different than what has been done before. This doesn't work every time, obviously—some institutions embrace the "we don't do that because we never have" mentality, and that's when you ponder other options. Sometimes your current teacher, school, or district will let you know that they have no strategies in place to meet your child's needs, and they don't foresee that changing anytime soon. Or, if it's a specialized program, they will know when it's not the best fit for your child. Take these words from the professionals seriously. You know that saying, "When people tell you who they are, believe them the first time"?

What if you as a parent are certain that a certain style of learning is best for your child? You are certain because this style, for example, Montessori education techniques, worked beautifully for two of your children. However, child number 3 is not one who functions best in that kind of environment. In fact, when given choices child 3 will likely choose to visit with friends or conjure up something creative, humorous, or even just plain naughty. When the director of the school states that this is not the best fit for his learning style, believe her. Despite your love for Montessori a force fit is usually not the answer.

(Joan Larson, M.A.)

Some factors to consider:

1. What needs are not being met in your child's current educational setting? Social/emotional? Academic? Creative expression?
2. Generate a list. What are some ideas for getting those needs met? Homeschooling? Changing schools? Partial homeschooling?
3. Which of the endless ideas are possible for your family? Take into account transportation, cost, time, etc.
4. Your and your parenting partner's education philosophies.
5. Your child's willingness to make a change.

TABLE 14.1 An nonexhaustive list of schooling options

Type of school	Type of schooling
Local public school	◆ Regular classroom with age peers ◆ Regular classroom with gifted enrichment pull-out program ◆ Gifted cluster-group in regular classroom ◆ Full-time gifted classroom ◆ Online public school
Local public school with acceleration	◆ Early entrance to kindergarten ◆ Early entrance to 1st grade ◆ Subject acceleration in one or more subjects ◆ Accelerated online learning in one or more subjects ◆ Full-grade skip
Local public school/homeschool combo	◆ Partial homeschool with child in school full-time (homeschool provider responsible for one or more subjects) ◆ Partial homeschool with child in school part-time (parent/caregiver provides alternate education during part of school day/week)
Open enrollment in nearby public school (Open enrollment may require test scores or audition, and may be unavailable when enrollment is capped)	◆ Full-time gifted program ◆ Language immersion programs ◆ STEM or STEAM programs ◆ Art programs ◆ Theater programs ◆ Music programs ◆ Dance programs ◆ Ecology programs ◆ Project-based programs ◆ Etc.
Charter school, where available (Charter schools are public schools. They are created by parents, caregivers, educators, or community members who are interested in providing a specialized education. These schools are created in agreement with and under the supervision of district, county, or state authorizers.)	◆ Montessori ◆ Classical education ◆ Language immersion ◆ STEM or STEAM ◆ Art ◆ Theater ◆ Music ◆ Dance ◆ History ◆ Ecology ◆ Project-based learning ◆ Etc.

(Cont.)

TABLE 14.1 (Cont.)

Type of school	Type of schooling
Private school, in person (Private schools can specialize even further than public or charter schools and have greater autonomy over how and by whom students are taught. Unless these schools receive public funding, they are not held to the same standards for providing special education services. They may, however, specialize in special education.)	◆ 2e specialization ◆ Gifted ◆ Special education only ◆ Religious education ◆ Arts education ◆ College prep ◆ STEM or STEAM education ◆ Classical education ◆ Etc.
Private school, online	◆ One-to-one instruction ◆ Asynchronous instruction ◆ Cohort instruction ◆ Flexible grouping ◆ Accelerated content ◆ Etc.
Homeschool (Parent/guardian takes responsibility for child's education, or parent/guardian signs on with homeschool co-op that provides structure and transcripts)	◆ Unschooling (child-led learning) ◆ School at home ◆ Classical homeschooling ◆ Roadschooling ◆ Worldschooling ◆ Eclectic homeschooling (mix and match of homeschool styles) ◆ Curated homeschooling (finding instructors and classes) ◆ Etc.
Dual enrollment college options (By application only. These can be boarding schools or day schools in which students complete high school requirements and earn a bachelor's degree in the same 4 years.)	◆ Full-time gifted programs in a college setting
Micro schools (These tiny, private schools are created by parents, caregivers, or educators who want to provide a small community of like-minded peers along with fairly individualized instruction. They can be offered in a place of work or in a home or other location.)	◆ Small cohort instruction ◆ Any of the above philosophies or disciplines

Parents and guardians have more power to make change than they realize. If your child's job of school is a job they wish they could quit, here are some options you may have (Table 14.1). These options are U.S.-based, as I have little experience with the laws and practices in other countries. They vary state by state, region by region. You may have access to some or all of these, or very few, depending on your location.

Some search terms to find out about the laws in your region:

◆ Homeschool laws in (your state, region, or country)
◆ Public school open enrollment in _____
◆ Partial homeschooling laws in _____
◆ Charter school laws in _____

The National Association for Gifted Children provides a glossary of terms in education on its website.

In the next sections, we'll look at some of the variations on school mentioned in Table 14.1. Keep in mind that this is not a complete guide to everything out there. Nor is it a guarantee that your school or district will be open to some/any/all of the ideas mentioned here. This chapter is intended to give you some information and a lot of ideas so that you can begin to gather your options and understand your jurisdiction over your child's education.

As I've mentioned a bunch of times already, try not to make decisions about your child's education unilaterally. Do your homework with your parenting partner(s) before presenting options to your child and be sure to only present viable options. Presenting a change as a fait accompli is rarely met with over-whelming success and enthusiasm. The more ownership you can give your child over the process, the more likely they are to put in the work to make the change successful.

⊕ Our oldest was entering 4th grade when we changed schools so she could attend a full-time gifted school-within-a-school. We attended information sessions, toured the new school, and she even shadowed a student for a day. We made the decision as a family to start both kids in the new school in the fall. (This was not the first of many decisions and changes we made on our non-traditional K-12 path for both kids. Of the 18 types of acceleration listed in the 2004 Templeton National Report on Acceleration, "A Nation Deceived," our family implemented 11 over the 15 years we had kids in K-12.) We stayed in touch with some families through Girl Scouts and many of those bright humans did very well staying in the local school district. The comparisons were naturally made, and sometimes it was hard for my kids to see the positives in their new situation when faced with the neat things they were missing out on. So even though we made most educational decisions as a family, regret and grass-is-greener thinking still happened.

Acceleration

Much fuss is made about acceleration. Someone always knows the worst stories of kids who were too young, too little, and just not ready. Sad stories of kids skipping grades and losing their friends. Even worse, stories of kids skipping grades and catching up with an older sibling. Cautionary tales of sending kids to college way too early (this is one of the main arguments for avoiding full grade skips). So many stories of drama and strife. What we don't hear about very much are the many, many success stories. Mostly because they are uneventful and relatively quiet stories of making school a better fit.

Acceleration comes in many forms. A few of the most common are:

◆ **Early entrance to kindergarten or first grade** – this is just what it sounds like. You approach the school with the request, and they will (hopefully) have a process in place to evaluate whether they think this is a good idea for your child. Schools tend to be more open to this if your child is closer to the age cut-off and will turn 5 (for kindergarten) or 6 (for first grade) within the first couple of months of school. If, through their evaluation process, they decide to try early entrance, there will be a system of check-ins and evaluations along the way to make sure it's all working out well.

♦ **Grade-skipping** – this, too, is exactly what it sounds like. Sometimes the family requests evaluation for a grade-skip, and sometimes the school recommends it. Rarely, a double grade skip will be considered. Even if the school is proposing the grade-skip, the family has the power to accept or refuse. If you're new to the idea or on the fence about your decision, it may help to start a pros and cons list (Table 14.2). You may want to do this more than once – the first one with just you or you and your parenting partner(s), the second one with your child.

Your for and against items may be similar to Kay's family's list, or you may have other concerns. Every family will weight the items on their list differently.

TABLE 14.2 Grade-skipping: for and against

For	Against
Kay knows all the content for 3rd grade already, so a skip would give them new things to learn	4th grade will go at the same slow pace, so even though the content will be new, Kay can't move through it any faster
Kay has a friend in the 4th grade class already	They might lose touch with the friends they have in their current grade
Kay will be able to participate in the summer program that is for 4th grade and up	Kay is pretty small for their age – they may have a disadvantage in sports later on
If Kay graduates a year early, they can have a gap year to travel or intern somewhere	If Kay wants to go right to college after high school, they will be younger than everyone there
Kay has always preferred being around older kids	Kay's classmates will mature earlier and drive earlier, and they might be into more grown-up things earlier
Kay will be in the same school with their older sibling for more years	Kay's older sib may not like the idea of their younger sib being in a closer grade
Kay will be able to access higher-level coursework offerings, like AP, a year sooner	If Kay stays in school longer, they may be able to take more higher-level coursework and earn more AP credits before going to college

◆ **Subject acceleration** – we talked about this in Chapter 10. Subject acceleration is a wonderful way to allow kids to access higher-level content without the full grade skip. Trotting down the hall for higher math is a free and easy option for schools. If the subject acceleration needs to happen between schools, like a middle schooler heading to the high school, scheduling gets a little more complicated. At this point, an online option might be implemented to cover the gap until the child moves to the high school full-time.

◆ **Dual enrollment** (high school and college) – for kids who are ready for college-level coursework, it may be possible to do dual enrollment in high school. The credits earned need to double as high school credit, so there is some careful organizing and course selection to do each semester. If the student is still taking classes at their high school, this can also create quite the transportation and scheduling puzzle (Wilkins, 2022).

Some states have a Post Secondary Enrollment Options (PSEO) program. High school students can attend a college or university in person or online while still in high school. The college must be enrolled in the PSEO program and students have to meet certain criteria with test scores and/or grades to qualify. PSEO allows students to earn college credit at no additional cost to the family.

College in the Schools(CIS) is another program that might be available in your school or district. CIS also allows high school kids to access college coursework, and in this program, classes are taught in person or online through the high school itself.

Advanced Placement (AP) classes are more common than PSEO or CIS, and also provide a pathway to early college credit. AP classes are taught by qualified teachers according to the AP guidelines. Students take the classes and then a final, standardized test. A score of 3 out of 5 or better on this test means the student did well enough to earn college credit if the college of their choice accepts AP credits. Not all 4-year colleges accept these credits.

Students may sign up for the AP exams without taking the full class.

◆ **Early entrance to college** – this may sound like the result of grade-skipping, but this is a different thing altogether. When a student has exhausted the high school's resources, they may apply to college. Local community or state colleges may have dual enrollment programs, like PSEO, that will fund this option. It is very similar to dual enrollment, except that the student does not have classes at the high school and is full-time at the college. Homeschool families can also access early college or dual enrollment by contacting the college directly and learning what the process for admission entails.

The Acceleration Institute at the Belin-Blank Center, University of Iowa, has a wealth of resources and in-depth information on the many types of acceleration.

Diagnostics: Getting Your Child Tested

Why Test?

IQ, or intelligence quotient, test scores can open doors to various types of programs, including full-time gifted schools, online programs, and gifted communities that cater to high IQ folks, like Davidson Young Scholars or Mensa (Davidson Institute; Mensa International). Certain kinds of tests can also give you insight into your child's strengths and challenges. A child's test profile that shows significant discrepancies between subtests could be a helpful indicator of twice-exceptionality. There are tests that can help you decide whether or not to accelerate your child, and there are tests that look for specific cognition, learning, and processing differences.

Some folks want to test just out of curiosity, or for the confirmation of their suspicions. I think, as long as you are careful with how you use the information you receive, it's okay to test to learn more about how your child thinks and learns. I do caution, as I did in the talking about gifts section in Chapter 4, that sharing some testing information, like IQ scores, with your child can cause them to pin their gifted identity on numbers rather than on characteristics and strengths. Sharing too much detail with the larger world can also set your child up for comparisons and judgment. Testing, in my opinion, should be considered a tool, not a badge.

Testing for the sake of testing can be detrimental to a child's self-esteem and make them wonder what could be so wrong with them that they need all of the tests. Conversely, not getting to the bottom of an issue means you may not know about or be able to access interventions and supports. Treat testing like a self-discovery process for your child. You can't find the right tool for the job until you discover what the job requires. Like if you were to show up with a hammer only to find that the job is changing a tire. What you really need is a jack and a lug wrench, or if you go all out, a lift and an impact wrench.

What Kinds of Tests Are There?
Ability or IQ Test
Ability tests and IQ tests measure a child's potential to do well in specific areas. They may measure visual/spatial skills, verbal reasoning, problem-solving ability, and more. There are several commonly used IQ tests out there, plus a bunch of lesser-used or out-of-date tests. When seeking an IQ assessment, do your research on:

- The provider – do they understand giftedness and twice-exceptionality? This can make a difference in the way they approach your child and the usefulness of their report.
- Type of test(s) used – is it one of the standards that will serve the purpose you have for testing? Check with the school or program you are interested in to make sure the test your provider uses is an accepted measure.
- Cost – testing can range from a few hundred U.S dollars to several thousand dollars. These tests are rarely covered by insurance.
- One test or many?– Some providers offer packages of testing. These may include IQ, achievement, screeners for

ADHD, autism, or learning disability. Some folks offer inventories of interests, social and emotional needs, etc. Be clear about what you are looking for and what you need.

Achievement Tests

Achievement tests are assessments of what your child knows. These can test knowledge in all core subjects, or very specific ones. You can assess things like reading fluency, reading comprehension, math level, science knowledge, etc. These tests can help you and your educational team decide on things like subject acceleration or a grade skip. Schools tend to have preferences here, too, so take care to match the tool to the job, or the test to its intended purpose.

Screeners

Screeners exist for a thousand things. Well, maybe not a thousand. Well, maybe more than a thousand. There are gifted screeners, which measure aptitude. Reading screeners that look for dyslexia, comprehension issues, etc. Screeners for autism, ADHD, anxiety, and many, many more. If you suspect a particular challenge, let your provider know specifically what behaviors, actions, emotions, or other signals have you seeking assessment.

Specialty Testing

A neuropsychological evaluation includes many or all of the above kinds of tests and screeners. If you know something is going on but don't know what, a full neuropsychological evaluation can be a great place to start. Sometimes tests occur over two or more days, so scheduling is a consideration. These full evaluations can be expensive, and testing for educational purposes is generally not covered by insurance.

There are many other kinds of evaluations you may want to pursue if you're not getting answers or if the answers you get don't fit what you know. For instance, if you think your child's hearing may be the underlying cause of their attention issues, you would go see an audiologist. If your family has a history of sight challenges, you see an ophthalmologist.

Sometimes it feels like every answer you get leads to two more questions. Finding and working with a gifted center or gifted parent coach who specializes in supporting families through this discovery process can be helpful. As always, ask all the questions and document everything. Ask for the full names of assessments and check on the credentials of the provider. And try to keep it light and fun for your child. Make it a pleasant experience, with an outing or an indulgence to look forward to afterward. Talk about how cool it is that people create these assessments to help us figure out what tools we need. Don't fret or coach your child on behavior or focus – the provider has experience with kids and will do just fine with whatever your child throws their way.

How Much Horsepower Do You Have? Advocating for Your 2e Child

There is a wonderful, short article by Deborah J. Paquette called *Stones Across the River*. In it, she uses the analogy of school work being heavy stones children need to get from one side of a river to the other. Most kids use a wheelbarrow and cross the river using a bridge. Some kids don't have a wheelbarrow or access to the bridge and try to swim the stones across, but this requires a great deal of strength and most of these kids get in over their heads and obviously need some help. Twice-exceptional kids may be very strong swimmers – their giftedness makes it possible for them to swim stones across even when their additional exceptionalities mean no wheelbarrow, no bridge. So they look like they're doing an average amount of work, when in fact they are swimming like crazy (Hoagies' Gifted).

I find this analogy very helpful when advocating with 2e learners for accommodations or modifications to their job of school. Just because these kids can keep their heads above water while carrying heavy stones doesn't mean they should have to. And what happens when the rocks get bigger and heavier and they still don't have a wheelbarrow or access to that bridge? They either let go of the stones or they sink right along with them. We don't want either of these outcomes for kids.

Parents and guardians who ask for modifications to their child's education are often met with the word "no." Some of the most frustrating responses I have received from educators and administrators are "we don't do that because we don't do that," or "no one has ever done that before and we don't want to set a precedent," "that isn't how the system works," or "we don't see evidence that this is necessary." These lines are delivered with firm assurance, no evidence of flexibility or compromise in sight. The person brave enough to ask is firmly put in their place, and no further discussion is welcome.

On the other hand are the parents and caregivers who don't know to ask for modifications or accommodations or testing for their child. They know their child is struggling, but trust the school to have the answers and the willingness to take all available steps to support the learners in their care.

Schools may volunteer to evaluate a child whose achievement has fallen far (2 grade levels or more) behind age peers. Unfortunately, 2e kids may take a long time to get to the point where they are significantly enough behind to warrant evaluation. Twice-exceptional kids are very often able to compensate for their challenges because of their unusually strong strengths. These kids will look absolutely average from 10,000 feet, but if you look more closely, you'll see the spikes and valleys.

If you know that something is making the job of school harder for your smart kid than it should be, it might be time to request an evaluation. You have some legwork to do first:

◆ Start your paper trail. Document the strengths and the struggles your child is experiencing. Save test scores, write brief descriptions of the challenges, include examples.
◆ Talk with your child's teacher. Make sure they see what you see, or learn what they are seeing that is different from your perspective. Send follow-up emails to add to your documentation.

◆ Request, in writing, a special education assessment for a suspected learning disability. If your child has a diagnosis, include that information in your request.

◆ Follow up to be sure your request was received. You'll want documentation, including the date you handed it over or mailed it.

◆ Ask the school what their process and timeline are, and check in with them regularly.

There are many great sources of information about special education law. If your child qualifies for special education services, there are laws, rules, and guidelines in place to help families access support.

Good special education services are individualized, intensive and expensive. Schools often balk at providing intensive services. Parents are often dealing with personal obstacles – lack of information, isolation, and emotions. What can you do?

You can use tactics and strategies to anticipate problems, manage conflict, and avoid crises. If you have a disagreement or dispute with the school, tactics and strategy will help you control the outcome.

(Wrightslaw)

What Is an IEP?

An IEP is an Individualized Education Plan. An IEP is a legally binding agreement that the school will offer specialized, goal-oriented instruction to support students with disabilities in reaching their educational and related goals. The IEP falls under the Individuals with Disabilities Education Act (IDEA) (Individuals with Disabilities Education Act). A child must have a diagnosed disability that interferes with their ability to thrive academically in order to qualify for an IEP. These can be physical, emotional, or cognitive challenges – there are 13 categories of disability that qualify. IEPs identify goals and include strategies for helping students achieve those goals. A goal might be behavioral, "When feeling overwhelmed, Vee will ask to use the quiet corner or will employ a calming strategy at their desk (5 senses check in, 5 counted breaths, etc.)." Or relate to schoolwork, "Vee will work toward a goal of having 90% of homework assignments turned in on time." Some goals extend outside of school, "By the end of the year, Vee will be getting to school on time 100% of the time."

Because 2e kids have strengths that can mask or mitigate their challenges, it can be tricky to get a diagnosis. For instance, a gifted child with a reading disability like dyslexia may be able to recall enormous amounts of information through memorization, so their learning challenge is only found when the workload exceeds their ability to use their strong memory to mask their reading difficulty. Even in cases when a child *has* a diagnosis that could make them eligible for an IEP, they also have to demonstrate a need for special education services. Like the child swimming the stones across, 2e kids may be too strong to look like they need help.

What Is a 504 Plan?

504 agreements fall under the purview of the U.S. Department of Education's Office for Civil Rights (OCR). These plans are all about removing barriers. They differ from an IEP in that they don't focus as much on goals, but outline modifications and accommodations that make learning accessible. Kind of like finding a substitute for the wheelbarrow and bridge in Paquette's story (U.S. Department of Education).

What Is a GIEP?

Some schools, districts, and/or states in the U.S. have what is called a Gifted IEP (GIEP). These are educational plans that focus on strength building and may include acceleration options, enrichment opportunities, or access to differentiated instruction (meaning doing different work, not just more of the same). These are not covered under the IDEA nor enforced by the OCR, but may be covered under state law. These plans require schools to have an identification protocol and gifted services in place, so they may come after identification and funding mandates in your state-level advocacy efforts.

Won't the Label Follow Them Forever?

Labels are useful tools in a lot of ways. Educators use labels as a kind of quick reference guide to the kinds of strategies and supports a child will require in the classroom. The shorthand helps teachers with 25 new students identify the kids who may need more time and attention. Labels also serve as a possible qualification for special education services and one of the legal agreements mentioned above. These agreements can specify that a child needs extra time on tests, a quiet space for writing tasks, or assistive technology in the classroom. These accommodations can then follow the student to college and help them self-advocate for additional supports from the college or university office that provides such assistance.

Some labels come with negative connotations, however. An Emotional Behavioral Disorder (EBD) label can strike fear in the hearts of classroom teachers because they don't know if they will have a quiet child too riddled with anxiety to speak up and ask for help, or if they will have a child with a short fuse and big temper that might pose safety concerns for themself or others. Similarly, an ADHD diagnosis can present as an inattentive daydreaming student or one who is bouncing off the walls.

Will the label be a liability down the road? I don't have a crystal ball (well, I do, but it's the kind you bring out for Halloween and not terribly effective for looking into the future) so I don't know how things will play out on the road ahead. What I see happening right now is young people embracing differences, learning more about themselves and wearing labels proudly. I think we adults can support this ideology of acceptance, and practice it ourselves. The more we normalize differences, the less our unusual kids will feel like they have to hide in conformity. If you consider a label to be a useful tool that gives access to other tools, your child will, too.

Homeschooling

The word homeschooling, like the word gifted, has a wealth of baggage that clutters conversations to the point where a piece of common ground is hard to find. It may seem old-fashioned or overprotective. The term implies a rejection of societal norms. The mention of homeschool evokes homespun dresses, slate chalkboards, and Mama holding a pointer stick and lecturing on grammar. In some families, this might be how homeschooling is done. Gifted and 2e homeschooling, however, is infinitely more global citizen-oriented. Rather than a rejection of the world, gifted homeschooling is an exploration of the world. There are even people who world school. That is, they travel the globe with their kids and teach them all about their world while still getting in the basics, like math and grammar. There may be a little rejection of societal norms, at least as far as it comes to socializing children so they fit in with their age peers. But it's certainly a different kind of homeschooling.

There are many philosophies of homeschooling, and your family can choose what works best for you. It's okay to start in traditional school and move to homeschooling, and it's equally okay to do the reverse. You have a lot more control over your child's education than you may know. (Some places have laws against homeschooling, so do your homework!) I recommend connecting with local and online gifted organizations that have a homeschooling group where you can ask all your questions.

My children were evaluated by a gifted education specialist in 2002. The results led to each of them being skipped a grade. Despite multiple meetings with school staff in preparation for the upcoming school year, the outcomes weren't ideal – particularly for my older child. The teacher created an environment so hostile to my kid that I was compelled to pull both children out and homeschool. I hadn't ever seen myself as a homeschooler, but my kids blossomed at home. They excelled in a setting that gave them academic freedom and demonstrated to them that their needs would *always* be supported.

(Teresa Ryan Manzella)

Gifted homeschooling can happen a lot of different ways and in many combinations:

◆ Caregivers teach a topic or two of interest.
◆ Family members teach a topic of interest.
◆ Co-ops with local families.
◆ Online co-ops with families from everywhere.
◆ Micro-schools.
◆ Online courses.
◆ Partial homeschooling (some classes in school, some elsewhere).
◆ Road school – learning while traveling.
◆ World schooling – learning while traveling abroad.
◆ Mentorships.
◆ Internships.
◆ MOOCS.
◆ Libraries.

Unschooling

Homeschooling can be a saving grace for families with multi-exceptional kids. If your child has become so traumatized or burned-out by school that they just can't function anymore, taking them out of school may be the way to get them (and you) out of the endlessly negative cycle. There is a technique called unschooling that is the first step in starting homeschooling after attending a brick-and-mortar school. Unschooling is like healing a broken bone. You can't put any weight on it for as long as it takes to become fully healed. No required school work, no classes, no assigned reading. Student-led learning only. Of course, there are routines that make the family function, like chores and curfews, etc., but the more you can let go, the more complete the healing may be. Then, as your child begins to express an interest in things, follow their lead and go at their pace.

This process can be excruciating for sequential adults who thrive on timelines and to-do's. It's a huge commitment on the part of the whole family. And there are plenty of families who cannot, under any circumstances, make this happen, like solo parents who must work outside the home and do not have anyone to stay with this unschooling child.

Partial Homeschooling (Blended Learning)

Partial homeschooling can happen in a lot of variations. The negotiation with the school to make this option work will look different for every family. Rather than going in for a meeting with partial homeschool in your back pocket as a last resort, put it squarely on the table as an option (if it is an option for your family, that is!). Do some research ahead of time to find out what the laws are in your area, and ask homeschooling parents what they know about the laws and rules governing homeschooling and partial homeschooling in your region. The clearer your plan, and the less work for the school, the better chance it will be a smooth process.

If the school is resistant to your plan, ask how they would improve upon it. Very often the biggest argument against these arrangements is transportation or the need for student supervision if the class the child is opting out of is in the middle of the school day. Sometimes, it's more about setting a precedent that they don't want – "If you do this, everyone will want to do it!" kind of thinking. Really, though, I think most parents want to let the school handle school, so setting a precedent and creating a flood of applicants for partial homeschooling are unlikely.

Let's look at a few ways partial homeschooling worked well.

🜨 If I knew then what I know now... How many conversations have I started with that very sentence? One of the things I coulda-woulda-shoulda myself about is homeschooling. We did partial homeschool for one year with each child, one in 8th grade and one in 12th. For the 8th grader, it was so she could do math at her own pace. We opted out of the gifted math class, signed her up for an online program, and negotiated space in the library for her to work during math time. Because she had taken ownership of her mathematical trajectory, she was ready and able to take AP Calculus in 9th grade. I know this doesn't sound at all like homeschooling, but no one wanted me to sit that child down at the dining room table and try to teach her math I never took. This is what gifted homeschooling can look like – find ways to let your child stretch their mental muscles in their topics of strength and interest. And it doesn't depend on what you know. For most of us, our kids will outpace us in one or more subjects, if given the resources and time to do so. What a wonderful thing! We are not limited by our own expertise or ability to teach, just by our willingness to curate opportunities and negotiate shared time, in the case of partial homeschooling.

For the 12th grader, it was a matter of making time for classes in her interest area. She wanted to take all the art history classes available to her, but she needed one more year of English credit and one more of Health. She was attending an art school, and the principal was completely on board with the partial homeschooling agreement. I consulted with my kid, filled out the paperwork our state requires, wrote up and submitted the syllabi and course outlines as per our agreement with the school, and then just let her do her stuff. For her Health credit, she grocery shopped, cooked meals, and discussed the nutritional values of things. She made her own doctor and dentist appointments and got herself to them. She worked hard to manage her chronic sleep deficit, and regularly reminded us to stay hydrated. "Hydrate don't die-drate" became a common phrase in our household. For English, she submitted a presentation proposal to a national gifted organization, was accepted, created a dynamic PowerPoint, and delivered a very cool presentation to an engaged and delighted audience. She handled the Q&A with aplomb. She enjoyed it so much, she presented again the next year as a college freshman.

🚌 My son D in 2nd grade had the option to go outside the classroom with four other students to work on higher-level math. He refused, as he didn't want to "do something different" from the rest of the class. I frequently volunteered at the school and witnessed him sitting in the classroom during math lessons with content I knew he had understood years previous. He also struggled with sensory overload throughout the long school day; he often said that he wished he could go to school only half of the day. Due to his lack of academic challenge and sensory issues, I requested to homeschool him in the afternoons during his 3rd-grade year. That allowed him to work on math, social studies, science, and cursive writing at home. D's 3rd-grade teacher thankfully was willing to work with me and let me know what the students were doing in science and social studies. I chose to use a different math curriculum from the school, and we worked through 3rd- and 4th-grade math in that year. The time together working on school-things was not always easy, but it made the morning time at school easier for D … and he was actually learning new things at home. I was fortunate that the school's principal was willing to let me part-day home school. I am a community college math instructor and, as I said, volunteered in the school, so the principal knew me. A self-contained gifted academy opened in the district the next year, and that met D's needs for the next few years.

(AH)

Philosophies of Homeschooling

In Table 14.1, we looked at just a few of the models and philosophies of homeschooling. I've been lucky enough to work and volunteer with many homeschool parents and caregivers, and I've learned a lot about the different models or structures. The only kind of homeschooling our family did was partial homeschooling, so I listen and learn with a healthy dose of admiration and awe to the creativity and dedication of gifted homeschoolers.

I won't go into the different philosophies here, partly because I don't have room and partly because I think you should hear from the folks who have been there and done that. If homeschooling is in your future, know that you do not have to know everything your child needs to learn. If you have an area of expertise and a pleasant way of teaching your child, go for it. For the rest, outsource instruction to the experts.

Let Them Drive: Trust Your Child

Our biggest advocacy story occurred when we removed our kindergartener from public school. After many unsuccessful attempts to advocate for his academic and social-emotional needs, we decided to begin our homeschooling journey. Ever since then we've been extremely thoughtful and mindful of who has access to our children. We've been proactive when searching for mentors, teachers and tutors who support our individualized education approach to schooling. For example, when we began our search for a piano teacher for our son, we advocated for his need to be self-directed, unpressured, and to move at his own pace. We found the perfect teacher for this and it worked until our son indicated through his massive explosion of skills that he needed to move to a more intensive music education. But, we couldn't sacrifice the necessary characteristics of the teacher; someone who was patient and kind, extremely talented and really knew when to push him and when to pull back. We found a great fit and our son is now a second-year piano performance major at a top-level conservatory.

This approach also meant that our children became aware of their own needs and how they work best. Our daughter advocated for a grade skip because both her academic level and her social development were more in line with older students. And while she is homeschooled, this resulted in her having access to both extracurricular and academic programming that better met her overall needs. She has also developed a very clear picture of the types of classes that work for her and why. She is the final decision maker in all of her academic programming. Our daughter continues to have a strong sense of self, a deep need for autonomy, and the confidence to express her needs and make adjustments as needed.

(Kasi Peters, M. Ed.)

Encourage Side Trips: Taking a Gap Year or Exploring Options

Sometimes you just need a break. While your child is a child and not supporting themself or a family, a break is not only possible, but sometimes necessary. As we talked about above, unschooling is a break from the rigid structure of school and a time to allow a child to direct their own learning. Unschooling can happen at any time in a child's school career, but there are some natural breaks. Summer vacation can function like an unschooling period, but only if it isn't overly scheduled. Taking a gap year after high school is another time a kid can unschool before making the next big decision. Sometimes kids take a break and are ready to jump right back into school, college this time, and occasionally they find a new direction they want to pursue. If your child was an early entrant or had a grade-skip, you may have a gap year or two built into the plan. For families whose kids graduate with their age peers, a gap year can seem like falling behind. Can you reframe it as a sabbatical or a hiatus? Something intentional and thoughtful? Why the rush?

New Pathways: Career Change

Remember the discussion of multipotentiality in Chapter 4? These creative, multi-talented folks have a world of options and only 24 hours in a day, so it can be heartbreaking to choose only one path. Our kids choose a major in college (or refuse to choose a major) and feel like that decision has set their course for the rest of their lives. The kids who opt not to go to college feel the limitations even more strongly – "I don't have a degree, so I can't apply for this job that will use all of my skills and talents."

Think about the people you know who have changed direction in their careers, maybe even more than once. You might be one of those flexible thinkers, yourself. You may have started down one path and learned about something new that caught your interest. You may realize your current career just isn't working for you and it's time to make a change. Whatever the reasons for a change, there is a world of options out there.

We can normalize this idea for our kids who are frozen at the very thought of declaring a major or starting their first "grown-up" job. The specific skills you learn and use in one career may not transfer, but the work ethic and professionalism certainly will. I heard a fellow named Josh Waitzkin speak at a conference years ago. He was the 9-year-old chess champion who inspired the movie, *Searching for Bobby Fischer*. He talked about the skills and focus he put into the game of chess and how he applied those to his second successful career in martial arts. He calls it transfer of level (Waitzkin, 2008).

This idea struck me as significant for how we teach gifted kids about their work. The skills they learn in one area are never wasted, even if they change paths. That was a comforting idea to me, a chronic multipotentialite, and one I have shared with others ever since.

Stop and Smell the Roses: Maintaining a Work/Life Balance

We talked in Chapter 13 about how the fast track isn't always the right track for your gifted or 2e child. Sometimes they will take you on a high-speed race because that's the way they roll. And sometimes they will seemingly stall out and struggle to get the most basic tasks done. This is when you help them find ways to lighten their load and find time to smell the roses.

Work/life balance isn't for everyone. Some driven few thrive on the intensity of single-minded purpose. Even those folks, I imagine, need a break from time to time. And our definition of the life part of work/life balance can be different from person to person. I find nothing in the world so relaxing as reading, so that's a big part of my self-care. Another person needs time in nature. Still another recharges their batteries by gaming online with friends.

- What does your ideal work/life balance look like? Is your child's idea of a good balance for them similar or different from yours?
- If you could have done school your way, what would that have looked like? What would be your child's ideal job of school?

References

Acceleration Institute. https://www.accelerationinstitute.org/ (accessed 30 September 2024).

Davidson Institute. "Davidson Young Scholars for the Highly Gifted." 7 March 2021. https://www.davidsongifted.org/gifted-programs/young-scholars/

Hoagies' Gifted. Stones Across the River. https://www.hoagiesgifted.org/stones_across_river.htm

Individuals with Disabilities Education Act. "Individuals with Disabilities Education Act (IDEA)." 5 April 2017. https://sites.ed.gov/idea/

Mensa International.. "IQ Test – FAQs – Mensa International." 1 February 2024. https://www.mensa.org/getting-your-iq-tested-faqs/

National Association for Gifted Children. "Glossary of Terms." https://nagc.org/page/glossary (accessed 14 October 2024).

U.S. Department of Education. "Protecting Students with Disabilities." https://www2.ed.gov/about/offices/list/ocr/504faq.html (accessed 1 October 2024).

Waitzkin, Josh. *The Art of Learning: An Inner Journey to Optimal Performance.* Simon & Schuster, 2008.

Wilkins, JoAnne. "50-State Comparison: Dual/Concurrent Enrollment Policies." Education Commission of the States, 21 June 2022. https://www.ecs.org/50-state-comparison-dual-concurrent-enrollment-policies/

Wrightslaw. https://www.wrightslaw.com/info/advo.index.htm

PART 5

Maps, Tools, and a Spare Tire

15

Bon Voyage

Journeys rarely go exactly according to plan (at least in my experience). The journey of raising gifted children is challenging, interesting, humorous, frustrating, overwhelming, delightful, exhausting, and a whole pile of other difficult and wonderful things. The key is to be ready for anything, and to change course as necessary. The idea of K-12 in neighborhood schools that adequately meet your child's needs may seem like a long-ago dream, but the road you are on will be filled with adventure.

♦ Remember to trust your gut.
♦ If school isn't working as it is, look at your options.
♦ Protect your family relationships.
♦ Find others who understand you and your child.
♦ Delegate some things to experts as needed.
♦ Let go of perfect.
♦ Value hard work and resilience.

Your child is so incredibly lucky to have you on their side, showing them how to live their lives, how to self-advocate, and how to advocate for others.

When you're stressed and overwhelmed and wonder if you'll all get through this all in one pieces (yes, the plural is intentional, but nice catch!), think of my long-suffering parents, who traveled Europe for 3 months with three gifted teens, 13, 16, and 19, in a

DOI: 10.4324/9781003467441-20

tiny station wagon. You can see by the looks on our faces that we were done. Imagine what the expressions on our parents' faces were!

FIGURE 15.1   Moooom? Are we there yet?

You can do this. I believe in you. Courage and strength.

Carol

Appendix A
Resources

Websites

Davidson Young Scholars
Programs (by application only), articles, and blog
http://www.davidsongifted.org

Gifted Homeschoolers Forum (GHF)
Tons of free, current resources, not just for homeschoolers
https://ghflearners.org

Hoagies Gifted
Treasure trove of resources
http://www.hoagiesgifted.org

Mihaly Csikszentmihalyi TED Talk on Flow
Well worth your 15 minutes!
https://www.ted.com/talks/mihaly_csikszentmihalyi_on
_flow

Minnesota Council for the Gifted and Talented (MCGT)
Your MN and beyond parent and caregiver community
http://www.mcgt.net

National Association for Gifted Children (NAGC)
Reliable resource for all things gifted education
https://nagc.org

National Center for Research on Gifted Education (NCRGE)
Javits Grant central
https://ncrge.uconn.edu/javits-projects

Project Northstar
Javits Grant research study on addressing needs of gifted in
rural settings
https://www.mcgt.net/northstar

Supporting Emotional Needs of the Gifted (SENG)
Articles library
https://www.sengifted.org

Wrights Law
Information you need when advocating for your 2e child
https://www.wrightslaw.com/

Books

Brock Eide and Fernette Eide, *The Dyslexic Advantage*. Penguin Random House.

James Webb et al., *Misdiagnosis and Dual Diagnosis of Gifted Children and Adults*. Gifted Unlimited.

James Webb et al., *A Parent's Guide to Gifted Children*. Gifted Unlimited.

Joy Lawson Davis. *Bright, Talented, and Black: A Guide for Families of Black Gifted Learners*. SCB Distributors.

Judy Galbraith. *The Gifted Kids' Survival Guide, 10 and Under*. Free Spirit Publishing.

Judy Galbraith and Jim Delisle, *The Gifted Teen Survival Guide*. Free Spirit Publishing.

Karen Rogers, *Reforming Gifted Education*. Gifted Unlimited.

Kelly Huegel, *GLBTQ: The Survival Guide for Queer & Questioning Teens*. Free Spirit Publishing.

Linda Silverman, *Upside-Down Brilliance: The Visual-Spatial Learner*. DeLeon Publishing.

Mary Sheedy Kurcinka , *Raising Your Spirited Child*. William Morrow.

Ross Greene, *The Explosive Child*. HarperCollins.

Susan Daniels and Michael Piechowski, *Living with Intensity: Understanding the Sensitivity, Excitability, and the Emotional Development of Gifted Children, Adolescents and Adults*. Gifted Unlimited.

Susan Winebrenner and Dina Brulles, *Teaching Gifted Kids in Today's Classroom: Strategies and Techniques Every Teacher Can Use*. Free Spirit Publishing.

Publishers of Books and Curriculum

Art of Problem Solving (AOPS) – Beast Academy
Free Spirit Publishing
Gifted Unlimited
Prufrock Press
Royal Fireworks Press – Michael Clay Thompson language arts

Appendix B
Supplementary Materials

Chapter 2

Who's who on our advocacy team

Who	Why	Where
Parents and caregivers	Parents and caregivers can be more outspoken about what's missing or needs changing when it comes to gifted education because it won't affect their livelihood	♦ Online forums ♦ Schools with gifted services or programs ♦ After-school and Saturday programs that attract gifted kids ♦ Non-profit organizations that serve gifted families ♦ Gifted support conferences ♦ Gifted homeschool groups
Educators	Educators can speak from the school perspective but may have some restrictions about advocating for change in their own district. Many gifted educators are also parents of gifted kids, which gives them an additional layer of insight to share.	♦ Schools that offer gifted services or programs ♦ Non-profit organizations that support educators of gifted children ♦ Universities that offer gifted certifications or degrees ♦ Gifted education conferences
Administrators	Whatever level of change you are working toward, having one or more administrators working with you is very helpful. They can bring the big-picture thinking to the table.	♦ Statewide administrator groups ♦ Districts that offer gifted services or programs ♦ Gifted education conferences

(Cont.)

(Cont.)

Who	Why	Where
Non-profit organizations	Having an organization behind your advocacy gives you: (a) more presence, (b) more resources, and (c) access to more potential volunteers and stakeholders	◆ Check with the National Association for Gifted Children to see if your area has an affiliate organization
Legal brains	Lawyers, researchers, and lobbyists bring specific and valuable skill sets to an advocacy team. Pro bono help from a lobbyist can save you a great deal of legwork and guesswork.	◆ Your state Bar Association may have leads on lawyers and lobbyists who do pro bono work in your area ◆ Other organizations that advocate for similar stakeholder groups may have legal services that they can recommend
Who is missing?	Additional stakeholders	

Advocacy planning calendar

Date	Proposed Advocacy Timeline
January	◆
February	◆
March	◆
April	◆
May	◆
June	◆
July	◆
August	◆
September	◆
October	◆
November	◆
December	◆
January	◆

Chapter 6

A family challenges and solutions worksheet

The challenge	Possible solutions	Discussion	Evaluation
	◆		
	◆		
	◆		
	◆		
	◆		
	◆		

Chapter 9

Pros and cons: school options

Options	Pros	Cons
Neighborhood school	◆	◆
Private school	◆	◆
Charter school	◆	◆
Homeschool	◆	◆
Online school	◆	◆

Chapter 10

Regulation suggestions: early grades by Cori Paulet

Category	Description/Example
BEHAVIORS you might see	◆
SITUATIONS where behaviors are more likely	◆
PREVENTION of disruptive behaviors	◆
CALMING help regain control	◆

Chapter 11

What my family can offer: volunteering brainstorm

If you know how to do:	*Offer to help with:*
Graphic design	◆ Newsletter ◆ Invitations ◆ Posters ◆ Social media posts ◆ School brochures ◆ Swag for events/teams/causes
Event planning	◆ Class parties ◆ School events ◆ District events ◆ Fundraisers ◆ Food/coat/clothing drive
Arts and crafts	◆ Art talks ◆ Museum field trip ◆ Virtual field trip ◆ Art activity ◆ Craft for fundraiser, donation, or holiday gifts, etc.
Science	◆ Lead an after school science club ◆ Plan a field trip to a lab ◆ Give an in-class presentation ◆ Connect the teacher with a scientist who can join the class virtually for an online conversation
Math	◆ Fundraisers ◆ Donation drives ◆ Small group help ◆ Sourcing alternate curriculum for kids who pretest out of a math unit
Theater	◆ Offer to help with the school play ◆ Be a guest judge for a competition ◆ Support small groups as a mentor in competitions like Destination Imagination and others
Engineering	◆ Lead a hands-on building activity in a classroom ◆ Mentor a robotics team ◆ Join the playground redesign committee
What you know	◆ Helping the school ◆ Teaching a group of kids ◆ Supporting the work ◆ Mentoring a group ◆ Creating a plan ◆ Lending a hand, a strong back, or a keen eye

Meeting notes organizer

Date: (Always add the date)
Time: (Time of day and location of meeting can help jog your memory or someone else's)
Place: (Phone call, hallway at school, classroom, etc.)
Reason: (Conferences, drop-in, scheduled meeting, etc.)
Attendees: (This is worth taking a few minutes to get spelling and job titles.) Em, Em's Parent, Math Teacher, etc.

Discussion item	Discussion notes	Action item	
Homework completion is a daily struggle	Tutor, Hardest First, different math class, medication	Math teacher will allow Em to do Hardest First strategy. Teacher will identify 20% of homework for Em to complete. As long as Em scores 80% or better on that portion, they do not need to revisit that homework. If Em's score falls below 80%, the teacher will assign review work.	